DRUID POWER

About the Author

Amber Wolfe is a master-level educator and psychotherapist in private practice. She follows an American Shamanic path, using the wisdom found in the Celtic forms of Craft, spirituality, and myth that are her heritage. She also honors the sacred teachings of Native American medicine elders who have shared their knowledge of the nature of this land.

She calls herself a *Ban Drui*, a term that has several meanings. Among them are Wise Woman, Druidess, White Oak Woman, and (as described by William Butler Yeats) a "Faerie Doctor." These titles represent her style as a writer, teacher, and therapist, whose work emphasizes the magick qualities of self-transformation and personal evolution.

Amber is a solitary practitioner of the Celtic tradition of the Craft of the Wise. In addition to three earlier books published by Llewellyn, she has created guided imagery tapes designed to evoke and support the quest for spirituality and Nature awareness. She is currently working on several books drawn from her work with both Celtic and Native American sources.

To Write to the Author

If you wish to contact the author or would like more information about this book, please write to the author in care of Llewellyn Worldwide, and we will forward your request. Both the author and publisher appreciate hearing from you and learning of your enjoyment of this book and how it has helped you. Llewellyn Worldwide cannot guarantee that every letter written to the author can be answered, but all will be forwarded. Please write to:

Llewellyn Worldwide
2143 Wooddale Drive, Dept. 978-0-7387-0588-0
Woodbury, MN 55125-2989, U.S.A.

Please enclose a self-addressed, stamped envelope for reply, or $1.00 to cover costs.
If outside the U.S.A., enclose international postal reply coupon.

DRUID POWER

CELTIC FAERIE CRAFT & ELEMENTAL MAGIC

AMBER WOLFE

Llewellyn Publications
Woodbury, Minnesota

Cover design by Kevin R. Brown
Cover background © Photodisc, ivy © Brand X Pictures
Interior illustrations by Kerigwen
Interior editing, layout, and design by Amy Rost

Llewellyn is a registered trademark of Llewellyn Worldwide Ltd.

FIRST EDITION
Twentieth Printing, 2021

Library of Congress Cataloging-In-Publication Data
Wolfe, Amber, 1950–
    Druid power : Celtic faerie craft & elemental magic / Amber Wolfe.
Rev. ed. of: Elemental power. 1996.
    p. cm.
Includes bibliographical references and index.
ISBN 13: 978-0-7387-0588-0
ISBN 10: 0-7387-0588-8
    1. Magic, Celtic. 2. Mythology, Celtic. 3. Druids and Druidism–Miscellanea.
I. Wolfe, Amber 1950-Elemental Power. II. Title. II. Series.

BF1622.C45W65 2004
133.4'3'089916—dc22

                                                                              2004048552

Llewellyn Worldwide does not participate in, endorse, or have any authority or responsibility concerning private business transactions between our authors and the public.

All mail addressed to the author is forwarded but the publisher cannot, unless specifically instructed by the author, give out an address or phone number.

Any Internet references contained in this work are current at publication time, but the publisher cannot guarantee that a specific location will continue to be maintained. Please refer to the publisher's website for links to authors' websites and other sources.

Llewellyn Publications
A Division of Llewellyn Worldwide Ltd.
2143 Wooddale Drive
Woodbury, Minnesota 55125-2989
www.llewellyn.com

Printed in the United States of America

Other Books by the Author

*In the Shadow of the Shaman: Connecting with Self,
Nature and Spirit*

*Personal Alchemy: A Handbook of Healing and Self-
Transformation*

The Arthurian Quest: Living the Legends of Camelot

Acknowledgements

I am grateful to the many people who have shared the gifts of their wisdom, their experiences, their support, and their encouragement to help make *Druid Power* possible. Special thanks to: Stardragon—sister and mentor; to Pech Rafferty—true brother, for teaching me to always look at life through "special glasses;" to my family for doing me the great favor of living with a writer; to Jon, Kara, and Jonathan Starr and the Avalon Touring Company; to "Miss Jennie" Temples, Patti Cake, Ryan, Laser, and Lady Candace—as well as all the rest of the San Diego Dragonriders; to Danny Doyle—a true bard; to Cud'n Jean Underwood—dragon-ken; to Jay Veneer—a dragon warrior; to Bruce and Jeanne-Jeanne for their technowizardry, and to the Dragonmaster himself.

Table of Contents

Druid Power
is gratefully dedicated to
all the Children of Danu.

Preface:
The Song of the Celts

I drift along the borders of consciousness to the dimension where myth and memory meet, to a place of long ago.

It is a crisp winter morning. Snow lies piled in clean white drifts against the tall stones at the top of the great hill of Tara. I am part of a small procession making its way up the hill. The procession follows a spiral path that ends at the largest circle of tall stones.

In the center of this circle is one immense stone, taller than all the others and covered with interwoven patterns. Intricate Celtic knot work is hewn carefully in the surface, and primitive runic symbols are carved around the base of this great stone. These carvings contain the sacred wisdoms and the ancestral stories of the people who have inhabited this land for many ages. They form a record for the descendents of these ancient, oft-forgotten folk, whose true histories are now blurred in the mists of memory and myth. They form a record of the past for the purposes of the future.

It has been a sacred ceremonial morning. A ritual rejoicing the return of the Sun's energy to the Earth has already been performed. Now most of the participants have left for the warmth of their hearth fires and the welcome pleasures of the holiday feasts.

Only a few of us remain on this chill, windy hill—a company of white-robed druids and I. Though I cannot see any of their faces, I know they have come to support my search for the sacred knowledge in the stone. They have come into the inner landscape of my mind, and they have cracked the secret codes of my memories.

I stand facing the center stone alone. There is no fire to thaw the deep, cold uncertainty that threatens to freeze me into immobility. I remind myself how much I have wanted to hear this stone speak.

I feel the wind die suddenly. An eerie stillness surrounds the stone circle; an unearthly quiet descends across the land. I can only hear the sound of my heartbeat as I step closer to this stone of destiny, seeking to understand the foundational secrets of its wisdom. As a further rite of passage, I seek a deeper connection to the element of earth. It is an element whose influence I have always felt guiding my development, yet have only recently begun to fully appreciate. Now I come, questing the power of earth through its sacred symbol, the stone of destiny.

The stone looms before me like a sleeping giant. I cannot decipher all of the symbols carved on its surface, but I feel their message deep within my tribal memory. I brush my fingers across these ancient carved patterns, but they only seem cold and worn with the ravages of times past.

I breathe warm air into the palms of my hands and lay them flat against the surface of the great stone. From deep within my heart I call forth a claim of kinship and a reverent connection to the creators of the sacred stone. I thrust the force of this heartfelt honor into the stone. I feel it pulsing through my hands and awakening a rhythm inside.

For a time, the rhythm of my heartbeat and that of the stone are one clear, shared vibration. Around me, the circle of druids—the hooded ones—begins to hum. The resonance of their tone shakes the Earth beneath my feet. I steady myself and stand my ground.

I call forth from the core of my Self and connect to the core of my culture. It reaches through me in shamanic connection to the core of the Earth.

I hear the banshees shrieking out in celebration. I hear the birth cry of a mighty tribe of people. I hear the battle cries of a thousand clans. I hear the cheers of countless victorious warriors.

I hear the sacred wisdoms and the ceremonial chants of Earth rituals echoing within the deepest chambers of my consciousness. I hear heroic tales being told. I hear the truths of Brehon laws vibrating across the dimensions of time.

I hear an ancient refrain stirring in my blood and bones. I hear the song of the Celts. I hear it clearly, and I join in its proud chorus.

Beneath that chorus I hear a subtle melody interweaving its resonant strain. I hear the music of the Sidhe. I hear the clear, fair voices of the Children of Danu in accompaniment.

It is the clear, perfect harmony of kinship. It is a melody of magickal alliance. I hear it reverberate around the world with power. I feel, in the magnetism of its tone, a force pulling the web of life together, creating a stronger weave.

I hear the exaltation of the past reclaimed, the present fully recognized, and the future rewoven for freedom. I hear the fierce independence songs of the Celts and, from deep within their chords, I hear the voice of Lady Liberty. I hear her calling out in clear refrain for the natural rights of humanity, for the inalienable rights of each individual human being. This sacred music vibrates to a crescendo, then softens into a gentle melody. It is the melody of democracy.

Just as the stone of destiny ceases its vibrations, just as all becomes silent once more, I hear the songs of the weavers working at their looms.

Introduction:
A Chronicle of Celtic
Consciousness

Several millennia before the birth of Christ, there emerged from the heart of Europe a tribe of people destined to change the face of the world for all time to come. So magnificent were the exploits of this tribe and so mystical its origins, that then, as now, it seems to belong to the realms of myth and legend. While this legendary tribe kept the secrets of its wisdom and power safe within the sacred traditions of the unwritten word, the classical writers of ancient Greece and Rome strove to chronicle the existence and experience of these people, described as Keltoi—the Celts.

Later, in the span of time now defined as recorded history, others sought to give definition to these ancient peoples. After the advent of Christ and the creation of an organized, catholic church, monks and priests of that new religion pieced together fragments of the Celtic oral traditions. Then, with the flourishes of their own new-found faith, these zealous scribes presented their versions, their often conveniently adapted descriptions of these peoples, the ultimately indescribable Celts.

For a relatively brief period of history, there was a fair time. The old ways of the Celt and the new ways of the Christian blended harmoniously in connection to the lands they shared and the civilized order they mutually strove to create. For a time, sagas of mythic Celtic warriors, mysterious stories regarding the powers of newly anointed saints, and heroic tales of the Galilean spread throughout the realms of the Celts with the ease of equanimity.

Then, as surely as darkness follows the light, a shadow fell across the lands of the Celts, bringing with it the graven silence of oppression. About a thousand years after the advent of Christ, a Dark Age came into being. The rulers of the Christian Church, who had originally come to convert others with the revealed truth of their messiah, were now in self-proclaimed, blasphemous possession of his holy powers. The structured forces of the Church sought absolute control, using dictates and dogmas to separate the common people from their tribal roots and ancient ways. The revered message of light and truth transformed into restrictive mandates of licentious tyranny.

For a time, the stories of the Celts were unspoken, save perhaps for the insistent whispers of the winds in the deep woods and the cry of the banshees from the barrows. Wars, pestilence, famine, and persecution moved through the lands of the Celts with an inexorable malevolence. Deep within the burial cairns of the honored mythic ancestors and high atop the tors of their ancient rites, the wisdom and the power of the Celts lay waiting in the mists for the wheel of time to turn in their favor.

In an age best not forgotten, the dark angels of fear and greed held reign over the lands of the Celts, plaguing the people in a desperate attempt to achieve final, destructive dominance over their tribal destiny. Simple altars, engraved with Ogham Script and rudimentary carvings depicting the spirit faces of field and stream, were demolished. The great trees of the sacred groves were felled. In their stead, elaborate places of worship were erected, often no more than expensive effigies of the conquerors' pride, wrought of once-sacred stone and wood. These were often bought with the blood of the common peoples, now taxed into destitution and submissive resignation, resulting from generations of starvation and deprivation.

Satisfied that they had obliterated all traces, all relics, and all records of the old ways that connected the Celts with their ancient power, the conquerors—once garbed as centurions, now clad as pious clerics in service to Rome—turned their attention to the domination of the Holy Lands, birthplace of their own religion. Diverted by the dark forces of their own divisive greed, these would-be conquerors failed to notice the reemergence of the Celts' most ancient sovereign ally, the pure power of Nature.

From within the unity of spirit that arises in times of threatened annihilation, the soul force of the Celtic peoples stirred into action. It seemed that the very elements of Nature conspired to remind these once-proud people of their noble legacy. When the dank smoke from the funeral pyres of destruction and disease had been carried away by the winds of change, the healing face of Nature was seen clearly once more, illuminated by the light of truth.

The power of the land itself remained steadfast and abiding, as solid and immovable as the circles of standing stones built in time immemorial to connect with the indomitable regenerative forces of Nature. That which had appeared to be dead now proved to be merely lying fallow, its seeds germinating deep in the bosom of Mother Earth and in the fertile ground of the Celtic spirit. Just as new growth had sprung forth from the stumps of sacred trees once hastily hewn to the ground, a remembrance reemerged among the Celts. They remembered their sacred connection to the soul of Nature, and, in that remembrance, they began to recall the soul source of their powers.

Humble friars worked in honored service to the land and the peoples, rekindling the light of faith and strength. Holy sisters emerged from the seclusion of their stone sanctuaries and began to practice the healing arts once more. This they did in defiance of their chosen religion, which had sought to maintain control over the primary processes of birth and death.

From within the impoverished villages, the rich traditions of recalled truths began to emerge. From behind the baronial walls of the landed gentry, new voices of revolution were heard across the land. Soon voices raised in shared purpose were shouting for the rights of the people. They joined to shout down the despotic rule forced upon everyone by the feudal system, and contrived by those who had usurped and abused the ancient, divine right of royalty.

Though few had access to the rare volumes of written history, and fewer still could decipher the letters therein, these people managed to create a foundational system of laws from which their rights as individuals could be regained. These laws were crafted from the remnants of their ancient druidic orders and from shreds of truth borrowed from the very civilizations that had sought to control and contain their expansive Celtic nature.

Though the times of persecution were not yet a thing of the past, their negative influence began to wane. The fires of retribution struggled in vain to consume the reemergence of the Celts. Voices of dissension rang out across the lands, but were silenced by a stronger chorus, a resonant strain from deep within the tribal consciousness of the Celtic peoples. Like the bards of ancient days, the troubadours of this medieval time sang out in celebration of passion, romance, and the power of love.

The Celts, once dominated by dogma that reviled the pleasures and values of human emotions, now recalled the beauty of their natural expressions. The false purity of pious posturing gave way to the real forces of pure love. The troubadours regaled the people with mythic tales once more. These tales were drawn from the ancient voices of their oral traditions, which had never ceased to be heard deep within their tribal memories.

As springtime transforms the face of Nature, bringing blossoms to branches once cold and barren, so too these mythic tales were newly garbed in the flowery vestments of romance. The proud warrior codes of the Celtic ancestors were now transformed into a pure order of chivalry. The descendents of fierce barbarians, who carved their way across the continent of Europe and established their strongholds on the sacred islands in the Atlantic Ocean, now became noble knights and gentle ladies. They too were destined to become the stuff of legends and faerie tales.

Honored even by their foes from times of antiquity for their generous hospitality, the Celts found themselves comfortably armored by this polished system of chivalry. Though it proved to be a thin veneer of civilized humanity, as the chronicles of their times revealed, it was a new beginning for these people still steeped in the old ways and born before the concepts of lawful, civilized consciousness came into being.

Even the mythic symbols of their wisdom, their legacy from dimensions beyond the measurements of time and place, were transformed to reflect a more refined order. The cauldron became the Grail; the stone of destiny was replaced by the shield; the spear of their primitive ancestry evolved into the sword of power; and the staff became the scepter, or, magickally, the wand. While this transformation of sacred symbols reflected a shift into higher realms of consciousness, it neglected to purely retain the connection to Nature that these symbols originally represented.

For a time, only the country folk, the people of the heath, recalled the powers of the ancient symbols, and retained their use in the daily crafting of their lives. The elaborate trappings of a new chivalrous society still belonged, for the most part, to the people born to wealth and power. Still, the beautiful blossoming celebration of love and honor sowed the seeds that would, in time, emerge as flowers of freedom for all of the people.

Realizing the power of love and honor, the Celts began to recognize the right of the individual to pursue a life of happiness, a revelation whose message would return in future times. This message would come later in revolutionary tones, as descendents of these Celtic codes and chivalric orders sought and obtained their own rights to be free and self-ruling.

For nearly 500 years, the powers of the Celts and their European cousins were caught up in the expansive growth initiated by the rebirth of civilization and the rapid evolution of learning that followed. The tender buds of the troubadour's spring burst forth into the full-blown summer of the Renaissance. Art, music, and poetry flourished throughout most of Europe and the British Isles.

The peoples of the old Western world were awakening to a new potential, a new power, and a new purpose. The drab shades of restrictive religions were soon discarded in favor of the colorful reflections of newly emerging spiritual choices and greater self-rule. The dark overtones of domination, which had shadowed the Celts for so long, faded in the explosion of light and color during this time of reformation.

In a manner reminiscent of his mythic forbearers, a Celtic king severed for all time the bindings placed on his realm during the Roman conquest. Though his motives were not purely of noble intent, his cut was true. In the healing process of those once-bound wounds were the regenerative forces of spiritual choices and personal liberties. Alas, these were still to be long in coming, and the scars of these bindings and their severance were destined to remain in the consciousness of the Celts far into the future, as shadowy reminders of sanctimony and separatism.

There followed a time of dichotomy. In the midst of their newly regained powers, the Celts lost contact with the memories of their own forlorn period of domination. They became caught up in the conquest of new lands and the acquisition of new sources of wealth. In an expansive wave, unparalleled in history, the Celts, now fueled by the red fires of their Teutonic cousins, extended their realm to include the greater part of the known world and beyond. While they created of an empire on which the Sun would never set, these descendents of mythic conquerors turned also upon themselves.

In what may be described as a tribal sibling rivalry, the Gaelic and Brythonic Celts made war upon each other. In alliance with their mutual Teutonic cousins, the Brythonic Celts forced their Gaelic kin into submission to what is now known as the British crown. The green ray of the Celtic legacy, which had reflected most vibrantly in the mystical nature of the Gaels, now clashed with the blood-red ray of the Britta.

Those of the Gaels who resisted the onslaught of the Britta were sent to fight in foreign wars far from their homelands. Others were forced to colonize the British Empire abroad. During this process of empire building, the Brythonic Celts separated from the origin they shared with the Gaelic Celts. The force of this separation was to be felt for centuries to come; its shock waves still reverberate to this day on the neighborhood battlefields of Northern Ireland.

The realms of the Gaelic Celt were soon relegated to the dominion of the Britta. Wales, Cornwall, and Scotland, bound geographically to the Brythonic regions, were first to yield. Ancient Ireland had been privileged to remain unconquered by the Romans, and enjoyed a thousand years virtually uninfluenced by outside forces. In her strength, this bastion of the old blood remained unconquered, even as the Anglo-Saxon sword spilled her blood and starved out her children.

In this shameful period of Celtic history (best remembered clearly to avoid its repetition), several events revealed the mystical, weaving hands of the Fates at work. During this period of blatant imperialistic expansion, the Celts—both Gaelic and Brythonic—established themselves throughout the world, in regions destined to become great nations. By methods of selfish design, at times both brutal and benevolent, these descendents of ancient warriors forged new civilizations, and, in relatively short order, they claimed these civilizations as their own.

For a time in this evolutionary history of the Celts, all their attentions focused on the establishment of their own free countries. These Celts, often forced from their homelands themselves, finally remembered the pain of subjugation, and strove to create new realms of freedom and democracy. Some, like the United States, became completely independent of the binding weight of the British monarchy. Others, like Canada and Australia, became part of the British Commonwealth, yet retained the rights of self-rule. The fierce Celtic legacy, which strove for personal freedom, manifested itself as a group of great allies, subject only to the needs of the people in their new homelands. Though the records of these newly established countries are marred by injustices toward their indigenous peoples, there remains an underlying positive connection that might yet serve the greater purposes of the planet.

While establishing themselves as new countries with untapped resources and unexplored regions to understand and govern, these peoples put aside their Celtic origins in favor of forging new identities as new nations. For a time, that which was considered Celtic drifted once more into the mists of legend, or was relegated to the outlying regions of Great Britain where the Gaelic Celts still held sway. Once again, the wisdom and the power of the Celts waited in the mists for the wheel to turn in their favor. This wheel was not so much the dimensions of time, but rather the evolution of consciousness and the destiny of an ancient connection to Nature.

In the final century of this millennium, the descendents of the fierce Celtic strain found themselves embroiled in terrible wars that raged throughout the world. From the ravages of these wars came a new realization of the need to preserve peace. Once more in alliance, the Gaelic and Brythonic Celt began transforming from the role of the forceful conqueror into a preservation force for freedom.

Though this transformational shift has been slow and, at times, most unsteady, it has occurred with an inexorable certainty of purpose. Throughout the regions now inhabited by modern-day Celts, there has begun an awakening of consciousness of a magnitude not seen even in the days of the Renaissance. Along with this newly awakened consciousness has come an assertive, protective connection to the lands that were conquered and colonized by the Celtic force of will.

Now, in the magick moment of present day, the modern Celts turn to the indigenous peoples as allies in the fight for the preservation of their lands. They also turn to the global community as a whole for the purposes of preserving this shared planet. Once admittedly willful, imperialistic, and warlike by nature, these modern Celts now clearly have the potential to transform those same traits into a fighting force, with the willpower to activate and maintain the preservation of this planet.

While this may seem, to those who do not know the Celts, a new way of being, it is, in truth, quite ancient. Within the codes of the Celts lies, still somewhat dormant, the remembrance of their sacred connection to Nature. The soul of the Celt and the soul of Nature are elementally connected. They have been in rooted shamanic connection to the Earth since this great tribe emerged with its own identity and began to establish its place in the history of humankind.

As the consciousness of Nature reawakens in the awareness of the modern Celt, so too shall the soul of the ancient Celt reemerge in sacred connection to the land. The ancient Celts, still figures of myth and legend for most of us, are, in fact, quite real and present in the world today. Despite the attempts of those who would claim they are a vanquished people, the Celts remain an indomitable force with great value for the present time.

The Nature consciousness of the Celts—the sacred, mystical awareness that connects them to the source of their power—has begun to reemerge in earnest. Within this realm of Celtic Nature consciousness dwells their true power and wisdom. Traces of this ancient wisdom can be found in the records of archivists, the digs of archaeologists, and the efforts of anthropologists and historians. While all of these fine sciences reveal valuable clues about the Celts, they do not enter into the realms of Celtic consciousness itself; they do not enter into the mind of the Celt. They do not enter into the archetypal forces of Nature, which are the basic elements reflected in the Celtic consciousness.

To access and activate Celtic consciousness, we need to enter into the realms of music, myth, and conscious mind. In doing so, we can connect with the symbolic record of their wisdom and their tribal codes. Deep within the melodies of Celtic music and poetry we can begin to hear the song of the Celts in true accord with the harmonics of Nature. Deeper still, within the archetypal tribal consciousness, original patterns, and symbolic codes of these legendary peoples, we can reclaim our sovereign connection to Nature, as did our Celtic ancestors. In doing so, we can reclaim what has been stored in memory, myth, and faerie tale for far too long.

As we journey into these sacred realms of symbolic myth and tribal memory, we might well find that the legendary Mystic Isles of Celtic fame and power lie waiting in the mists of our own consciousness, waiting for the wheel of self-evolution to turn and awaken us to the "time of doing."

Some Introductory Notes on Elemental Power

In this volume we will seek a deeper connection to the consciousness of the Celts through the mediums of Jungian active imagery and shamanic journey work. As keys to our journeys, we will use the four basic elements of Nature—air, fire, water, and earth—plus a fifth element, spirit. These elements will be correlated with Celtic symbols and mythic figures or deities to deepen the experience of accessing ancient tribal codes.

In addition, because we are entering this mythic realm through the mind or psyche, we will coordinate each element with aspects and strengths that have applicability and value for our lives today. By coordinating the elements of Nature with the elements of self-nature, we begin to make a more sacred, in-depth, and shamanic connection to our personal power, as well as to the empowering energies of the planet.

For those of you unfamiliar with the processes of shamanic journey work, you may approach these experiences as you would dream work or as personal faerie tales. You may view these as personal records of your inner adventures in the realms of deep-mind and symbolic consciousness. Before we begin to get a feel for the energies of each element and explore the experiential modalities of the shamanic journey, we will spend some time simply getting to know the Celts a little better.

It is my hope that this volume will awaken you to the deeper meanings of the Celtic myths with which you may already be familiar, and inspire you to seek out your own sources of Celtic myth and mysteries. It is not my intention to retell the ancient traditional Celtic myths after the sacred manner of the bards. Instead, it is my intent to provide a new way to access the codes, the patterns, the frequencies of energy that accompany these myths—the elemental powers—and their symbolic representations.

This may be compared to playing ancient music on modern instruments. The melody remains the same, but the vibrational pattern of the music is amplified and expressed in a new way. The experience is expanded and evolved to attune with the shifts and growths of modern human consciousness.

When we have explored the elemental realms through the experiential journeys, we will move deeper into the development of our personal power. We will explore new and ancient ways of working with energy and power more directly and more effectively. We will explore the natural laws as they apply to the exchange of energies in our daily interactions and in our extraordinary experiences, such as ceremonial and ritual workings.

Finally, we will begin to work at the loom of our lives and that of the planet. We will learn what it is to be a weaver of energy, power, and light. Throughout this volume, bear in mind that the consciousness of the Celt always has been, is now, and ever shall be active.

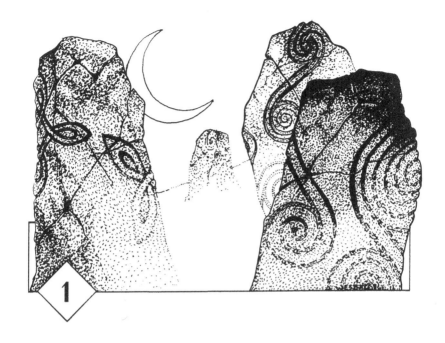

Elemental Power:
The Mystical Connection

We begin this chapter by connecting with the magick of imagination.

The Celtic Otherworld:
An Experiential Guided Imagery

Take a moment to imagine—or to remember—the ancient times, the Celtic times. Open your mind to expanded dimensions, to inner vision. Open to the experience within. Imagine that you are walking through a primeval forest thick with oak and ash trees. Above you, the sunlight streams down through a green canopy of interwoven branches and shimmering leaves. Below you, the ground is deep, rich soil over solid rock. Dense carpets of moss cover many of the great stone boulders. The moss softens the sharp edges of the stones that jut forth from the low, rolling hills rising gently from the forest floor. Lacy late-summer ferns move away gently at your touch as you move through the forest.

You make your way to the foot of the largest hill and rest for a moment against an ancient tree. It is a great gnarled oak growing out of a wide crevasse between two large boulders. You run your fingers over the boulder closest to the tree and find three short lines carved into the stone. You can barely see them under the moss and lichens growing on the stone. You touch these marks gently, taking care not to disturb the natural camouflage covering them.

You breathe a sigh of contentment, for you know you have found an ancient sacred place. The three lines carved in the stone are wizard marks. Wise Ones have been here before.

This place is a gateway between the worlds. It is a place where the veil between this world and the Otherworld is quite thin. It is a place where some are given the honor of stepping through that veil for a brief time, then allowed to step back, transformed by the power of the experience.

You feel the joy of anticipation, but you remind yourself to observe the proper form for making such an Otherworld journey. You reach into an old leather pouch tied on at your waist and take out the small treasures that you have brought for the keepers of this sacred place.

Carefully, ceremonially, you place these treasures into a narrow crack in the stone where a large root of the oak tree has pushed its way out of the ground. One by one, you offer your tiny gifts—a boar's tooth, a bit of copper still tinged with green ore, and a pale violet crystal from the faraway islands in the great Northern Sea.

You wait to see if your gifts are accepted. You wait to know if your request will be honored and you will be allowed to glimpse the realm of the Otherworld.

For a time you are aware of only the sounds of the forest. A light breeze stirs the leaves high up on the branches above you. You can hear the gentle trickle of water not far away, and see the silver glistening trail it makes streaming softly down the stones. The water makes its way into a small pool surrounded by ferns and wildflowers. From deep in the forest a whippoorwill calls out and is answered by its mate.

A mist has begun to rise; it glides silently across the forest floor and gathers around the ancient oak where you are waiting. It thickens, enveloping the ferns and the low underbrush around you. The outlines of the trees grow dimmer and dimmer now, blanketed by the misty veil. Crystalline lights shimmer across the surface of the mist as shafts of sunlight reach through from above.

You look up to see a golden eagle flying high above the tallest trees in the forest. The eagle circles above you. Its cry pierces the silence of the forest and beckons you to a new realm.

With joy and gratitude, you stand and stretch out to reach the sky. You will yourself to be one with that golden eagle—flying free.

Suddenly you are soaring, skillfully riding the winds. You are away, up in the sky. You hear the eagle's cry again and realize it is your own. Your great wings carry you out beyond the rolling hills and dark green forests below. You are swept up into the clouds and enveloped in silvery white mist.

You dive down through the clouds only to find that the landscape has changed. You find yourself flying over a vast body of water that surrounds a series of islands shrouded in mist and cloud cover. You sweep down for a closer look and catch a glimpse of gold and silver spires reaching up through mists that covers the islands below. The islands seem to float on the surface of the water, drifting along with the clouds that cover them from view.

You fly into the cloud cover and are swept away by strange currents. Mysterious forces pull you into the mists, and you enter as in a dream.

Images pass before you from out of the mists. Mythic warriors of ages past and present bravely defend their land. Wizards of the once and future times perform their wonders. Harpists play magickal melodies, and lovely maidens sing haunting refrains. Weavers work upon massive looms with threads of mysterious fibers. Wise Ones meet in sacred groves, while children play in sweet sunlit meadows.

The golden gods of Nature call out in salutation as you soar through their domains. You hear their laughter ringing in your ears, vibrating into the depths of your spirit. You hail them as you pass, sending greetings to your ancestors now dwelling in this golden realm.

Lifted higher by the winds, you are swept up into the clouds once more. For a time you can see nothing but the clouds surrounding you, and you can hear nothing but that golden laughter on the wind. The laughter is growing strangely louder now, and you feel yourself winging downward, closer to the Earth. You break through the clouds in a steep dive and find the landscape familiar once more.

Familiar, but seemingly different.

As you fly towards the familiar hills and forests, you see them in a new light. For a brief moment, the landscape all around you seems awake and alive. As you sweep down through the tree branches, you call out in honor and recognition. You feel a surge of joy from within, and all of Nature resonates in response.

You land with surprising grace at the foot of the gnarled oak where you began. You glance around to get your bearings and catch sight of many wondrous things you had not seen before. Tiny lights sparkle from the forest. Some swirl and dance across the small pool of water. Others rustle through the ferns or glimmer from deep within the roots of the tree. You reach out to touch these magickal lights, but they are gone. Only the sound of laughter rings out through the wood.

From out of the forest a wizard steps. He is one of the Wise Ones who dwell in this sacred wood. He laughs again to see your startled expression; his eyes twinkle with delight as he speaks directly to you.

"I see that you've had a peek," he chuckles.

He touches you gently on the forehead and says, "Perhaps now you'll be wanting to know a bit more about where you've been, and perhaps where you're going, as well."

The wizard sweeps his arms open wide and brings his hands back together with a loud clap. The oak, the forest, the mists, the ferns, the pool, the moss-covered stones instantly fade away.

The wizard smiles with mysterious amusement and slowly fades. As he does, he whispers no louder than a breath on the winds:

It's all one and the same, you see,
Where you've been, and where you'll be.
Understand that, and you'll fly free.
If Celtic quest is what you seek,
'Twill take far more than just a peek.
Awaken your mind, give your brain a tweak;
Learn and listen...'til next we speak.

The history of the Celts and mysteries of the Celts share an intricately interwoven relationship. It is often impossible to determine where the line between fact and fantasy might be drawn. Yet, this is truly in keeping with the philosophy of the Celts.

For the exploration of the Celts and their mysteries, we too shall have to pass through the dimensions of our own minds. We will journey where the magick and the mundane blend to create the Celtic myth. As we do so, we may come to know the mythic aspects of our Selves, as well.

We begin by examining the elemental power of the Celts and their mystical connection to the web of life we call Nature.

It is said that when the Celts invaded Italy and sacked Rome, they were amazed and somewhat amused to see the many statues representing the pantheon of Roman gods and goddesses. These all-too-human representations were quite absurd to the Celtic point of view of the mystical and divine. To the Celts, the realm of deities and the realm of Nature were created from the same essentially nonrepresentational elements. To the Celts, the divine is reflected in all aspects and all elements of Nature in a basically nonhierarchal relationship with humankind. The mystical philosophy of the Celts is based on an active interconnection of all realms and life forms, however animate or inanimate they may appear. It is an essentially shamanic philosophy, and one in which the direct power manifest in Nature is activated through humankind.

Humankind, in totemic, shamanic relationship to the land, is able to call forth the elemental energies and powers of animals, plants, rocks, trees, and all other aspects of what we call Nature. To the Celts, Nature is eternally and essentially inseparable from Self.

This is perhaps most clearly revealed in the Celtic view of reincarnation and metamorphosis. In the Celtic philosophy, all life is part of a continuing chain of existence. In this chain, many interwoven links represent the many forms and dimensions in which life may reflect itself.

The traditional interwoven Celtic knot-work designs are symbolic representations of this philosophy. These designs represent life eternally interweaving in and upon the dimensions of itself. They show life flowing into life, shifting form and dimension as easily as the changing light shifts its reflections upon the water. The shifts from one dimensional form to another, which we might now refer to as the transformations of life, death, and rebirth, are accomplished with the effortless ease that the rising winds uses to ruffle the leaves on the trees.

All things, all forces, all aspects, all elements that reflect in Nature are part of the same interwoven flowing pattern in the philosophy of the Celts. All dimensions, seen and unseen, are part of a continually shifting cosmology. The Celtic Otherworld, a realm of myth and faerie folk, is considered to be a contiguous overlay upon the land. However, it is not seen as being external or separate in any way. It might best be described as an inner landscape eternally reflecting within the consciousness of humankind.

Fundamental to the psychology of the Celts is the abiding belief that upon what we might now refer to as death, the essential spirit returns to the elements of Nature. From this elemental reconnection, the spirit may move in and out of the many reflected dimensions or worlds until it passes into another form or body, and begins to be a new link in that eternal chain of existence.

This philosophy of eternal recreation easily explains the famed Celtic fearlessness in battle. Furthermore, the Celtic mystical philosophy contains no real evidence of what we now call retributive justice or, in New Age jargon, karmic debts. Instead, it reveals an eternally recurring cycle of life forms, which leads to a spiritual perfection without the punitive threats of purgatory or hell.

In the Celtic view, there is no heaven or hell as such, but the Otherworld, which is a realm of refinement, not reward. It is a realm that may be visited without the physical transformation of death, though it requires an essential shifting of consciousness to reach. There is also, in the mystical philosophy of the Celts, a conceptualized underworld. Though it shares a certain chaotic quality with the later concepts of purgatory or hell, it is neither. Instead, it is a realm best understood, in terms of Nature's growth, as lying fallow.

Naturally, the impetuous Celts did not lie fallow well, as their expansive history has shown. Perhaps the impatient qualities of the Celts contributed to the later concept of an underworld being less than desirable. This also explains the famed self-sacrificing gallantry of the Celtic nature; such a refined action would surely result in the choicest realms of the Otherworld being reached.

Another essential aspect of Celtic mystical philosophy is the belief in the *genus locorum* or *geni loci*. This is the belief in "spirit of place," which we may now call *devic* deities. To the Celts, all forms of deities emerged from these spirits of place and from their tribal gods. These, in turn, may once have been persons of great mythic qualities who had achieved the status of Otherworld realms. These deities might have emerged directly from the dimensions of Other-world to aid and empower humankind, and to regulate the elemental forces of Nature.

With the basic philosophical acceptance of deities eternally coming and going, it is easy to see how the influence of Christianity reflected so strongly in the Celt. It was not the spiritual wisdom of the Christian religion that confounded the Celt, but the hierarchal exclusivity of its structures and, most profoundly, its separation from Nature. Fortunately, that separation from Nature appears clearly destined to disappear in the rapidly awakening light of truth and the reconnection of humankind (Celt or not) to Nature.

The ancient Celts were so clearly bound to the tribal gods and spirits of place that their sacred oath still rings true with its wisdom for us in present time. That oath said, "I swear by the gods of my people!" "Teutates," once considered the name of a great Celtic tribal god, is now considered by some linguists to be an abbreviated form of that Celtic oath.

The proof of the power invested in these tribal gods and spirits of place is shown in the records of Celtic deities that have been clearly identified. Of approximately 374 Celtic god names, just four or five occur only once, and these only twenty or thirty times (Piggot, Stuart. *The Druids.* New York: Devin-Adair, 1949).

It is also interesting to note how this multitude of minor deities echoes the spiritual philosophies found in Northern India. There too, all of life is viewed as part of a continuous flow, yet a wide variety of deities is provided, presumably onto which one may anchor a more mundane concern or request. The Indo-European origins of the Celts have been presented by anthropologists and ethnologists for some time now, and this multiple-reflecting divine flow is yet another indication of the Indo-European connection.

However, I find that the Celts reflected a deeper connection to the spiritual powers of the land itself. To the Celts, the land is the true sovereign. The land is the mundane reflection or the essential manifestation in which all dimensions meet. An ancient Celtic tradition held that the land itself—or, more appropriately, herself—provided seven sacred gifts: nurturance, growth, harvest, abundance, truth, law, and victory.

When the Celts failed or fail to honor the true sovereignty of the land, then all the elements of Nature are seen to be forsaken. The result of this broken connection is the loss of any one or all of the seven sovereign gifts. Considering the condition in which Nature finds herself today, it is no small wonder that many of these sacred gifts seem to have been withdrawn in places on this planet.

Fortunately, Nature is both self-healing and forgiving when she is remembered with honor. Any person following the many ways of Nature throughout this great, wide world could tell you this truth. This truth is essential to the spiritual philosophy of the Celts, then, now, always.

This Celtic philosophy, which expounds the sacred queenship or sovereignty of the land, has given rise to the concept that the Celtic culture is matriarchal. This is, in truth, not an accurate representation at all. The Celtic culture was and is neither matriarchal nor patriarchal. The Celtic cultural philosophy is essentially *matristic*, which means that the core of the philosophy, as well as the culture, reflects a mother-centered point of view. The mother in this case, around which all life still revolves, is Mother Earth.

I diverge here to make a point upon which I will elaborate in a later chapter. It is a misconception to view Celtic philosophies in terms reflecting the duality of "either/or." In the Celtic view, what appears to be opposite is seen to be a polarity, rather than a duality. Duality represents opposing points of view or separatist divisions, such as either and or, rather than both. It is a static point of view, eternally divisive. Polarity is the dynamic, eteranally balancing "dance" of energy, sparked by the forces of creation. In turn, polarity sparks the forces of creation in Nature and in self-nature. Polarity is the continuous catalyst for force and for form.

In the Celtic view, what is male and what is female are seen to be in dynamic relationship with each other in order to create life itself. Neither male nor female may be defined as being the constant consort of the other (though at times in Nature it appears that way). Instead, the relationship of male and female is seen to reflect in harmonious concert with each other. The Celtic culture in its original form reflected a truly egalitarian philosophy. Its spiritual philosophy reflected an enhanced view of the female aspect as the symbolic representation of Mother Nature.

In the ancient rites of the Celts, the king or chieftain often mated ritually with a selected queen or priestess (and occasionally with an animal, such as a white horse) who symbolized the sovereign Goddess—Mother Nature herself. This rite symbolized the sacred relationship of the male force—the Sun, Lord of Light—with the female force—the Earth, Lady of Nature (and Nurturance). This symbolic ritual is reflected in the mundane relationships of the Celts, as well.

This essential equality remained until the patriarchal influences of the Roman world and the Christian religious structures, with their eastern desert philosophies, emerged on the scene. People who emerge from places in which Nature is generous and nurturing in her abundance invariably have a spiritual philosophy that reveres the female aspect, but not at the expense of the male.

The enhanced view of the female found in Celtic philosophy and mythology is no more or less a balance for the powerful image of the Celtic male. Indeed, it may be said that with the Celts (then as now), both genders have decidedly chauvinistic tendencies. When all forms are seen as equal parts of a great, interwoven pattern of life, pride in Self is more easily understood.

The concept of matriarchal rule in regard to the Celts probably arose from a misconception of the Celtic triple-aspect Goddess. This goddess trinity, called the *trois matres*, is the form most often recovered in symbolic or physical form in Celtic mythos and mundane sites, such as burial cairns and sacred temples. She is seen to be three goddesses in one, symbolizing aspects such as Maiden, Mother, and Crone; creator, nurturer, and destroyer; the seasons of growth in Nature; or the phases of the moon.

In keeping with the ancient beliefs of the Celt, it is most likely that the Triple Goddess symbolized the seasons of growth. It has been theorized that the Celts did not originally hold an idea of four seasons, but had only three. These were most likely correlated with what we now call spring, summer, and winter. In the colder climates from which the Celts emerged, fall was not a distinct phase.

Later, as the Earth warmed and the Celts moved, a fourth season became more apparent. Still later, as the druids learned to measure the relationships of the Sun and the Earth to the stars, the solstices and equinoxes became the official marking points for four distinct seasons.

Originally, though, only three seasons were recognized, as far as we can tell. One very strong indication of this is reflected in the ancient name of the Celtic "wheel of the year day," which signaled the coming of winter. This day, which many now call Halloween, was then called Samhain, So'ween, or Summer's Wane.

The aspects of the Goddess were seen to reflect the aspects of Nature. Spring was the Maiden/creator of birth. Summer was the Mother/nurturer of growth, and included the times of harvest we now call fall. Winter was the Crone/destroyer of life. These triple aspects are perhaps more easily understood in terms that apply to personal power. The power of the Maiden is budding; that of the Mother is full blooming; and the power of the Crone is withdrawn—waiting, but not absent.

It may also be said that the Celtic Triple Goddess represents aspects of the human psyche, influences on personal traits, and the processes of self-development.

The Maiden aspect is free-spirited, active, natural, instinctive, physical, overt, and reflects the external energies of the individual. Borrowing somewhat generally from astrological systems, the Maiden is the sun sign. The Mother is receptive, rational, mature, thoughtful, nurturing, and reflects a balance of internal and external energies in an individual. She represents the astrological ascendent or rising sign. The Crone (whom I prefer to call the Grandmother) is reflective, devotional, sedate, intuitive, covert, spiritual, and reflects the internal energies of the individual. Astrologically, she is represented by the moon sign.

You will notice that I give this Triple Goddess no name or names. This is for two primary reasons. First, it is very important, particularly in regard to the Celtic philosophical viewpoint, to understand most clearly the essential forces that these three aspects symbolize, and, in turn, understand the sacred wholeness represented by the triplicity, the combination of forces that is Nature. Second, these aspects of the Goddess emerge in many Celtic myths with many different names, as do the gods. These different names reflect the differences in tribal mythos only, and not any significant shifts in aspects. As we delve deeper into these aspects in later chapters, we will discuss these nuances and these different names.

For now, we can best recall the succinct wisdom of Dion Fortune, who said, "All gods are one god. All goddesses are one goddess, and there is one initiator." The initiator is the Self in sacred connection to the life forces of Nature and the elements we personify and deify as goddesses and gods.

In the Celtic mystical philosophy, there are two basic gods who make their appearance with nearly the same frequency and in the same consistent manner as the Triple Goddess. These two gods reflect the aspects of the solar/light/warrior king and the dark/tanist/wizard, respectively. They appear most often as the Lord of Light and the Lord of the Underworld. Remembering that these do not represent merely a convenient duality, such as good or evil, we can begin to understand the forces that these Celtic gods do symbolize.

It is perhaps easiest to view these gods from the beginning as representing the external and internal forces of Nature and human nature. It may be said that the Lord of Light represents the potent, fertile periods of active growth. The Lord of the Underworld represents the fallow, inactive periods when growth is not occurring on the land. Simply put, the Lord of Light is expressive and extrovert in Nature; the Lord of the Underworld is latent and introvert in Nature. The Lord of Light represents the rational, physical, and mundane realms; the Lord of the Underworld symbolizes the intuitive realms of mind and psyche.

In Celtic culture, the Lord of Light would be represented by the active, forceful warrior, the fighter, guardian, chieftain, and protector of the tribe. The Lord of the Underworld would be represented by the mystical, contemplative teacher, wizard, wise man, priest, and keeper of the magickal traditions.

Together, in balanced, dynamic relationship, these two aspects create the Celtic ideal—the poet warrior. At odds with each other, however, they cease to be a useful polarity and can succumb to being a battle between what is rational and irrational, controlling and uncontrollable, or protective and destructive. Notice that either part of each of these pairs may apply to either of these god aspects. Either god can be rational or irrational in his natural aspect. It is the dynamic polarity that maintains the balance here, just as it is within our Selves.

In seeking to represent these Celtic deities in a manner more suited to our current times, I found that an interesting balance occurs when the *trois matres* take on a fourth aspect to symbolize the addition of a fall season:

Maiden = Spring   Mother = Summer
Crone = Fall   Hag = Winter

If we divide each of the gods into aspects we can call youthful and mature, we can create a balance of eight deities where we once had five:

The Child of Light = Spring   The Lord of Light = Summer
The Apprentice Priest = Fall   The Lord of Wisdom = Winter

I present these as food for thought and as a reminder that the greatest strength of any system of wisdom or spiritual philosophy is its ability to evolve into the present, not its resistance to being removed from the archives of the past. I also hasten to say that the same can be said of our Selves as vessels of wisdom and spirituality.

It's best to recall that the nature of the Celts was and is expansive, exploratory, and experiential. This noble—or, dare I say, mobile—nature is best symbolized by the next deity whose frequent and dramatic representations place her in a category by herself. This deity is the horse goddess, Epona, symbol of mobility, freedom, power, speed, prowess, strength, endurance, support, and courage. Needless to say, these were all aspects honored by the Celts.

Although this horse goddess is often presented as symbolic of the land, I feel she is more clearly symbolic of the people. Perhaps she might best be described as the shamanic steed that carries the Celts into the realms of the Otherworld, for she often appears in just that role. She might also represent the shamanic connection of humankind to the animal world, and in this regard be considered a totemic symbol.

In the images recovered by archaeologists and mythologists, she is a strong female figure riding on a large, powerful horse. In that form, she may well represent the forces of Nature herself, harnessed by the skills of the Celts. Perhaps she represents the driving forces of Nature that carried the Celts into places and positions of power throughout the world. She may even represent the combined forces of male and female as a matristic version of the centaurs or an earthy form of the pegasus.

It is well known that the love affair between the Celt and the horse is deep and abiding. The horse was a measure of wealth and power for the Celts. Beyond that, the horse was a sacrifice made to anoint a new ruler or to symbolically impregnate the land with fertile power. Despite these ancient rites or the real images found of this horse goddess, I find that, for me, her evolved image as the horned horse, the unicorn, holds the most interesting symbolic key to her essential mystery.

I wonder if this goddess represented as or with a fine horse isn't most clearly a representation of the individual, personal Celtic connection to the mystical realms of the Otherworld consciousness and the elemental powers of Nature. I have found that the manner in which the horse presents itself in mythic tales or in magickal imagery tells a great deal about the purposes and the powers being expressed and utilized. Because of this, my considered opinion regarding the horse goddess is that for the Celts, she is a true connector to the elements of Nature and self-nature. The manner in which this connection is made is individualistic and unique, just like the Celts.

Shamanic Steed:
An Experiential, Guided Imagery

Imagine that you are in the same primeval forest you entered not so long ago. As you reenter the forest, all of Nature greets your arrival. Sunlight streams in through the trees illuminating this, the sacred wood. You walk past the now familiar gnarled oak and the great stone boulders. Woodland violets perfume the air with a sweet, mystical fragrance. You catch sight of these tiny, brilliant-hued flowers almost hiding inside the roots of the great trees that you pass along your way.

You move silently through the forest until you come to a lovely clearing and woodland glade. It is a small, round meadow surrounded by a grove of ancient trees.

Just at the edge of the grove on the far side of the meadow, you see a horse born of myth and legend. You coax this horse to step out from the shadows of the forest and into the light at the center of the clearing.

You call forth this fine steed from within your Self.

Slowly your horse steps forward and moves near the center of the meadow. Your steed is just as you have fashioned it to be. Perhaps it has wings or the single horn on its forehead to mark its ancient origin. Perhaps it is a war horse or a noble hunting mount. Perhaps it is a young, gentle steed, a sweet pony suitable for being ridden by a child of light.

Your steed steps forward and moves fully into the center of the clearing. The Sun bathes this mythic animal in warm, golden light. You see that your steed is just as you expected; it is just as you require to serve you on your present journey.

You walk out to the center of the meadow to greet your new steed, your sacred ally for journeys into the shamanic, Otherworld realms of Nature. Together, you and your steed shall brave the elements and become one with the elements of your Self.

With a gentle touch, you assure your steed of your positive intention and the security in knowing it is your right to ride into the magickal, Otherworld realms. You connect and communicate with your steed as you make preparations for the ride. With a final stroke of assurance, you mount your shamanic horse.

As you do so, all of Nature animates around you. The grove of trees resonates with a rapidly increasing intensity. The sound becomes light, encircling the meadow with multihued bands of color. Their brilliance vibrates into the center of your being, lifting your spirit high.

Your steed rears, then leaps up, taking flight. You are carried up into the blue above you on a trail of rainbow lights. Sky blue deepens to cobalt as you are carried outward toward new dimensions. Below you, the world fades from view, shifting its shape to a blue-green egg floating in the sea of space.

You climb higher now. The world is invisible to your eye. Now the massive Sun is only one of an immeasurable number of stars twinkling in the vast midnight-blue depths of infinite space. You ride still higher, still faster, still farther into the unknown dimensions of the universe beyond description. You can no longer make out individual stars. Their lights have merged into a great mystical pattern.

From where you are now, you can see the sparkling bands of pure light forming an immense crystalline web. So vast is this web that you can see where it is only from your point of view. Where this web begins and where it ends is immaterial, for you are always as you are now, at the center of its power. The web moves and vibrates to an eternal rhythm; you feel its music within your soul.

You are mystified for a moment by this beautiful crystalline web. With reverence, you see that it is shining in the light of a truly celestial source of power. You notice also that the web is illuminated from within the interconnected threads that form its weave. You can feel the resonance of the life force within the web, as all worlds and dimensions weave together. You see light and life interwoven, determining the nature of the universal web—guided only by source itself, experienced only from the source of Self within.

You guide your steed into the bands of light forming the crystal web. For a time you ride in the purest flow of light and life force. You empower your Self and your life purpose directly from the energies of this highest light.

When you have accepted healing and power from the crystalline web, it begins to change once more. Threaded bands of light become clusters of sparkling stars. Star clusters divide into galaxies, centered around great suns. All galaxies float away into the boundless blue-violet dimensions of space. There is a vast silence.

You are left with one now-quite-familiar galaxy as you ride your steed toward the blue-green hills of Earth.

As you reach the dimension surrounding the planet, you see the many shapes of the land. You see the many faces of the Earth—the faces of Nature herself. You rein in your shamanic steed and pause to reflect on the many shifting shapes of the world to which you belong. You pause to watch the changing faces of Nature as she dances in the light of the great Sun above. As she swirls and dances to a universal melody, the Earth reflects the changing rhythms of Nature and all humankind.

The Sun appears in the east. A new light arises, illuminating Nature with a gentle glow. From out of the Sun's rays a youthful rider appears, beginning his journey across the surface of the land. He is fair and golden, this springtime Child of Light. As he rides, he reawakens the life force of the planet beneath him. The planet responds and transforms herself into a springtime Maiden filled with life and promise.

As he traverses the dimension of Nature, this Child of Light transforms to the full growth of his power. He becomes the summer Lord of Light—guardian, activator, protector, and generative force for the life of the planet.

Earth responds in kind to this transformation of the solar light. Nature blossoms at high summer into the fullness of her power. She becomes the Lady Mother, the creative nurturer. She brings forth the fruits of light to sustain her children.

As the Lord of Light journeys still farther across the realm of Nature, his light becomes dim, but not diminished. As his light shifts, he throws his power fully into the bosom of Nature. His dimming rays of light enter the Earth and join with the inner light and heat of the planet in autumn. The solar rider has become Nature's Priest, sworn to maintain the sacred connection of the light of the land. The land transforms quietly, her face reflecting the harvested wisdom of the Crone in the season of fall.

With promises of return, the Solar Priest turns inward and journeys into the depths of space, seemingly gone from the embrace of the planet. He journeys into hidden realms and becomes the ancient Lord of Wisdom. He waits, this winter lord, for rebirth of his power, for resurrection of his flight.

Nature turns inward also, her face cold and wintry, seemingly dead. She becomes the Hag, nursing seeds of the future, plants in the cold, still ground. She is Nature warming the forces of life deep within herself, defying death with faith in the power of transformation. She swirls and dances once more to a universal melody.

The solar lord arises again, seemingly born from the inner dimensions of Earth's far horizon. He arises and reanimates the face of Nature with his warm, pure light. Child of Light and Maiden of Spring once more, the Sun and the Earth begin their sacred dance again and again and again.

Now, as the winter sleep has turned to springtime dance, you ride your shamanic steed back to your own world of Nature. You reenter the sunlit clearing encircled by an ancient grove of trees, deep within your own primeval forest. You rest for a time in that golden meadow, musing on all you have experienced.

When you are ready, you release your steed to graze in the shadows of the grove surrounding this, your magickal meadow. Your steed moves deeper into the forest with one long, last look to let you know where it may be found when you choose to ride again. It will be ready when you are to journey into the realms of Otherworld, all worlds and dimensions beyond clear definition.

You rest for one long moment, listening to the resonant melody of Nature. You listen for the almost imperceptible vibration of the crystalline web. You remember that you may always receive from the light and power of that web. You know you can receive most clearly from that of which you are an integral part.

You know you can receive from the source of all light and power, so long as you reach out from within your Self, connecting the internal with the eternal. You know that the external is but a manifestation of the melody and the dance. You know that you may journey inward to Otherworld realms, so long as your mind is open, your spirit clear, and your heart pure.

When you are ready, you may return to the present time and place. You know that your shamanic steed and your primeval forest await and abide inside your conscious mind, eternally ready for your return.

Rest now and reflect on what you have experienced. Note the nature of your imagery. Note also the way your inner visions made you feel. You have already begun to connect with the mystical Celt within your Self.

Druidism:
Its Connection to Nature
and Self-Nature

We begin to trace the elusive figure of the druid by first exploring the inner dimensions where myth and memory are reflected.

Druidic Self-Discovery:
An Experiential, Guided Imagery

 Take a moment to focus your awareness on your inner vision. Expand the dimensions of your mind's imagination. Begin a journey of self-discovery.

Imagine that you are in a small cave many thousands of years ago. It is very cold outside. Icicles hang from the top of the cave, and freezing winds shake the great bearskin that covers the entrance.

Inside the cave you sit very close to a small fire. You shiver despite the thick blanket of furs that are wrapped tightly around you. Winter has come very early, and you, who are called the "Wise One," must decide whether or not your family clan must move on, or stay and attempt to weather this unexpected turn of Nature.

You toss sacred herbs on the fire as an offering to the spirit keepers of your clan. You send prayers to the Wise Ones who have come before you to this ceremonial cave. You place gifts of meat and soft rabbit skins beside the fire in the hope that your ancestors will honor you with their wisdom. You gaze into the flames and wait for the signs to appear. As you do so, you rock and chant ancient tones. Your mind begins to float free, and the visions emerge.

You see herd animals moving across snowy ground, and fierce wolves attacking those too weak or cold to walk any farther. You see a small band of hunters watching from behind stone boulders. They are far too few in number to compete with the wolves for the much-needed meat.

The image shifts, and you see many of your family clan sick and dying of starvation. You see predators invading your camp. These predators are sometimes human, sometimes animal, but the destruction is the same. They are driven to kill for their own survival.

You toss more herbs on the flames and pray for more visions. You reach for images for which you have no words. You request a sign that will tell you how to keep this disaster from befalling your family clan.

Images form in the flames, and you see the hunters once again, watching from behind the boulders. This time, though, there are many hunters. Some you know as part of your family clan; others are from other clans who live nearby. Still other hunters are unfamiliar, but their faces show them to be friends and not foes.

The image shifts, and all the hunters are seated in a large circle around a center fire. They talk and feast together. The women share their own wisdom, and the elders swap secrets as well as reminiscences. Children from all the families run merrily about, rosy-cheeked and full of life. The spirit keepers of all the clans are strong and smiling as they watch from the Otherworld.

You feel the power of this vision. You hear the voices of the spirit keepers echoing in your mind, sending you the message that will ensure the survival of your family clan and that of many others, as well. Though you may not yet know the word for what you see, you recognize the power of a shared alliance. You see the makings of a tribe.

The flames burn softly now, almost fading into the ashes along with your visions. You stand and give thanks to the spirit keepers and to your ancestors for their wisdom. Outside, the wind has stopped blowing. The sky is filled with bright stars that twinkle with greeting as you step from the mouth of the cave.

You notice, perhaps for the first time, that some of the stars are in clusters, some are far apart from each other, and a great band of stars seems to travel all across the sky. You wonder at the meaning of this, and pause to reflect for just a moment.

It is growing colder, and your people are waiting for news of your vision. There will be much to do, gathering the people together. The Wise Ones of all the clans will have to meet, as well. They will certainly want to tell of their own visions. Perhaps these visions will be shared, since the spirit keepers are in accord. There will be many new things to consider. You know that you and your family clan will face a new beginning. You know that all the people will have to make changes. With the spirit keepers' blessings, those changes will bring power.

You take one last look at the cold night sky before you head for your home and the warm fires of your family clan.

Not far away a wolf howls mournfully. You take a piece of dried meat and leave it on the ground as a sign that there will be meat for that greatest of hunters. The spirit of shared abundance walks home with you this wintry eve, and you are honored with its wisdom.

෧෨෭෧

Take a moment to rest and reflect on what you have seen. Take another moment now to let that ancient, shamanic image slip away into the memory banks of your mind. Now shift your focus to a more classical time of druidic discovery.

Imagine that you are at a massive stone circle atop a spiral tor. The tall, blue-gray stones thrust up from the vibrant green hill and reach into an azure sky. The midsummer sunlight has brought a myriad of wildflowers bursting forth from the ground. Their scents and colors blend in a dizzying display of Nature's radiant joy.

Sounds of laughter drift up the hill from the forest below. Smoke and the smell of suppers cooking rise from many fires. You have spent many hours already in this stone circle atop the tor. You are ready for the pleasant company of the people camped in the forest and for a share of their evening feast. You make your way down the tor, following the spiral path that led you up. You stop just long enough to gather a handful of wildflowers and bid farewell to the spirits of this beautiful sacred hill.

When you reach the forest, you find that everyone is bustling in preparation for the evening's activities. There are many "Wise Ones" gathered here, many drui coming together to share what they have learned. Many have brought their retinues with them, curious combinations of servants, students, and scholars. It amuses you to note that it is not always easy to tell which is which or who is who.

Some of these drui are easy to spot. They wear grand, flowing robes and elaborate symbols of their orders and rank. You stifle a laugh as you watch one particularly important-looking figure expound about the wisdom of his latest revelation, completely unconscious of the fact that his richly embroidered garments are brushing the edges of a cooking fire. You are forced to laugh aloud as a quick-thinking servant pours ale on the fine garments to drown the fire that creeps along the hem. The Wise One continues expounding, oblivious to all but the sound of his own words. You exchange an amused glance with the servant and move on to the next group of drui.

You can hear the sound of several harps melodiously ringing throughout the gathering. Accompanying them are the lyrical voices of the poets sharing song and stories that preserve heritage and power. Their voices merge into a rhythmic ceremony of remembrance. You listen for a while, then move on.

The next group of drui seems to be intent on understanding the mysterious charts and tools of another drui who has recently returned from the lands far to the east. You glance at a chart as you pass by quietly, and are surprised to see a pattern of the sky at night. It is very much as you have observed it from atop the high cliffs near your home. There are some differences in the chart, but you have heard that the sky's pattern is different in other parts of the world. You wish to ask these drui about this and other marvels such as those encountered in the East. However, you must observe protocol and wait until you have been selected, and have yourself chosen to be a student of the drui.

You move on to the next group of Wise Ones exchanging their wisdom with one another. There are many women in this group, more than in most groups, so you know that these drui deal with the healing arts. They are discussing a fever that had been all too common among the people the previous winter. Many died of this fever, but some survived its raging fire. These drui share their experiences, looking for a common thread in the treatments used to defeat the disease.

One woman insists that the fierce disease can be defeated by destroying all the belongings and bedclothes of the people who had died of the fever. Some agree that this measure helped them, too. Others are mystified at this, unable to link these together. You listen as the woman tries to explain her knowledge of how this will help and her admission that she doesn't truly understand why.

You move on, taking note of all you see. You record all you see in the realm of inner vision and encapsulate the experience.

The next group of drui is intent upon arguing some deeply vital point of law and procedure. Much of the discussion is on the subject of what is or is not justice. The rest is on how to persuade the people to use a strong system of laws instead of always resorting to a sharp sword blade.

There is a burst of laughter as one of these drui recalls a scathing that had been performed on a particularly rash young chieftain. These words of censure were delivered after the chieftain had demolished a carefully designed plan for an alliance that the drui had painstakingly devised. One of the drui makes a statement about the power of the word, and the others nod in agreement.

You make your way past another group of drui who are drawing marks in the ground and discussing what each means. Several others examine a set of stones and some wooden sticks carved with the runic symbol writing of the northern peoples. You watch fascinated as a pair of these drui carries on a full conversation with no words, merely the subtle movements of their fingers. You consider the advantage of having a silent language made up of signals alone, particularly if these signals are kept secret from most.

As you think about all you have seen, you begin to hear the sound of chants and magickal intonations. The sound drifts through the forest, subduing all other noises, great and small.

You turn to see the most mysterious of the drui lighting the ceremonial fires in the oak grove not far away. You can just see the flames flickering from within the center of the grove. The pale robes of these mysterious drui reflect in the firelight as they move in procession toward the same path you had traveled on the tor.

All is quiet as they move past the rest of the Wise Ones gathered in the forest. These mysterious drui carry torches to light the fires atop the tor as soon as darkness falls completely. You wonder about all you have heard of these most mysterious drui. Some call them slayers; others call them saviors. They are the Wise Ones said to speak directly to the gods. Because of this, they are given the power of life and death over the rest of the people, and over the other drui, as well.

Some say these mysterious drui come from many different realms, many walks of life in this world and the Otherworld. Others say they emerged from the land or the sky. Some say they came in from the sea. A few maintain that their origin is divine, and that they are all the same.

As the procession of mysterious drui passes by where you stand, you notice an Otherworld quality about them, which you cannot quite define. You notice also how human they are—how very, fully human, with all of the possibilities and potentials that includes. The procession of drui makes its way out of the forest and begins its climb up to the top of the tor. Some other drui follow this procession quietly, keeping a respectful distance, but staying in full view of all. Others follow in the shadows, choosing to remain unseen. The matter of the mysterious drui attracts both shadow and light, you have been told—for balance, it is said, but rarely understood.

You have had much to look at and much to consider thus far on this journey. You are ready to rest and reflect on your experience. Take a moment to find that gentle place of quiet reflection within that forest where the Wise Ones have gathered.

You catch a whiff of something delicious, and are reminded why you came down from the tor in the first place. You turn to see a small campfire set apart a comfortable distance from the others. At that campfire is an old couple, a man and a woman who seem quite familiar to you. You are startled by the sense that they have been with you all along, yet perhaps they had merely been at each group of drui you visited.

The old man laughs and beckons you to join them. The old woman offers you a cup of warm brew as you take a seat beside their fire. You notice the same Otherworld quality about these Old, Wise Ones that you saw in the mysterious drui now almost out of sight in the stone circle at the top of the tor.

Unable to contain your curiosity any longer, you insist on knowing why these two Wise Ones—who are so obviously of shared quality with the mysterious drui on the tor—are not up there, too.

The old woman dismisses your question with gentle authority in her voice. She chides you for believing that the tor is the "highest" place.

> *Away if you must, be fleet of feet.*
> *Fire, ash, and dust when you greet the elite.*
> *Gold and silver n'er rust, make your Self complete.*
> *Had you not the trust, you'd have the best seat.*

The old man puffs on his pipe and blows the smoke out slowly, as though he were sharing it with an unseen guest. He studies you intently for a moment with the eyes of a dragon, then speaks.

> *Neither riches nor position will guide you to knowing.*
> *Only with passion can knowledge keep growing.*
> *No order, nor rank, nor gilt for bestowing*
> *Can wisdom awaken, or truth start flowing.*
> *Discover your Self, your own seeds keep sowing.*
> *For the power of the drui dwells within your self-knowing.*

The old woman takes an egg from out of her apron pocket and holds it up for you to see. She speaks gently.

> *This shell is your Self now, don't you see?*
> *It protects what's within quite practically.*

Yet when it is time, when you are ready to Be,
Then the shell must be broken so you may be free.

With that said, the old woman cracks the egg into a hot pan resting on the fire. As the egg sizzles, you wonder at the meaning this has for your life. You wonder if you can release your boundaries and reach the power of your own inner wisdom.

You know that you can.

❦

Take a moment in your realm of imagination and reflect upon what you have seen and felt. Have a private talk with the Wise Ones you met on this journey. Muse within your mind about the different images of the drui and the many paths to power. Decide which ones seemed most personally powerful; these are the ones you feel most passionate about, the ones you already reflect in your daily life. These are the kinds of wisdom with which you are willing and wanting to be involved.

Perhaps you are pulled to the image of the ancient, shamanic Wise One who uses knowledge for the benefit of the family, the clan, or the tribe. Perhaps the solitary student atop the tor reflects your style. Perhaps one or more of the groups of drui attracts you most. Perhaps they all do, in their own way, because they all reflect parts of your Self. They are images of your inner wisdom. Seek within. Discover your Self as the drui.

Understand that the true nature of what is called druidic is that of experiential, experimental involvement with as many dimensions of mind, knowledge, and wisdom as you can reach. Know that there are no instant druids, just as there is no kind of automatic wisdom. A truly druidic philosophy is one that constantly grows and changes.

Druids have never really disappeared; they have simply adapted their ways to meet the times in which they are living. Wherever there is an open exchange of ideas, discoveries, and a shared atmosphere of knowing, the drui still survive.

Remember that as we study these ancient figures of myth and mystery. You may find them to be far more real and present than you had expected. Retain your magickal inner images of the drui to bring out their best aspects in your Self. Reflect on these images and see the magickal, druidic aspects of your Self and Nature.

With your newfound steed, let us now ride into the realms of Celtic philosophy and mysticism that often become elusive and difficult to track. We will begin with those most mysterious figures who represent a true blend of mythic and mundane form. These figures of mystery are the druids—the teachers, healers, magicians, bards, counselors, sacrificers, priests, judges, and scientists of the Celts.

The origin of the word "druid" is as much a matter of speculation as those who were referred to by that name. Some theorize that the word "druid" is derived from the Sanskrit meaning "to see" or "to know." The word for this in Irish is "drui," and in Welsh, "derwydd." Others suggest that "druid" arises from the same words that mean "oak," such as "dervo" in the Gaulish, "daur" in the Irish, or "derw" in the Welsh. These are considered to reflect the well-known druidic view of the oak as a sacred tree, symbolic of the strength, magick, wisdom, and Earth-connected powers of their spiritual philosophy. Further sources present a variety of root words, often from defunct languages, which equate their words for wisdom with the word "druid" in the same arcane relationship in which both tree and knowledge are equated. These correlate "druid" with words and phrases that refer to the "tree of life" in the Kabbalah and with the "tree of knowledge" in the Judeo-Christian Bible.

Because no real agreement on this matter of word origin appears to be forthcoming, I suggest a somewhat whimsical, yet applicable, meaning for the word "druid." Considering the importance of the oral tradition and the significance of the sound of words in Celtic-druidic philosophy, I suggest, with a bit of bardic boldness, that "drew-it" reveals a great deal about who the druids were and what they were about with their wizardry.

The druids represented the intelligentsia of the Celtic culture for millennia. In many ways, they were the mapmakers of both the mundane and the metaphysical. Using what must be regarded as among the first methods of scientific technique, the druids sought to study, speculate, and structure their observations of the world (or worlds) in which they lived. Because of their efforts and observations, systems of wisdom were developed to both preserve and impart knowledge. Their establishment of druidic "colleges" and their interactive relationship with the people suggest a truly balanced blend of theory and application.

Our primary sources of information regarding the nature of the druidic orders and practices are the mythic traditions and the records of classical Greco-Roman writers who sought to explain the roles of these mysterious figures. These sources show the druids as skillful bridges between the dimensions of the Otherworld and the daily routines of life. This combination is in keeping with the theories that point to a shamanic origin for druidism. This further links its inception to Indo-European Nature magick in general. More specifically, it links them to that equally mysterious figure, the Siberian shaman, symbolic ancestor of all people of mystery and wisdom.

The actual origin of the druids and their practices probably will never be known. This in itself is very much in keeping with the Celtic spiritual philosophy described earlier. The druids shifted the dimensions of their wisdom and evolved their roles in concert with the changes in Celtic culture as a whole. That ever-changing role most likely began as one of shamanic mode. The druid was the overseer of knowledge who lived close to Nature, attuned to her mysteries, and was able to "walk between the worlds" of wisdom to empower the whole of the tribe. However, the druid was not as separate from the tribe like the "classic" shaman, nor as central to it as the "medicine person" or modern physician. The druid, like the Otherworld itself, represented an overlay of mystery that was both contiguous to and interwoven with the many dimensions of life.

It is significant that the identity of the druids began to shift towards a more structured, hierarchal role as the influences of classical Greco-Roman culture grew stronger. Though some of this shift may reflect the classical writers' efforts to define the druids in terms of their own priests, it also reflects a point where a separation from Nature began to develop. Along with this separation came a role that was far more removed from the people of the tribes.

It is not known at precisely what point the druids began to divide themselves into specific hierarchal orders, but the functions of these orders are reasonably well known. This is in no small part due to the fact that Irish druidism was minimally affected by Greco-Roman influences, and thus was able to retain its position far longer than in other Celtic areas. By exploring a variety of ancient and modern writers, we can gather that the druids were divided into three or four primary categories in regard to their functions. These categories we may generally call priests, professors, physicians, and poets. We use these modern terms since they best describe the forms into which "druidism" has evolved in current times. Classical and neoclassical sources describe these categories in variable terms, such as:

- **Vates** (ovates) who interpret sacrifices, natural phenomena, and make divinations as well as diagnoses.
- **Bards** (bardoi) who were singers and poets.
- **Draoi** (druids) who observed, structured, and taught wisdom.
- **Equites** (seneschai) who devised and advised based on moral philosophies and natural laws.

The last two were sometimes seen as one category.

Once again, the definitive nature of the druids eludes us. No two sources seem to agree on exactly who or what these figures of mystery were specifically. I feel this is because their roles were relative to the requirements of their people at the various points in the evolutionary process of the Celts. Perhaps it is most useful to stress that the druids were the learned ones of the tribe who approached their roles in a sentient, scientific manner. I believe, at least to begin with, they did this without making the separations into categories such as holy or secular. These separations came later in much the same way that the old country doctors have become a variety of specialists today. The druid, like the "Renaissance Man," has been relegated to a past in which it was still possible to both obtain and retain most of the wisdom existing in the world at that time.

In this current age, which blends information, communication, technology, and consciousness, "druid" becomes more of a verb than a noun. Now "druid" can signify a special approach to whatever field we find ourselves involved in today. This, I feel, is far more in keeping with the true spirit of druidism than most of the modern forms that profess to practice according to ancient druidic traditions. These forms are generally drawn from traditions constructed during various periods of Celtic and druidic revivals. Of particular influence are those in the eighteenth century, empire-building phase of Britain. While they were quite valuable for their archival contributions, their supposedly traditional methods were far more imperialistic than empirical.

The less-positive aspects of the legacy left by the eighteenth-century constructs echo in current times when various modern "experts" on druidism claim to have an on-going, exclusive connection to this or that seat of druidic power. I think it is absurd to believe that anyone anywhere can have proprietary rights to the elemental forces of Nature from which the powers of druidic practice are derived.

There are a few modern examples of organized druidic practice that strive to meld the fragments of historic information with mythic and symbolic wisdom, to create a flexible format for a new spiritual philosophy based on these old ways. So long as these modern forms continue to evolve with the changes in human consciousness, they will reflect an essentially druidic way of knowledge. Druidism is an active part of the eternal present, continually weaving already acquired wisdom into patterns that allow future information to be included.

Druidic traditions, to whatever extent they existed, would have reflected the active consciousness of the Celts. The druidic way was—and is still—explorative, experiential, expansive, and expressive. Druidism reflects an ever-evolving relationship with whatever wisdom it is examining.

Druidism began with natural shamanic roots and branched out into many forms of knowledge. We can say that those branches are separate, but in truth they are not; they are connected to the same source from which they grew. The forms these branches take are an expression of that source, as it evolves in an interactive relationship with its environment. When we seek wisdom by reaching out from a strong, grounded sense of wonder, we are being that growing, evolving tree of knowledge. We are also being the tree of life, seeding new growth with our own development. This we do from within the center of our Self. We evolve from the supportive "trunk" of personal wisdom, which is formed from our life experiences.

The great oak, so sacred and so synonymous with the druid, has roots that reach deep into the Earth. It has a sturdy trunk that shapes itself in order to develop a harmonious relationship with its environment. This oak also has numerous far-reaching branches of many sizes and shapes. These, in turn, grew out of strong, wide-spreading limbs, which were designed to support the growth of that tree to its fullest potential.

Here is a little bardic ditty to help activate your image of this analogy:

Oak as Druid as Wisdom

Study carefully how the oak grows,
And you will know what the druid knows.
Roots in the past, both myth and prose,
Strong trunk of thine, not these or those.
Limbs that can move when the wind blows,
Branches on high, each grows and grows.
Nurture carefully how the Self grows,
And you will know what the wise oak knows.

Regardless of the differences in the way the druids are viewed, there remains a shared acknowledgement that their legacy is active in our lives today. In the mundane sense, the druids left us with a heritage of new and enhanced foundational systems, such as calendars measuring the planetary cycles, mnemonic alphabets, cypher codes, and symbolic scripts that enhance human communication as well as our connection to Nature. Their special legacy to us is an oral tradition designed to preserve and program wisdom for generations of Celts yet to be born.

It can be said that the druids were among the first to actively create an effective form of acquiring knowledge and accessing multi-dimensional realms of consciousness. The way of the druid is the way of the spiritual weaver, linking the mind of humankind with the heart of poetry and the soul of Nature. The druids were, and are still, active explorers of human and planetary consciousness. Their spiritual philosophy regarding the dimensions of life and Nature speak clearly to us in regard to the ways in which we shape the nature of our Self.

From medieval sources translated in more modern times, we are able to glean enough information to formulate a basic bardic-druidic spiritual philosophy. In this general, druidic view, we are told that the principal nature of things is in three categories: power, matter, and mode. Science is made up of three aspects, each a process and a product: life, intellect, and affection. Wisdom derives from object, mode, and benefit. Memorials or spiritual practices result from a combination of affection, distinctive sign, and reverence for the better. (See Murry Hope's *Practical Celtic Magic: A Working Guide to the Magical Heritage of the Celtic Races.* Northamptonshire, England, UK: Aquarian Press, 1987.)

These ancient definitions are still quite meaningful and relevant today. To understand them more clearly, we can update their terminology for current use (and not succumb to creating something that is merely more jargon). This is done in an effort to blend ancient mysticism with modern physical, metaphysical, and psychological science, in order to increase the applicability of these theories.

The Druidic Nature of Things

In the druidic view, the nature of things is in three categories:

Power = Force, energy, or action.

Matter = Form, manifested with energy.

Mode = Frequency, pattern, or vibrational rate of energy.

In a more personal psychological view, the nature of Self combines the principles of:

Power = Motivation (the driving force, catalyst; the why).

Matter = Manifestation (the desired form, result; the what).

Mode = Method (the distinctive pattern, style; the how).

Science, the acquisition and application of information, combines aspects of:

Life = The reflective interactive state of being aware.

Intellect = The contemplative processing of information.

Affection = The consciously chosen, experiential involvement.

Science, in personal and psychological aspects:

Life = Self-esteem, self-evolution.

Intellect = Self-evaluation, self-education.

Affection = Self-expression, self-enhancement.

Wisdom, the evolution of information into knowledge, includes:

Object = Theory, hypothesis, inspiration, idea.

Mode = Method, analysis, testing.

Benefit = Application, viability, validity.

Wisdom, as a personal psychological process, includes:

Object = Conceptualized goal, vision; the what.

Mode = Activating steps, styles, processes; the how.

Benefit = Resulting changes, both expected and realized; the why.

Memorials, a spiritual regard for life, combine:

Affection = Higher love, universal attunement, devotion.

Distinctive Sign = Intuitive guidance, shamanic connection.

Reverence for the Better = Faith, hope, trust, evolution.

Memorials, in personal, psychological terms, combine:

Affection = Positive regard for personal development, empowerment; the what.

Distinctive Sign = Realization and activation of personal power and potential; the how.

Reverence for the Better = Acceptance of personal power and potential; the why.

We can now summarize our expanded definitions into several decidedly druidic statements.

The nature of all things evolves from a catalyst force or power that manifests as matter or form, according to and reflecting specific patterns or modes.

Science is a process involving an interactive relationship with life, an activation of information through the use of intellect, and a conscious affection for the experiences chosen.

Wisdom results from the study of an idea or object of inspiration that has been analyzed and tested according to certain modes or methods. These determine the viability of the original object in regard to its potential benefit and application for the good of all.

Memorials regard the spirituality of life with a true affection for the higher love reflected in universal attunement, made known through distinctive signs emerging within realms of intuitive guidance and through shamanic connections made with reverence for the better, and faith in the positive evolution of spirit.

The nature of Self is determined by the alchemy of our personal motivations and desires. These motivations and desires give power to personal form. These forms of Self reflect our unique, distinctive patterns. It is our way of expressing who we are, as both the personal self and the Higher Self—a blended alchemy.

Memorials, personally made in regard to spirituality, derive from devotion and affection for the higher love reflected in our Selves, often encouraged by distinctive signs from our intuitive guidance; our awakened shamanic connection to Nature; and our trust, faith, and reverence for the better aspects of life.

In case you are wondering if all this weaving and reweaving with words tells you more about the wisdom of the druids, let me remind you of one essential druidic tenet: the power of the word is most important in the preservation of knowledge and the perpetuation of wisdom. The oral tradition instituted by the druids has ensured the survival of their philosophies and the continuance of their systems as nothing else could have.

It is apparent to me that the ancient druids had incredible foresight in regard to the acquisition and distribution of knowledge. In their wisdom, they clearly understood that written systems could be vulnerable to the destructive actions of others, and easily be made inaccessible to the masses.

The power of the spoken word has a harmonic effect that vibrates directly into the mind of humankind. This vibrational force can be easily transmitted through the dimensions of time and consciousness. This transmission is particularly effective and durable in poetry, stories, myths, and songs, because the words of wisdom presented in these modes create lasting images which, in turn, evoke deep responses from within the heart and spirit of humankind. Each word or collection of words has a magick melody that attunes the consciousness of humankind to a higher dimension. The words in myth, poetry, and song link entire cultures to the realms in which their collective wisdom originated and are retained. The druids were and are many things of value to us still. As composers of our Celtic tribal memories and consciousness, their music remains, ringing true throughout time.

Tuatha de Dannan:
The Tribe of Danu

Here we begin to be acquainted with those wherein whom history and mystery meet to form legend and myth. As we move ever more deeply into the tribal consciousness of the Celts, we enter a realm where history, myth, and magick become one. It is at this point that we reach beyond tribal memory into cultural collective consciousness. Here what is truly, purely Celtic shows itself distinctly. Here the Celtic pattern is free of all the overlays that were cast upon its surface. Here the influences that have sought to interweave themselves into this fine fabric and failed are no more than fragments, with no substance at all.

It is within this realm that we find the original patterns of Celtic consciousness—the archetypes of the Celt. Here we find the elemental fibers, the threads that create the weave of the Celt in pure connection to Nature. Here we find the elements of Nature in their original form—the archetypes of Nature. Here we find the elements of Nature and the elements of the Celt reflecting a shared origin, a shared consciousness, and a shared sense of sovereignty. They reflect a spiritual symbiotic relationship, a mystical connection. Here we find the elements of Nature and the elements of the Celt interwoven in an archetypal pattern. Here we find forming a mythic fabric that gives definition to the cloth from which the Celts are cut.

As we trace the pattern of this fine mythic fabric, we find the threads of Celtic history, the fibers of Celtic consciousness, and the weave of Celtic wisdom. As we step back to observe the full dimensions of this fabric, we find that it reveals a tapestry of legendary quality. On that tapestry we find the mythic figures who represent all that is purely, powerfully Celtic. We find the Tribe of Danu. They are clearly present there, these mythic ancestors of the Celts, the Tuatha de Dannan—the elemental power of the Celts.

The de Dannan are the essential key to Celtic consciousness. All sources of Celtic wisdom, lore, mythos, and magick converge these, the *aés dana*, people of the arts. They are the masters of their craft, regardless of what it may be. They are the champions—the wisest, the finest, the best of the old blood. Their origin, like that of the druid, remains shrouded in mystery, accessed only through the realms of Celtic myth and consciousness. Their origin—indeed, their very nature—may seem mysterious, yet they are the true, spiritual ancestors of the Celts.

In James Bonwick's classic work of 1894, *Irish Druids and Old Irish Religions*, he quotes a predecessor of his. "McFirbis, 200 years ago, wrote, 'Everyone who is fair-haired, revengeful, large, and every plunderer, professors of musical and entertaining performances, who are adepts of druidical and magickal arts, they are the descendants of the Tuatha de Dannans.'"

With this poetic description in mind, let's begin our own look at the de Dannan.

Reweaving the de Dannan Myths

Myths and speculations about the druids pale in comparison to those concerning the de Dannan. These speculations are quite interesting, but in the end quite immaterial. With this truth in mind, I add my own speculations about the de Dannan.

The de Dannan were Celts. They were simply too typically Celtic, too archetypally Celtic, to be anything else or anything more, if they ever once were. I believe that the de Dannan were the cutting edge of the Celtic expansion in more ways than simply geographic.

There is no doubt that the de Dannan were of a magnitude of magnificence beyond that of most other Celtic tribes. However, pioneers of any sort invariably have that star quality that often leads them to become legends, even in their own time. This is particularly effective when it is planned, and I believe the de Dannan planned their own legends. A tribe of people that makes a mass invasion of a new land on a sacred, Celtic festival date, Beltane (May 1) and immediately proceeds to burn its ships, thereby creating a "mystical" fog to conceal its numbers and weapons is a tribe of people that knows exactly what it's doing.

Anyone who has any degree of familiarity with the invasion tactics and the subjugation strategies of the Celts would certainly recognize the methods employed by this all-too-Celtic tribe. Thus, emerging from the mists, the de Dannan began their takeover of Ireland from the Fir Bolgs, a much more primitive people, possibly even aboriginal. Is this pattern beginning to sound vaguely familiar—vaguely Celtic? Remember, I said Celtic consciousness, not Celtic conscience. (Celtic conscience is just beginning to evolve.)

So, the de Dannan took Ireland at the plains of Moytura, and for a while it was theirs to rule. I'm inclined to believe that it still is, since no other tribes that followed (all of which were Keltoi) ever managed to take Ireland with such style. No other tribe managed to make such a deep, direct impression on the land, on their own conquerors, and on their descendants for several thousand years. One of the many things that can be said with any certainty about the de Dannan is that they were truly ahead of their time. They were also wise and clever enough to maintain their powers, even in the face of their eventual defeat.

It is a matter of historic record that the Celts are often more than benevolent to those they have just brutally vanquished. Therefore, it's likely that the Milesians (the Gaelic tribe who took over from the de Dannan in typical, bloody, Celtic style) would have graciously honored their once foes, now simply vanquished allies. I can't believe, though, that these conquering Milesian Celts (the Gaels) would have honored the de Dannan so well as to have allowed them to hold sway mythically, unless the de Dannan were also Celts and probably Gaelic at that. Most importantly, the Milesian Celts were sincerely in awe of the de Dannans' abilities—their arts, their crafts, their magick.

Now, as the myths would lead us to believe, that Gaelic bard par excellence, Amergin, divided Ireland into two parts. All that was above ground belonged to the conquering Celts, the Milesian tribe. All that was below the ground belonged to the vanquished Celts, the de Dannan, the tribe of Danu.

If we take this division literally, we will miss a vitally important link in the chain of Celtic existence. However, if we look a bit more closely at what these myths try to tell us, we may find that Amergin had a wisdom that far exceeded that of Solomon. (Solomon, as you may recall, solved a disputed maternity by suggesting the baby in question be divided, literally, in half. Naturally, the true mother of the baby relinquished her claim immediately to save the life of her child. Thus, the great wise King Solomon knew to whom he should grant the maternal rights.)

Amergin, as a bardic druid, would have known, even more surely than his Milesian tribe, just how significant the powers of the de Dannan were. He would have known also how elementally important it was to obtain and maintain a connection to the land his tribe had just conquered. He would have known how to divide the land and still grant the maternal rights to the tribe that held the claim and power most purely.

Remember that all of the Celts were matristic; all had the *trois matres* of Nature in their spiritual philosophy. However, perhaps only one tribe claimed descent, guardianship, or simply a more direct, mystical connection to the mother of all Celtic gods—Danu, essentially Nature herself. Remember also the divisions of the male gods of the Celts. The Lord of the Underworld is the quintessential magician, druid, tanist, wizard, and shaman. The Lord of the Underworld works in a more mysterious, subtle, underground way with the forces of Nature.

So Amergin relegated the realms of magick, the realms of the Lord of the Underworld (from whom the Celts claimed descent anyway) to the de Dannan. The realms of the mundane, the realms of the Lord of Light, the warrior king, became the realms of the Gaelic, Milesian Celt. In one wise move, mythic in quality, Amergin placed the elemental power of the lands in the hands of the very tribe that held the keys to its magick doors and the doors of the Otherworld, as well. The de Dannan knew, beyond any shadow of a doubt, how to access, awaken, and activate the powers of the elements in their native land. These powers, druidically speaking, represented the elements of Nature, the elements of Celtic nature, and the elements of self-nature. Amergin preserved the magick.

As the myths tell us, the de Dannan went to live with the Sidhe (pronounced, I believe as Shee). The Sidhe, I believe, is a description of a *devic*, elementally powerful place, a place of deep shamanic connection, a place of magick. It is most likely that the Sidhe were populated by one of several primitive and possibly aboriginal inhabitants. More than likely, these places of power had collected a variety of inhabitants throughout the ages of Ireland. Perhaps the Sidhe, like the heart of Danu, had been sanctuaries for the people and the spirits of Nature for a long time.

Remembering the importance of the *genus locorum*, the spirit of place, the de Dannan were placed in the wild, natural, elemental powerful points throughout all of Ireland. They became the people of the Sidhe—not the Sidhe, but the people of the Sidhe.

You may wonder how such a fine, fair folk as the de Dannan could have been so summarily rousted by their kind, the Milesians. It's most likely that the de Dannan had become depleted by their continuing disputes with the Fomorians, their sometime allies, sometime foes. The Fomorians have been presented as evil in opposition to the de Dannan, the Good People. This, I believe, is no more than a Celtic shadow dance. The Fomorians were most probably Celtic as well, of a more earthy strain than the de Dannan, possibly Scots, but more likely of ancient Scandinavian line.

The fact that the Fomorians figure so predominantly in the de Dannan mythology, even as the classic bad guy, speaks quite clearly of their Celtic connection to the de Dannan. After all, why would the de Dannan empower the Fomorians with all the qualities necessary to a truly worthy foe if they weren't first related somehow? On the whole, the Celts seem only really satisfied with the worthiness of their opponent when that opponent is closely related to themselves in some form or another. History has borne witness to this long enough to make it quite clear.

It's interesting to speculate that if the Milesians had arrived in Ireland before the second battle of Moytura—in which the Fomorians and the de Dannan fought themselves into mutual submission—that it may have been the Milesians who were defeated. I suppose the Fomorians would then have had another go at the de Dannan. Had the Fomorians won, which was just as possible, then it might have been that one-eyed, evil wizard Balor who divided Ireland, instead of Amergin, the foresighted bard.

However, it was time for the Gaelic Celts. The Fomorians disappeared into the myths of time, relegated to the eternal role of the de Dannan's primary enemy. The de Dannan found themselves to be the rulers of the Sidhe, those primitive, elementally powerful places in Nature, similar to the same places in Central Europe from which they had emerged.

We can view them now in one of two ways. Either the de Dannan were consigned to some state of underground arrest, or they were granted the sanctuarial privilege of returning to the elements of Nature, to the Sidhe, in order to preserve their sacred arts. I'm inclined to believe the latter. This would explain how the elemental wisdom and power of the Celts was so clearly preserved from harm until its magickal secrets were safely assumed to be nothing more than folklore or faerie tales. Then and only then would it have been the time for the de Dannan to move into the mythic realms of the Otherworld. From that Happy Plain of consciousness the de Dannan could watch with amusement as their own magickal descendents finally awakened to find the elemental gifts of power they had been willed to receive.

These mythic gifts of the de Dannan, often called the *gifts of faerie*, are the powerful elemental heritage of all the Celts. Those gifts are the keys to the realm. This realm is the one wherein history and myth, the mundane and the magick, become as one with the elements of Nature and the elements of Self. It is a purely Celtic realm, but others of Nature are welcome there, if they can find it. Those who do—Celt or otherwise—need only use the keys to open the doors to the inner realms of the Otherworld, the dimension of the "Other Wise."

Of course, this requires the will to burn your ships when you get there. No retreat, no surrender, and no defeat.

The Keys to the Realms: The Gifts of Aés Dana

The mythic keys, the sacred gifts of the Tuatha de Dannan are:

- **The sword**, from the de Dannan point at Finias,
  now Munster: fire.
- **The cauldron**, from the de Dannan point at Murias,
  now Connaught: water.
- **The stone**, from de Dannan point of power at Falias,
  now Ulster: earth.
- **The spear**, from the de Dannan point of power at Gorias,
  now Leinster: air.

There are also four elements you may access with these keys:

- **Fire**, which grants you courage, faith, strength, and,
  if it doesn't consume you, the power of protection.
- **Water**, which brings you healing, transformation, and,
  if you let it flow through you purely, the privilege of
  inner wisdom.
- **Earth**, which provides you with structure, sustenance,
  and, if you don't try to possess them, the secrets of abundance magick.
- **Air**, which supplies you with communication, focus, illumination, and, if you can perceive them, the codes to intellect.

There are some who say that the keys are activated by simply matching each of the four elements with each of the four gifts.

- The sword "matches" with fire.
- The cauldron with water.
- The stone with earth.
- The spear with air.

This is a useful point at which to begin using the keys to the realms. Still, it only seems fair to say that point is a bit off center. To fit the keys into the locks, you will have to realign a few here and there.

Fire will grant you direct access with the sword, but fire is like that. It lets you in, but can you take the heat? Fire represents sensation.

Water can be found in the cauldron, but you'll have to go through the fires that keep it warm in order to get into it. Water represents intuition.

Earth provides you with abundant welcome when you touch the stone, so long as you can hear its song in the air beside it. Earth represents connection.

Air never holds the spear, but will transmit its illuminating message, after a fashion, in the shadows where it was cast by fire. Air represents perception.

You really didn't expect the de Dannan to keep it simple, did you? If things aren't symbolically complicated enough, here's another element. This one I have added, with poetic license or bardic right, to represent the whole of the other four, as well as the whole of itself. It is the element of spirit, to which I assign the gift of the crystal.

Absolutely the crystal amplifies your experience of spirit, but only according to your intent. Also, you can make your crystal any color you favor, or all of them, as you choose. Dark and light, cloudy and clear—they are all present in spirit, as they are in your Self. Spirit represents transcendence.

The Gifts of Faerie:
A Ceremony of Personal Empowerment

 The following ceremony gives you the elemental form for personal empowerment, using the symbolic keys called the gifts of faerie.

As you learn more about the elements, both mythically and personally, this ceremonial form may be expanded to include your own symbolic images for empowerment. These images may include inner landscapes, allies or inner guides, mythic figures, images of Nature and her mysteries, deities of shared or personal design, and any other aspect (mundane or Otherworld) that deepens your elemental connection to power.

If you prefer a set, ritual form, devise your own design in detail and follow it repeatedly until the associations are made between the mythic, symbolic, and mundane self-structuring aspects. This is very much like learning by rote, but it makes the association set clearly in your mind.

If you prefer a flowing, ceremonial form, experience it as fully as you can to awaken the association.

Use movement, music, and atmosphere to ingrain the symbols and images regardless of whether you use set ritual or flowing, ceremonial form. In so doing, you will develop new pathways in the mind and uncover old ones. In time or occasionally right away, you will find that these symbols activate ancient memory codes and tribal consciousness. These will lead you to the dimension of the mind where powerful, shared symbolic images—the archetypes—are stored. This dimension may be defined as being "on the border" of what C. G. Jung called the Collective Unconscious. On this border of consciousness we can use shared and/or personal images to define that which is ultimately impossible to define completely.

Take a moment now to move your awareness to a place of private ceremony. All you need is your clear intention for positive, personal empowerment and your inner sanctuary of imagination.

For this ceremony I suggest you stand facing a mirror. This is to remind you that the elements that you are honoring are inextricably linked to the inner dimensions of your Self. Perhaps you are used to connecting with elements at specific cardinal points; for example:

Fire	South
Water	West
Earth	North
Air	East
Spirit	Above, below, within

If so, you may continue to do this as long as you do not limit your access to the internal powers these elements represent. It may be argued that these elements are part of Nature, and therefore somewhat external in the mundane sense. However, it is in their link to our inner Self that the keys to power exist. Besides, if you think that Nature is external or somehow separate from your Self, you have lost the thread to the mystical connection of the Celts.

If you are not yet comfortable working in front of a mirror, simply close your eyes and look within yourself. That's where it's all happening anyway. The following is my suggested form. Feel free to create your own form and words.

Begin with the element of fire and respectfully say:

I request the activation of the element of fire.

I request that fire activate the power of protection in my life.

I request that fire activate the power of faith, confidence, and courage within my Self, within my life.

I honor all the many forms the element of fire takes.

I respect that fire can consume as well as create power, so I request the strength of body and mind to use the element of fire in a positive, balanced manner.

Call forth personal images of your Self that fully manifest the qualities represented by the element of fire. Call forth images that you personally associate with these qualities and with the element of fire. (Do this as you become familiar with mythic and symbolic representations of fire.)

Focus your awareness on the inner experience of feeling strong, brave, protected, and confident. Pause to absorb the positively empowering aspects of fire. Note your inner images, but do not become sidetracked with them.

Now respectfully say:

I request the activation of fire for the specific purpose of (state why you need this power activated) *in my life.*

I honor that the right use of power is a sacred responsibility

I accept this responsibilty fully in my use of this element fire.

Now pause to reflect on your reasons for wanting what fire activates. Be as clear about your intentions as possible. If you're not sure, but you feel intuitively that your request does involve right use of this power, then say:

I request the activation of fire for (specific purpose) *as I feel guided to do. I have faith that my intentions are clear and that I am following the wisdom of my inner council—my Self.*

I hold myself responsible for the right use of the element, fire.

As a gesture of good faith, I request that the highest aspects of truth and light be activated within my Self to guide my use of power.

I accept that power is a sacred gift in all its aspects and elements.

56

I accept this gift of power and the responsibility it requires.

*I honor the activation of the element fire as an ancient art, the
Craft of my ancestors, and the gift of Nature.*

*I honor this heritage by using the ancient symbolic gift—the key
to the element of fire.*

*I honor the Wise Ones who brought this gift of power to me and
to all those who come before and after me.*

*I accept the sacred duty to use this symbol wisely, for I know that
its elemental power is real.*

Now focus on your inner vision, and form an image of a magick
sword—the gift of the de Dannan—symbolizing the powers of fire.
Reverently say:

*I request the use of the faerie gift that activates the elemental
powers of fire.*

I request this sword for (state your intended use). *I await the
fulfillment of my request.*

Now pause and reflect once more on the reason for your request.
This is the third time you have stated your request. It represents the
sacred triplicities found in Celtic and Christian philosophy. You may
also imagine the three requests meeting the needs for this elemental power in body, mind, and spirit.

This is an appropriate association for the present time. It also
activates the conscious (and, some say, unconscious) aspects of your
mind more deeply than a single request.

This is important. If, while you pause and reflect or even before
this, you cannot call forth the symbol associated with the element,
go back and honestly review your reasons for wanting to activate
and utilize this element. Perhaps your reasons are clear, but your
emotions are not. Remember that the right use of any power
requires an ability to be compassionately detached. Otherwise, how
could you make an objective decision? If an image doesn't form or
you can't seem to focus on the symbol, you have probably not
found that objective detachment. Think it through and try again.

Sometimes you get no real sensation of the element, such as feeling yourself "ignited" with courage or physically "fired up" in a real
sense. If this happens, you are probably too focused on the words or

the mental images. Perhaps you have become too detached from the experience.

Remember the passion in compassionate, and don't be afraid to feel power—elemental and strong—within your Self.

More often than not, the sensations and the images will come swiftly. Sometimes these will come in a rush of different sensations and images. Try to focus on the most suitable sensation. This will be the one that makes you feel "right" about your Self and your request. Focus on the symbolic gift associated with the element. Hold the image clearly and say:

> *I accept this sacred gift of faerie, and I welcome its ancient power.*
>
> *I honor its service to my life and to the greater service of the highest light.*

Now hold fast to your image for one more moment. Recall the sensations that the element created within you. Resolve to keep these activated within the expanded dimensions of your mind while you restructure the patterns in your life for which you have requested the element of fire.

Finally release the images and sensations from the "front" of your mind. Imagine these being transported to a deeper inner dimension from which they may have more effect. Respectfully say:

> *In gratitude, I dismiss any unseen guest who has helped me activate this element of fire within my Self.*
>
> *I thank the Fair Folk for their gifts, and I thank the Wise Ones for their wisdom.*

If you have used any other mythic, ancestral, historic, personal, worldly, or Otherworldly allies (also called guides, spirit keepers, et cetera), this is the time to mention them. In this way you are naming your key images with the activating power of sound—and the power of the word is well known, druidically.

Close this ceremony by saying:

> *With gratitude, I thank my Self for allowing this elemental empowerment into my life.*

Check back in this chapter to find the aspects and symbols associated with the remaining elements. Review the basic form of the ceremony and the instructions, then create your own. Hint: activate fire; attune with water; connect with earth; access air; and evoke spirit. This trains your brain to develop associations that specifically reflect the nature of each element.

This ceremony provides you with a basic format to follow while creating your own ceremonies. You can certainly amplify the experience with as many ceremonial objects, symbols, drawings, or general magick paraphernalia as you want. It is your "rite" to do so. I do advise that you not let these substitute for the symbolic imagery created within your mind. That is truly where the magick of the multi-dimensional link as self-expansion occurs.

The real power of imageries is that you can be sure you have them with you—or within you. You can use them whenever you need. After all, you can't usually whip out a sword and perform a ceremony whenever you feel the need to activate the element of fire within your Self. Imagery provides you with built-in keys to develop your personal power. After you have "trained your brain" or pro-grammed your associated keys, these imageries will shift and form with ease according to what you need. Indeed, the presence of cer-tain associated imagery emerging in your inner vision will become cues for you.

For example, perhaps you are in a conversation with someone you have just met. This person seems pleasant enough, but you notice the imagery inside your mind beginning to reflect swords or images of the element fire. Check your physical sensations. If you still feel strong and confident, this image may indicate an elemen-tal affinity between you and that person. If you find that you feel uneasy, the imagery associated with fire may indicate a need for caution or personal protection. If so, focus on the imagery you have until you have a chance to learn more about the person or the situation. These images will provide you with a dimensional lock or a smoke screen in your mind.

Another good analogy for this is jamming the frequency, as in the blocking of radio waves. Another is that of a test pattern on a television station. It is impossible to get a glimpse of what's being shown inside your mind if you've got the symbolic "test pattern" held up on your screen. It's also not possible to tune you in if you've jammed your own frequency with the static of the mundane. Take the time to consciously clear your mind. Detach and observe your own experience. This will clear the lines of inner communication, deepening your connection to the inner realms and to the realms of spiritual journeys.

The images you activate in your mind are transmitted in much the same way that radio waves and television signals are carried. They are virtually imperceptible unless you have the equipment either to send them out or pick them up. There are more people who can do this than you may realize, though few are aware of it most of the time. Most people are aware of what we call shifts in elemental power; they simply don't have a system for defining it or using it.

For example, most people would probably not pick up an image of a sword if you projected that on your screen of inner vision. However, they would know that you had seemed either guarded in your manner or even aggressive, depending on the intent with which you held your image of the sword.

Be assured that what you deliberately, cognitively restructure within your mind will reflect in you and in your life. Focused concentration on an image sets up a psycho-physical current in your brain that will change the nature of your brain "signals." Ideally, these signals make the change in your Self much easier for you to accomplish.

For now, concentrate on using your imagery on yourself, and resist playing mind games on others. It is often quite useful to train your brain with others who are fully informed and like-minded. Just remember that some of your symbols and images will be, by nature, quite private, personal keys to power. Private images are like private prayers; be certain of whom you're working with before you share them.

If, after you have worked with the symbols and elements addressed here, you want to use tangible representations along with the intangible ones in your imagery, do so according to your own design. After all, ritual and ceremonial items are nothing more or less than symbolic representations of what we hold to be sacred.

Remember, it is the message of the symbol that is sacred, not its material form. Also remember that although you may not always have your material ceremonial items, you do always have that most powerful of all tools—your mind. Ceremony is another way of making a connection to the vast dimensions of mind and imagination. Ceremony wakes up the brain and expands the mind. Use ceremony and ritual to reach new realms within the Otherworld of your mind.

When archetypal images become deeply associated, they become keys to the powers they represent. When they become true keys for you, they will unlock your own "doors of perception" and show you a whole Otherworld of dimensions to explore within your Self.

It is quite possible that the memory records of all time and evolution are locked deep within the DNA codes. Perhaps codes for the future are there, as well, and we may find that the future is now. However, most important to your personal empowerment is the use of these keys to weave a positive present for your Self. Use experiences of the past and goals for the future to weave the "now" of your life with true power.

When you are able to do this without getting buried in the past or "spaced out" in the future, you will understand why the concept of the eternal present is so important. The eternal present reminds us that what once existed has always existed in elementally the same way. What has changed is our form of expressing the energy, power, or frequency in a different form.

Be on the lookout for modern symbols and archetypal images that reflect the same elemental power as the ancient images did and do. Try to put all of your images and symbolic keys in perspective. They are experiential catalysts for your personal evolution and empowerment. They are not externally powerful, except through your use of them to change yourself. The power does not reside in an object or image. Power is within your Self, and it is activated by your relationship with it.

Working With the Archetypes

An example of working with the archetypes in a positive relationship can be seen in the following section, which I refer to as "Q and A with the Wizardry." Q and A technically refers to questions and answers, but I'm told it also works well for quality and assurance. Because this Q-and-A form of working with images raises many questions, and because there is so much confusion about what is currently called "channeling," I'll attempt to define this in as straightforward a manner as possible.

Let's start with a simple psychological technique called the Empty Chair. It's quite easy to do. You pull up an empty chair beside or in front of yourself, and imagine that someone to whom you have something to express is actually seated in it. As you become comfortable doing this, you may find it quite easy to get a clear image of how that person might look, sound, act, and react if they were actually in that chair. If you've never experienced anything like this, I suggest you first try an image of someone with whom you feel comfortable. This can be an excellent rehearsal technique for working out what you want to express, or just figuring out what it is that you really want. When you have done that, you will be far more able to express yourself and your wants.

Now let's take this another step. Suppose the person you choose to "imagickally" project into that empty chair is an historical figure. More than likely this will be someone about whom you know a certain amount. It may be someone you have studied or simply a figure who inspired you somehow. Imagine having a conversation with this figure as though he or she were right there.

You may notice that the feel of the conversation with this figure is different than a conversation with the image of an individual currently (and comfortably) in your present life. Historical persons invariably come to be historical by the near-mythic qualities of their lives and actions. In becoming historical, they have begun to be associated with that same dimension where history and myth begin to merge. As we have discussed, this dimension is particularly active within the Celtic philosophy and remains so within the mind of the modern Celt.

We love our heroic, historic, mythic, larger-than-life figures. We can't wait to relegate them to the realm of legend and symbolic status. This is often criticized by those who do not understand that it is a way to store the elemental power—the archetypal, original pattern or type that the figure represents. This keeps the legend alive and active within our minds, and accessible to use for personal inspiration and empowerment.

The next step is to work with mythic figures or deities. Once again, for the Celts, these are not so easily defined. Suffice it to say that mythic figures in Celtic philosophy are those for whom no historical evidence is required, nothing mundane is needed to preserve the power that these figures represent. They occupy the dimensions where the mythic becomes archetypal, and are therefore quite powerful.

For example, it doesn't really matter to most of us whether Arthur, Guinevere, and Camelot ever historically existed. What matters is that the mythic messages they represent stay activated within our tribal codes. That mythic message, reduced to elemental simplicity, is to not lose touch with the true sovereignty of the land. It is also a mythic message that has taught the values of chivalry and ideals for noble living for more than a thousand years in Celtic culture.

The Camelot mythos has become ingrained within our tribal codes, even surviving its many shifts in form as various invaders changed its original format to suit their needs and to reflect the changing times. For instance, the figure of Lancelot did not appear until the time of the French troubadours. Also, the detailed stories of the Round Table knights took shape as concepts of chivalry and Christianity grew stronger in Celtic culture. Images change as philosophies change and vice versa, affecting both cultural and personal codes.

When you work with a mythic figure in your empty-chair technique or just within the musings of your mind, you are using a key to unlock deeper parts of your Self and to gain access to your inner wisdom. Sometimes this is just the technique you need to get a clear, objective look at a situation in your life. It can also be an excellent way to sort out information and focus your thinking.

The more you do this and the more creative you become at animating your imagery, the more the dimensions of your mind and imagination will activate and expand.

At times, this experience becomes quite interesting, particularly when you have become comfortable using this technique.

For the following section, I used pencil and paper to record the process of communicating with the archetypal wizard and friend of dragons, the Merlin. It is interesting that Merlin's figure has survived in our codes in a number of forms. Most clearly archetypal of these is that of what Carl Jung called "the wise old man." The Merlin represents a powerful mythic pattern that blends magick with the mundane (the Merlin is reputed to have been half human, half faerie). What better way to represent the blended dimensions of the mind that result in changes that are "magick"?

The subject of this Q-and-A session was sorting out the many mythic and historic accounts of the Celts and the de Dannan. When I "invited" the Merlin to have a seat in the empty chair (my inner vision) this time, I was astounded at how quickly the information came together. I could barely write fast enough to keep up.

Please note that this technique of writing out the inner conversations is done by keying into a strong, mythic-quality archetypal figure and holding fast. This is more advisable than simply requesting that someone "from the other side" communicate with you and merely waiting with a sharpened pencil. (This form was popular at the turn of the nineteenth century. It is a small miracle that "something" from the "other side" didn't turn up more often.) There is still a great deal we don't know about working with expanded dimensions of the mind. Because of this, it is always advisable to be specific about the unseen guest you invite to sit in your empty chair.

This is an internal experience, not an external one. Remember, magick and mysticism are only truly found within your Self.

Q and A with the Wizardry

Q = Wolfe, A = the Merlin (for purposes of this experience)

Q   What about the true Celts?

A   Ah, yes, Celts. More of an elemental origin, as most natural blends are, with earlier Celts in the British Isles having more influence. Ah, access, you say—more access to "faerie folk."

Q   Faerie folk—the de Dannan?

A   The Tuatha de were already a blend. They belonged to a time of greater interdimensional choices.

Q   The Tuatha de Dannan could blend as they chose to? They could shift in life or at death, what?

A   Not death, transformation. The Tuatha de had skills of shifting dimensions, wisdom from realms you call faerie—not linear, though, spherical realms. Some were present, material, but shifted; some were not.

Q   I'm lost! The de Dannan could shift dimensions—go to other realms? But the realms, some were not material anymore? Or the de Dannan were, but then weren't? Which? The de Dannan or the realms?

A Why do you favor the false simplicity of either and or when both is a much truer concept?

Q Bad habits die hard. Can we get back to the Celts? If de Dannan were already a blend, was part of that Celt?

A The Tuatha de defined the Celts. I assume this confuses you, as well. The Tuatha de defined themselves. In so doing, they defined the Celts.

Q So the Tuatha de Dannan were not faeries—it's not accurate to call them faeries, correct? But it's not entirely accurate to say they were part Celt? Yes, I'm confused....

A It is more accurate to say that the Celts are part Tuatha de Dannan. It is more correct to say that the Tuatha de Dannan are of the faerie realm. In point of fact, rulers of that realm. They had been of that realm for a rather long time, in mortal terms.

Q That realm—which once was material, but then wasn't—was this the realm the...well...was it called Hy Brasil or Atlantis or Avalon or what?

A It still has many names. That provides a certain measure of security for its inhabitants, can't you see?

Q Yes, like the Vikings calling the greener lands Iceland and the icy lands Greenland.

A An interesting comparison. Basic, but sound. Quite expressive of the Nordic strain, I must say.

Q Hmmm...yes, Nordic faeries are not so complicated either. Anyway, why did the de Dannan live in this realm? Is this symbolic, or are we speaking in mundane terms?

A I'm surprised you would ask such an obviously linear question. Most un-shay-manic, I must say.

Q Yes, yes, I know the symbolic stuff is an important part, but, well, I just don't really know what to think about all this.

A   You may think whatever you like. It's a conscious choice. Do I smell something burning, or is it simply my imagination?

Q   (Deep breath.) Yes, me. This does fire me up. Can you please just describe this business with faeries and Celts in mortal terms?

A   How boring! But nevertheless, I shall. Just keep that Pendragon under wraps, will you. I've had quite enough of that fire already. What was the question?

Q   (Another deep breath.) The question is…the questions are….

A   One at a time, please.

Q   (Deep breath, and another) The first question is: what were the de Dannan doing in that realm with many names?

A   They were being trained. Rather like special forces. Isn't that one of your favorites?

Q   Yes. Please continue.

A   The de Dannan, as you say, were quite gifted. They found the realm most desirable. So, as was their custom, they decided to rule it.

Q   Aha! I knew they were Celts!

Λ   As I was about to say, the children of Danu were trained for the purpose of rethreading the loom of memory. They were quite apt pupils. You are correct to call them by the name *aés dana*. Many of them became druids quite naturally.

Q   Let me catch up here….

A   Please do.

Q   Next time, you be mortal. As I was about to say, the de Dannan trained in this realm and became, well, many became druids. Was this the realm from which the druids originated?

A   Let's just say it was a realm that held great attraction for the druids. It had a magnetic effect on most of them. They… uh…often collected there.

Q   More mysteries?

A   Eternally. Shall you endeavor to explain them?

Q   Yes, that's what I do.

A   It would be easier to unravel all those Celtic knots.

Q   That's next. But for now, I'm starting to get a picture.

A   The miracles of modern technology never cease to amaze me.

Q   And this picture goes like this—stop me if I'm wrong.

A   How can you be, if you're describing your own picture?

Q   I see a highly advanced tribe of people finding a place where there were other, even more advanced people. I see this resulting in…well…a high-bred vigor.

A   Well said. Who are we talking about? I fell asleep.

Q   I see the de Dannan training with some highly advanced teachers, the druids. Okay so far?

A   Did I say anything to stop you?

Q   Okay, okay. The druids came to this mysterious realm because it was…well…a kind of center for wisdom. Then the de Dannans arrived and were rewarded for their efforts by becoming the teacher's pets, so to speak. The druids trained the de Dannan so they could train the Celts—or the other Celts, the Children of Don. That's what you mean by rethreading the loom of memory, I think. But why the de Dannan? Was it more than the fact that they got there first? Couldn't it have just as easily been the later-arriving Celts?

A   The de Dannan were chosen by the druids long before. They didn't simply happen upon the realms of mystery. They were guided there, naturally. There were many druids already in positions of power who had visited the realm in question. They selected the most appropriate tribe, and the de Dannan were ready, alchemically speaking. They had the most pure line to work with. So many other tribes had become quite unsuitable—too many unwelcome influences, too much energy wasted on conquering everything in sight.

Q   Too many unwelcome influences?

A   One does tend to pick up all manner of things when one travels in foreign regions.

Q   And this realm wasn't a foreign region?

A   Not foreign to the Celts. In modern terms, you might say that it was simply reserved, not open to the general public. They were quite boisterous, you realize—most difficult to work with at times. Still are, I believe. Besides, that particular realm was already filled to its capacity. That capacity, I might add, was swiftly being reduced by quite natural causes.

Q   Ah! I see what you're driving at. This realm was the mysterious sinking island, the lost civilization, right? Was this Atlantis?

A   It was certainly in the Atlantic at one time, perhaps it still is, more or less, according to what you believe.

Q   Well, what I believe is that Atlantis or that same island by any other name was real and probably a lot less mysterious than everyone wants to make it now. This being the case, how did the de Dannan choose Ireland?

A   Let's say they were in the neighborhood, anyway.

Q   All right. But why do these stories about misuse of sacred crystals and twelve mysterious beings leaving Atlantis persist in occult circles? Why have so many spiritual gurus picked up that message on the hot line, so to speak?

A   The crystals are symbols. You're quite fond of symbols, are you not? Crystals and symbols have one rather interesting property in common. They provide a means of amplification equally well for whomsoever should choose to work with them.

Q   Meaning...?

A   Meaning the wise ones become wiser, and the stupid ones become spiritual gurus.

Q   Whoops! I wonder where that puts me?

A   That remains to be seen. Life is its own test. You chose to take it.

Q   I think I'd better go back to school; it's much safer there. Life
     is hell.

A   Life is not hell, lass. Life is school.

I suggest that you experiment with this Q-and-A form for yourself.
Try using an image of the wizard you met in the forest, the
shamanic wise one in the cave, the Old, Wise Ones of the drui, and
of course, your image of the Merlin.

Note which of these produce the most richly active and experiential imageries for you. Note also how each of these image types
relates to you in different manners. This will give you clues as to
your inner processes, strengths, and needs. For example, the Merlin
in the previous Q and A was quite effective because of my own
affinity for the brain-storming strength of air.

A special word of thanks goes here to Kara Starr, author of The
Camelot Adventure: Merlin's Journal of Time, *for her friendship
and encouragement, and for her help in showing me new pathways to
the wizardry. She is a gift to Celtic wisdom and a true Lady of Avalon.*

The Elements:
Reflective Musings

In this chapter, we begin by musing on the nature of the elements, and learning to breathe life into our personal connections with them. As always, note your personal reactions. They will tell you the nature of the relationship you already have with each element. They will also tell you what each element can do to establish a stronger relationship with your Self and with your personal power.

Fire: Sensation

Fire is the element of strength. It is the force of faith and the power of protection.

Fire leads us to purification of our Self and of Nature. It is the inescapable force that draws us into personal and planetary evolution.

Fire activates the life forces. It is the rhythm, the sensation, and the heat of personal power.

Fire creates the spiritual warrior in service to the highest light of truth. It is the force that brings us to the true purposes of our lives.

Fire clears the path that begins and ends with the Self. It consumes all our obstacles to faith and trust.

Fire bestows courage through trials of strength and faith. It reduces all deadwood to ashes, and strengthens the essential nature of our Self. Fire strengthens Nature and self-nature.

Fire is the catalyst of the upward spiral. It is what empowers battles for truth and the preservation of natural balance.

Fire gives us strength and courage to fight for the preservation of quality in life. Fire holds the line.

Fire is the element of the guardians, the protectors of truth and light. It is the energy of J. R. R. Tolkien's Gandalf who declares, "I am a servant of the secret fire."

Fire inspires us to connect with others in mundane, worldly ways as well as in draconian, Otherworldly ways. It gives us the need to offer and accept the power of touch.

Fire enables us to charge and recharge our energies through physical sensations and experiences. It is the element of physical challenges and sexual energies.

Fire drives the physical body, and directs within the etheric or metaphysical bodies through the physical. It is the alchemy of physical and metaphysical touch, exchanged purely, which connects us to the sacred fires of spirit.

Fire may be vicariously conceptualized initially, but must be personally experienced ultimately. It is the private catalyst of our self-creation.

Fire is the eternal force, melding the internal with the external of our lives. It is the creative force that produces and reproduces the Self eternally interacting with others, as shadows or as allies.

Fire provides the light with which we may determine the difference between an ally and a shadow, both in relationship to ourselves and to others. It sanctifies our relationships with others and strengthens our path to Self. It purifies or consumes our relationships with others and with our Self.

Fire gives birth and rebirth to us, like the phoenix arising from the ashes of self-transformation. It gives us the power to change our lives.

Fire sends our life force forth from the childhood womb of warmth, protection, and security. It transforms our birth gifts of power into active manifestations of personal faith and courage throughout our lives.

Fire forges us as living swords of power in service to the highest light. It keeps the creation fires of our being alive and energizes the alchemy that is our essential, personal Self. Fire gives us the continuing courage to become and to be our Selves, despite our own attempts or those of others to change our essential nature. Fire is the element with which we "do our own thing."

Fire initially provides us with the energies of rebellion, then refines it into a revolutionary spirit. It hones our blade through the positive expressions of faith, courage, and strength.

Fire is the double-edged sword, directly purifying and protecting all that is positive. Fire consumes that which attempts to use its powers negatively. It is the tip of the blade and balance of the hilt.

Fire requires a purity of purpose and of heart from its warriors. It is the purest Self, but not the purist.

Fire warriors accept themselves as natural, human beings. It brings us the humor with which to honor our imperfections and the lessons they teach.

Fire shows us our strengths by revealing our vulnerabilities. It guides us as we crawl, trips us when we try to run away, and supports us as we stand, empowered by the acceptance of our sacred strength.

Fire encourages us to restructure our lives toward a clearer, purer purpose. It often painfully provides us with the lessons of our lives in order to give us the qualities of humility, compassion, and patience. Without these experiences, fire becomes an element that might be far too ruthless and rash. Fire transforms rage into reason through the purification of release and renewal.

Fire forces us to accept that which is the essential power of our life force. It forces us into the full realization of pure power far beyond the range of our senses.

Fire brings us awareness of that which is beyond our ken. It personalizes our connection to the source of all life forces by thrusting us into situations where we must reach beyond ourselves in order to survive and grow.

Fire teaches us how to ask for help and how to accept help when it is given. It teaches us how to offer help and how to provide help with purity of purpose.

Fire provides us with our first full physical experience of that which we call "God." It is force. It is action. It is strength. It is creation. Fire makes us feel godlike, cocky, and grandiose, then it brings us to our knees with compassion and self-control. Fire makes us clear in our self-confidence.

Fire is the procreating force for personal truth, the protection force for personal development, and the preservation force for our personal power.

Fire gives us the inspiration to express truth, even in the most repressive circumstances. It protects our inherent spirit and guards our essential Self. It is fire that enables us to hold on, even (and especially) when we seem to stand alone. Fire is the faith that assures us that we are never alone, never separate from the source of all life.

Fire creates and consumes. It is the power of life, the kiss of life, the heat, the energy, the force of life. Fire is the celebration of life in all its many transformations. Fire is birth that brings us the power of personal rebirth, and regeneration.

Fire is the gift of full self-acceptance received when the journey of self-challenge has reached full circle. Fire is the gift that inspires the next phase of the journey of self-transformation.

Fire is the passion of motivation.
—Stardragon

Fire: Basic Breathing Exercise

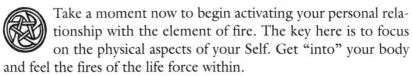 Take a moment now to begin activating your personal relationship with the element of fire. The key here is to focus on the physical aspects of your Self. Get "into" your body and feel the fires of the life force within.

Breathe deeply, deliberately energizing your body, mind, and spirit with each breath. Inhale slowly, purposefully, and hold each breath for a few moments. Exhale slowly, deliberately releasing stress and tension from your body and mind.

Repeat these breaths several times, energizing your Self, body, mind, and spirit, with each breath.

Breathe again and shift your focus to the physical sensations of your body. As you inhale, flex and tighten your muscles. Feel the strength of your body increase as your muscles are activated. Now breathe only through your mouth and feel the activation increase.

Hold your breath and tighten your muscles a bit more. Feel yourself physically strong and powerful. Now release your breath slowly and relax your muscles gently. Repeat this process several times until your body feels activated, poised, and strong. Notice that your mind has also become both alert and relaxed in concert with your body.

Breathe naturally now and shift your focus inward. Reach inside yourself to find that place of strength where body and mind are in balanced accord.

Focus on the rhythm of your breath. Keep it steady and strong. Feel the power of the life force moving throughout your body. Feel the heat of physical activity. Feel the fires of life within your Self.

Fire is the most physical and primal element. Fire makes you want to dance, get physical, touch and be touched.

It is the fire of your Self that brings you strength and willpower to activate, with pride, the full potential of your life. Honor your personal strength and celebrate your inner fire.

Use this fire exercise for increased physical energy and personal confidence. Activate the fire within and empower your Self. Honor your physical body for its many gifts. Ignite faith in your Self and celebrate your strengths. Feel strong. Feel proud. Feel the fire within.

Honor the life force and strengthen your connection to its power. Know yourself physically, and empower your life with pride in your body.

Activate the gifts your body brings you. Move with increased body awareness and honor your physical prowess. Accept your physical strengths with true pride and heartfelt gratitude.

Focus on the positive and find personal empowerment. Honor your capabilities and catalyze your potential for power. Activate your personal power and operate at full capacity. Feel proud of yourself. Get into your body. Get physical. Activate your life force.

Fire up and get fully into your life. Become strong and stay strong. Be an active participant in your life—in all life.

Water: Intuition

Water is the element of emotion. It is the power of inner knowing and the sacred force of self-healing.

Water is the element of intuition. It is the inner teacher who instructs subtly by shaking our emotional equilibrium. Water is the element we use when we finally learn to honor how we feel inside.

Water is the element with which we measure the ebb and flow in the tidal patterns of our personal lives. It is the element through which we express the flowing changes of our emotions.

Water is the element of initiation. It carries us through the transformations of our lives like a ship through a system of locks and canals. It is the element upon which we must wait as we make our way through the life series of self-transformational gates. Water is self-initiating.

Water is the element of the personal discovery. It is the lure of emotional attachment. It sends us seeking ever more deeply into the untold fathoms of our personal emotions. It knows how we really feel, despite our attempts to conceal this, even (and especially) from ourselves.

Water tempts us with a little taste from the Grail, then requires that we search within ourselves for the rest. Water is the eternal Grail of life.

Water will suddenly shower us with an outburst of cleansing emotions or the replenishing power of self-nurturance.

Water can leave us feeling bloated and dependent. It can dry us out and create a thirst for new adventures in self-exploration.

Water is the element on which we travel into our Selves. It seeks that fine, private place within where true self-healing can occur.

Water is the element of healing counsel. It is the inner priest, sending whispers of advice across the surface of our feelings. It is the inner priestess brewing the alchemy of our emotions deep within the cauldron of our being.

Water is the element of emotional release. It is the element that causes the cauldron to boil over when we do not pay attention to its needs or our own. It is the element that sends tidal waves across the sea of our emotions. Water seems to take us by surprise until we realize, with a shock, that we had felt it coming on all along.

Water provides us with an internal barometer, a temperature gauge, and a measuring cup. It will teach us, by example, time and time again. It will do this until we tire of the erratic patterns of floods and droughts in our lives.

Water is the element with which we finally learn to measure and maintain our emotions.

Water is the cup that we learn to fill gently to the brim, to sip from slowly as it foams to the top, to carry carefully with measured step to a place where we may enjoy its contents at our leisure, and to receive its nurturance in our full acceptance of its power.

Water is the element of receptivity. It makes us aware of our inner flow of feelings, needs, and fears. Water is the essential element of our survival. It is the element we must learn to live with harmoniously.

Water insists that we learn when to "go with the flow," when to harness its forces, when to ride on its power, and when to simply float on its surface.

Water shows us the mysteries of our inner currents. It remains submerged, invisible, until we allow it to carry us into the depths of oceanic consciousness.

Water is the pathway element of the realms we call subconscious. Water carries us into the mysteries of its depths, then casts us forth into quiet lagoons of peaceful pleasure with gentle waves of feeling flowing softly around our inner Self.

Water sends messages from the epicenter of our emotions. It is the eternal wave, sweeping back and forth. It is the never-ending ripple spreading across the surface of our consciousness.

Water reaches into the realms of planetary consciousness. It allows us to feel the planet weeping. It gives us the resolve to heal, to clear, to purify and nurture ourselves first, and thereby, purify and nurture the planet. Water shows us how to cleanse and to refresh.

Water is the eternal fountain. It is the sacred spring bubbling forth, ever clear, contaminated only by our callow lack of self-care.

Water is the element of eternal hope. It is the hope that springs eternal from the source of all healing.

Water comes to us purely with its mystical powers. It heals all wounds with the alchemy of emotional self-acceptance. Water carries us to the inner mother, nurturer of our nature and of Nature.

Water is the element of the womb. It is the element of our gestation. It is the medium of our emotional rebirth. It supports us as we develop a true awareness of our Selves. It allows us to form attachments to our feelings, and receive the nourishment of inner knowing.

Water is the element of unconditional love, of positive self-regard, and of pure emotional understanding.

Water sweeps us out from inside ourselves. It forces us to face our personal realities, to reveal our inner realms of being, if only to ourselves. Water is the element of naked truth. It is the voice declaring that the emperor is wearing no clothes.

Water rocks us to sleep with a lyrical lullaby. It sounds the alarm insistently when we succumb to slumbering for too long. It is the snooze alarm, ever ready, ever alert to signal us at appropriate times.

Water is the vessel that carries us to mystic realms of inner magick. It is the magick element of personal ritual, retained in the mundane within our emotional bodies.

Water is the element of memories that sustain and nostalgia that nurtures. It is a pool of sentimentality that remains clear so long as we do not wade in it too long.

Water is the element of dreams. It is the power of the personal, inner journey. It is the force, the insistent flow that compels us to search for the magick within ourselves.

Water is guidance from within. It transforms the magickal spirit guide into a mundane emotion for ease of transportation.

Water is the shape shifter that reflects our inner feelings onto our outer form.

Water is the mist, the fog, the storm that leads us to the place where we may meet our Selves.

Water is the element of reunion and clear renewal.
—Stardragon

Water: Basic Breathing Exercise

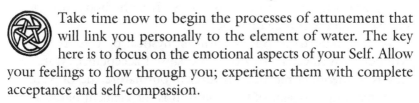 Take time now to begin the processes of attunement that will link you personally to the element of water. The key here is to focus on the emotional aspects of your Self. Allow your feelings to flow through you; experience them with complete acceptance and self-compassion.

Breathe slowly and deeply, in and out through your nose. Let each breath bring cleansing, clearing energy into your total being. Let each breath bring deep, inner healing. Feel your breath bring you soothing, centering energy. Feel peace entering your emotions.

Inhale and feel the healing flow infusing your entire being. Hold your breath gently. Savor the soothing calm and inner quiet. Exhale slowly and feel yourself detach from daily tensions.

Pause for a moment before you inhale again. Reflect on your increased state of relaxation. Repeat this process until you feel a sense of inner peace and quiet detachment.

Breathe naturally now and become the quiet observer of your own inner processes. Become familiar with your feelings. Experience the flow of your emotions as naturally as you experience the flow of your breath.

Consider the state of your emotions at this moment. Reflect on what you are feeling deep within yourself. Reach beyond the daily expectations and experience the reality within yourself.

Breathe deeply and release any thoughts and distractions.

Find that quiet place deep inside yourself and observe your emotions with calm acceptance.

Perhaps you feel anticipation or even impatience. These are no more or less than obstacles placed upon you by the avoidance of your deepest emotions. Perhaps you are allowing your Self to escape into expectations or even illusions. These are mental processes that both protect and prevent you from reaching into your deepest inner flow. These processes are needed at times. At other times they can trip you up on your journeys inward.

Breathe again and detach from your expectations. Watch as you reach within to connect with the flow of your inner being. Feel compassion for all your emotional frailties. Observe your Self with loving acceptance. Watch yourself as you observe yourself.

Feel your awareness flow outward from deep within yourself. Expand your awareness until it encompasses the whole of your being.

Now, with detached observation, ask yourself these questions.

How am I really feeling about myself?

How are my emotions flowing through me?

Do I feel needy? Is there an emotional thirst within myself?

Can I accept my emotional needs without self-judgment
and personal criticism?

Can I allow myself the all-too-human fragility of having
emotional needs?

Can I allow myself the privilege of meeting those needs?
Can I allow myself the transformative gifts of self-healing?

Can I begin by acknowledging my right to quench my
emotional thirsts?

Can I accept my emotions as healing indicators of my needs?
Can I honor these emotions for bringing me into full
awareness and compassionate attunement with the flow
of my true feelings?

Can I learn to let my emotional processes move through me
with a natural pattern of ebb and flow?

When my emotions are low, can I maintain my connection to
self-healing and trust the tidal patterns of transformation?

Can I trust that the tide will turn? When I am feeling
emotionally high, can I remember—with compassionate
acceptance—the times when I felt low, frail, and needy?

Can I accept that the ebb will naturally follow the flow?
Furthermore, can I learn to let the flow of my emotions
serve me rather than subjugate me?

Can I honestly recognize any responsibility for self-attunement, and accept the authority I have over the emotional
processes of my life?

Can I become like the receptive moon, gently guiding the
emotional tides within my life?

Breathe in and receive from the transformative, healing flow of
life. Breathe out and release any obstacles to complete emotional
attunement.

Know that there is but one flowing river of life and healing, of
which you are an integral part. Know the flow of your life in its
purest and most perfect form.

Learn to trust your inner flow. Learn to trust the flow of life.
Lovingly keep it clear and running free.

Earth: Connection

Earth is the element of manifestation. It is the power of practical wisdom and the structure that sustains our growth.

Earth connects us to the organized pattern of the mundane world. It is the reality of everyday existence. It is the routines and rituals that make us real. Earth is the element of reality.

Earth makes the simple profound. It is the profound truth of necessity. It is the simplicity of doing what must be done. Earth is the element of the everyday hero, the hunter, the chieftain, and the clan mother.

Earth is the element of abiding patience. It is making do with what you have while you work towards what is yet to come.

Earth is the element of abundance. It is the power of prosperity that persists in balance with the cycles of Self and of society. It is the element that provides, so long as provisions are made for it.

Earth teaches us how to care for ourselves. It is a budget. It teaches us about self-accountability. It is the element of responsibility. Earth is the adult we thought we wanted to become when we were younger, yet resist as we grow older.

Earth is the establishment we rebelled against in our youth. It is the foundation from which we sprang full force into life without casting even a brief backward glance.

Earth is the element to which we return when we realize how important our connection to home and family can be. It is the element with which we define our home, our family, our planet, our Selves. It is the element with which we may create a new foundation for ourselves and for the family of humankind.

Earth gets things done. It is the power of persistence and the force of form and function.

Earth is the manifestor, plain and simple—or intricate and complex. It is the material force of changes and creation. It is the outcome of all efforts, be they elaborately contrived or simply efficient. It is effective while remaining completely unaffected.

Earth is the element of gray flannel suits and sturdy shoes. It reminds us that all our rituals and regalia are so much stuff and nonsense, required only by our need for the superficial sense of security they provide.

Earth is the element of self-recognition. It calls us to task and sometimes to the carpet. It is the element of a British school head-mistress, a mother superior, and a no-nonsense nanny.

Earth encourages us to achieve. It requires us to behave to the best of our abilities functionally, socially, and with humane wis-dom. It shows us the sacred duties inherent in being human in its fullest potential.

Earth is the element we often fail to appreciate for its true value at first, but it forgives us when we realize its value and return to honor its influence in our lives. It welcomes us as prodigal children who seek the ancient secrets of sustaining life for ourselves, for our families, for our societies, for the family of humanity, and for the planet we share.

Earth is the element of sacred choice that comes with the accep-tance of personal, spiritual destiny. It is the full understanding of the forms we have chosen for our lives and for the life of our planet.

Earth is the element with which we assume authority and respon-sibility in our own lives, and in so doing, become the creators of our own destiny.

Earth is the clockworks of all forms of spirituality. It is the cog that keeps the wheel of true spirituality turning ever toward the light. This remains true even when that wheel seems most threat-ened by the corrosive rusts of rules and dogmas that have been externally created.

Earth is the element by which we regain our connection to nat-ural spiritual wisdom. It is the revealed truth that comes to us unmasked, as we face our lives directly, head on, for what they truly are.

Earth teaches us the ancient rites of power, the secret ceremonies that connect us to the real inner workings of what we call magick.

Earth is the element of celebration, ceremony, and ritual tradi-tions. It is the cornerstone of our traditions, and encourages us to build upon its foundations to ensure our own growth. It is the cor-nucopia, the horn of plenty. It is the feast table heavily laden with the fruits of our labors. Earth is the harvest of plenty. It is that which we share and that which we store for future growth.

Earth teases us with glitzy gifts and lulls us with luxurious indul-gences. It challenges us to retain our honor in the midst of tantaliz-ing temptations. It tests our abilities to deal with access to excess.

Earth is the element with which we learn the deep wisdom of moderation in all things.

Earth places our indulgences on a budget and ourselves on a schedule. It is the bountiful element that insists that we find the true sources of wealth and power.

Earth is the element of rulership. It teaches us to structure the mastery of our own game. It teaches us how to play effortlessly by first requiring diligence, skills, and extensive practice. It shows us all the moves, yet refuses to make them for us. It is the element of the coach, the professor, the boss, the mentor.

Earth expects our best performance and provides us with the opportunities to show our stuff. It is the energy of those special moments when we know that what we're working for is truly worthwhile.

Earth is humble gratitude. It is the grace of accepting the experiences of our lives as part of a greater pattern.

Earth is the loom on which we weave the fabric of our existence. It is the material fibers, the mundane forms that the threads of our lives take individually and as part of a greater weave.

Earth is the element with which we select and structure our personal life patterns. It encourages us to select the strongest, most practical fibers, and to select from the traditional patterns. It also sends us threads of gold and silver with no practical uses whatsoever.

Earth teaches us to relax and enjoy our lives. It shows us how to make that which is routine become ceremonial rituals of honor. Earth is Zen.

Earth is the element of simplicity that forms the core of all our structures. It is the glue that holds it all together when the pieces don't quite seem to fit. Earth makes the ends meet.

Earth is the center element of our existence. It is our personal force field of gravity that holds us fast to the planet. It keeps our feet planted firmly on the ground. When our world seems topsy-turvy, earth turns it right-side-up again.

Earth is the element of magnetic force. It roots us to the planet in sacred, shamanic connection to its deepest, abiding powers.

Earth is the inner compass. It always remembers the way home.

Earth is the element of endurance. It sustains us so long as we do not strain its material limitations. It keeps us resupplied, so long as we carefully structure the distribution of its abundant energies.

Earth is the real element of recycling, regardless of the material we use or the forms we may choose to take in the process.

Earth allocates and abides. It is the ancient keystone of power.

Earth is the element of satisfaction in a job well done.

Earth is your home away from home.
Please behave accordingly.
—Stardragon

Earth: Basic Breathing Exercise

Take some time now to begin programming your personal connection to the element of earth. The key here is to focus on the managerial, organizational, and structural aspects of your Self. Examine the patterns of your life logically, with an eye toward determining what is and is not manifesting effectively in the all-too-personal experience that is your life.

Breathe in deeply through your nose. Fill your lungs completely. Expand your chest and diaphragm consciously. Breathe in until you reach your full capacity to receive this essential nurturance.

When you have inhaled fully, pause very briefly and consider your ability to structure the simple patterns of your breathing. Consider your ability to similarly structure the patterns of your life.

Now exhale fully through your mouth, consciously expelling any self-limitations or negative expectations that may prevent you from effectively determining the patterns of your life.

Repeat this process several times until you begin to feel grounded and self-aware. Focus on the quiet power of positive, centered self-awareness. Notice how effectively you can begin to restructure your sense of Self, simply by consciously managing the way you breathe.

Begin another pattern of measured breathing. Inhale to the count of four. Hold your breath for four counts. Exhale to the count of four. Pause for four counts before you inhale again.

Focus on measuring, managing, and maintaining a steady pace with your breath. Experiment with a measure of four counts for a few breaths, then shift to a higher number. Try several different measured counts and determine which pattern is most effective for you. Make certain that the measure you choose suits your natural pace. Choose the measured pace that neither artificially strains nor superficially activates your natural breathing pattern.

When you have determined the measure of your breathing, continue at that pace until it becomes a natural pattern for you. When it does, you may stop counting. If you should lose focus, simply resume the count until you reconnect with the pattern.

Know that in doing this simple breathing exercise, you have truly begun to take the measure of your Self and the patterns in your life.

Now breathe naturally. Don't be surprised to find that your breathing pattern has shifted to the one you have chosen for yourself. Begin to trust your innate abilities to measure and manage what is truly effective for your Self.

Consider now, how simple it seemed to change your breathing pattern, but how complex the prospect of changing your life appears to be. Yet, is it so complex?

Is it merely a matter of measuring, experimenting with, establishing, and finally managing the patterns you have determined to be most effective for your Self?

Consider that the patterns of your life can be measured with the same processes as those used in determining the simple structures of your breathing. For example, if your life patterns are hectic, fast-paced, and seemingly out of control at times, the result will be like having a constant pattern of shallow breathing. If you are hyperventilating on life, you may well find yourself stressed and disorganized most of the time. This pattern makes you a slave to external structures while your internal processes strive to keep up the pace.

If this is happening in your life, stop. Examine your patterns. Consider first if the pace and the pattern of your life are of your own choosing. Take the measure of your life, honestly and logically. Determine which patterns are imposed upon you from external sources and which are self-imposed (or self-inflicted).

Make an honest assessment of what you have to do, what you don't have to do, and of what you have consciously chosen to do, regardless of whether it is required or not.

Now reach a little further within to take a deeper measure of your personal life patterns. In so doing, realistically determine what it is you are striving for. Reexamine your life patterns in the clear light of personal truth and choice. Ask yourself what it is that you truly want from your life, from yourself.

If you are fairly clear on what you really want, then you can effectively determine whether or not your life patterns are structuring your success. If you are uncertain about what you ultimately want, then you must ask yourself who or what is actually determining and managing the patterns of your life for you and why.

These are hard questions, but necessary ones if you want to take more power over the patterns in your life. Know that you do have the ability to choose far more in matters of your life patterns. The first step—and the last—is taking your personal measure.

When changing your life structures seems to be impossibly complex, remember the simple pattern of measured breathing.

Remember:

> You determine how much you can take in or receive.
>
> You determine how much you can hold onto and for how long.
>
> You determine how much you can let go of or release.
>
> You determine how long you can wait before you begin again.
>
> Most importantly, you determine what is the natural pace for your Self.

Air: Perception

Air is the element of communication. It is the power of perception and the medium of mental expansion.

Air is the element of inspiration. It is the creative force of the intellect expressing the mind of humankind.

Air is the element of focus in the midst of chaos. It is the sharpened awareness of clear thought and the sure strength of concentration.

Air is the element of illumination. It is the means by which we may receive and transmit messages of enlightenment. Air is the sacred frequency of the gods, clear of the static that is the mundane world.

Air is the element of the Muse and the sacred power of the bards. It is the element that allows us to communicate with all the inspirational dimensions of our Self, with all the universally inspiring dimensions of the Self.

Air is the element of evolution as it relates to the transformation of human intelligence. It is the means of communication. It is the Morse Code of DNA, which directs the development of the mind of humankind. Air is the genetic runway of "airport Leary."

Air is the upwardly spiraling current of mind and brain potential, fully realized anew with each original thought as it occurs in our own mind, echoing in the mindfulness of the All.

Air is the element of consciousness. It is the receptive flexibility of awareness. It is the vehicle of a caring conscience expressed in the positive thoughts, words, and deeds of our lives.

Air is the element of imagination. It is the magick realm of inner space. It allows us to ride the dragons of our fantasies and create our personal universes in a manageable form.

Air powers our personal flights into fantasy, fiction, fact, and form. It freely grants us the gift of wings. It is also the element by which we learn to fly, ever higher, ever more freely.

Air is the element on which we may soar into spirit. It is the pathway to the many spheres of conscious mind, the many dimensions of universal intelligence.

Air is the grand planner, the architect of our self-design. Air is the element with which we redesign our lives.

Air is the element of clear expression. It is the force of clarity in the moments of pure, personal truth.

Air gives us the ability to think. It is the sacred gift that both plagues and empowers us with possibility.

Air carries the blessed curse of unlimited potential. It is a pimp, a pusher, a priest demanding sacrifices to experience divine inspiration in its many forms.

Air gives us the power of choice. It is the element of discrimination, which is the staff of truth and the magick wand of choice.

Air allows us the luxury of being able to think before we speak, before we act, before we acquiesce.

Air allows us to experience dissonance in the subtle seduction of homogeneous harmony. It is the bloodhound of personal discernment that picks out our unique scent and style. It reminds us of our unique powers of individuality.

Air is the element of personal liberty, untouched and sacred, impervious to the many influences that constantly urge us to change our minds, more often than not in accordance with the thoughts of someone else.

Air is the inalienable right of free-mind in humankind. It empowers freedom of expression. It is freedom of choice unbound, unlimited, unpatentable, and unimpeachable.

Air is the element with which we may open or close our minds as we choose to do so.

Air gives us the joy of personal inspiration and the creativity of personal expression.

Air is the element of humor. It is the bardic jest, the spear point of satire, the crystalline clarity of comedy. It is the element of laughter. It dispels the lethargy of our lives and prevents us from languishing in self-despair.

Air is the element of music, from the hectic harmonics of the mundane to the celestial tones of the spirit, the divine. It encourages us to make our own kind of music and sing our own special song.

Air is the element through which we hear that different drummer. It is also the element with which we learn to keep time to the chorus and keep in step with the band.

Air is the element that reaches into the cracks of our mindsets and allows the true light of illumination to be perceived. It is also the mental caulking that keeps us snug and cozy in our stagnant complacencies.

Air is the winds of change against which no self-imposed artificial structures can stand.

Air is the wizard of Oz, the master of illusions, and the mesmerizing arts of mind control. It is the element with which we apprentice ourselves to the magickal craft of personal recreation.

Air is the great equalizer. It creates the same potential in the prince as it does in the pauper. It gives us perfect and equal brain capacities. It gives us equal access to the operational manuals for our lives. It also shows us clearly that these operational manuals are self-created and self-taught.

Air gives us all that we need in order to take flight and to maintain a steady course even during the stormy times of self-transformation.

Air allows us the power to create a new image for ourselves. It allows us to stay focused on that clear, new self-image, and to use that as a homing beacon of light, even in the darkest hours of confusion and distraction.

Air is the element of the mantra. It is the wing and the prayer on which we must sometimes make our way home. It is the tune we whistle in the dark and the chorus we chant in the celebration of the light.

Air is the voice of Nature—heard, recorded, and expressed through the mind of humankind. It is the universal language.

Air is the profound power of positive thought. It is the element of expansion into realms as yet unknown.

Air is the element of multidimensional linking. It is the channel of choice and the communication medium of clarity. It is the element of radio free-mind that sends its messages out into the spheres of the universal Self.

Air enables us to link all times into an eternal present. It is the element by which we connect our personal experience to the universal, mythic experience.

Air is the element of the myth maker, the Muse singer, the magickal child, and the mystical sage. It is the element that carries them—all in one—into the realms of spirit.

> *Air is that upon which we may coast,*
> *fly, or dance, Tippy-toes.*

> —Stardragon
> (post-humous quote)

Air: Basic Breathing Exercise

 Take the time to begin developing your personal ability to access the element of air. The key here is to focus on the mental aspects of your Self. Sharpen your senses. Remind yourself that you are a rational, creative, thinking individual.

Right now, I want you to solve a problem with thought. Make a decision, quickly, about an issue. This issue can be as complex as how to instantly resolve the tensions in the Middle East or as seemingly simple as finding a word to rhyme with purple. It can also be an issue in your life that needs a decision. Whatever the issue, give it all you've got right now.

Concentrate fully. Focus on this issue exclusively. Get those thinking powers turned on. Use that magnificent bit of gray matter that is your brain. Let nothing distract your thought processes. Quickly now, the clock is running. Think about it. Think very hard.

While you're grinding those mental gears, let me ask you: are you holding your breath?

Uh huh, just as I thought. Let's try something else.

I want you to place your hands close together. Make them very close with each fingertip of one hand almost, but not quite, touching its mate on the other hand.

Concentrate on this position carefully. It doesn't count if you actually touch fingertips. If you do, you'll have to start over, and there's only a little time. Best do it the right way and right away.

Focus now. Are you doing it properly? Steady now. It's not as simple as it seems.

It will be much easier if you breathe into it. You were breathing just then, weren't you?

So what if you were holding your breath the first time? So what if you held your breath both times?

So what if you had to make a series of intense decisions in a hurry? So what if you had to think fast for an extended period of time?

So what if you had to concentrate fully on each move you made each time you made one?

So what if you had to hold your focus sharply for several very studied motions or actions?

What do you think happens when you continue to hold your breath? What do you think causes more mental exhaustion and creative depletion than almost any other factor?

It's self-inflicted mental suffocation.

More often than not, when we have to think fast or concentrate fully, we unconsciously hold our breath while we're doing so. This may give us a false sense of having put all we have into what we are thinking or doing, but this is an illusion.

Instead, we actually take away from what we have to work with—a fully focused, energized mind. It's a bit like setting up a complex computer program that we have the capacity to complete, then unplugging the machine before it has finished processing the problem. Perhaps the computer can be reconnected and the program retrieved, perhaps not. Even so, the processes involved in setting up again take time and energy that may not be readily available. Consider how much more may be accomplished if the source of energy remains constant and flowing.

Creative thinking, focused concentration, and intense mental activity all require one readily available source of energy. That energy comes from the simple act of breathing consciously to activate the physical processes of our brain. These physical processes, in turn, amplify the mental processes of our mind.

Consider how often your breathing (or lack of breathing) reflects a negative, depleting relationship with your mental processes. When your thoughts are racing, your creative inspirations flowing, and your concentrative abilities are fully activated, these processes need fuel. Too often these processes are forced to run on fumes or faith. Too often we succumb to the seductive challenge of being able to produce hot-shot, on-the-spot decisions. Too often we strive to think fast, rather than stopping briefly to think thoroughly. Then we wonder why it is so difficult to focus, to think, and to create.

When we learn to pause, breathe, and energize our thoughts and inspirations, we gain both greater clarity and increased capacity. If this seems simplistic, that's because it is profoundly so.

Breathe with sharpened awareness and focused concentration. Your thought processes will reflect accordingly. Breathe erratically, and your thoughts will reflect accordingly.

Breathe energy into your thoughts, ideas, inspirations or decisions. The more energy you can consciously breathe into your mental processes, the more manifest they become in your life.

Breathe to activate your brain. Remember that the brain is the organ of the mind. To access the capacities of the mind, you must first train, not drain, your brain.

Allow yourself the luxury of thinking things through gently and completely in a relaxed manner as often as you can. Develop a meditative relationship with your own mind. It is from within this meditative relationship that the true source of all creative endeavors arises. The source of clear inspiration awakens in the musing of a clear, energized mind.

Honor your mental capacities for their many gifts. Enjoy expanding your mental horizons consciously, positively, and perceptively.

Spirit: Transcendence

Spirit is the element of the eternal. It is the force that transcends form and the power that pervades the All.

Spirit transmutes all energy into matter and returns it to energy once again. It is the many vibrational frequencies of life.

Spirit is the great mystery. It is the undefined meaning of all being. Spirit has no paradigm. It is the element of the foreign and of the familiar. It is the alien and the ally, both of whom we know intimately.

Spirit is the element of the unseen guest. It is the element with which we create our gods, and from which, in turn, we are created.

Spirit is the element of sanctity in all areas and aspects of our lives. Spirit is the holy element. It is the power of holism and the force of universal harmony. Spirit is the wonder worker, the wise one, the fool.

Spirit is the element of the Old Ones. It is the multidimensional realm that transcends the mundane and energizes the etheric.

Spirit is the element of inevitability. It is the force that spins the planets around the suns in galaxies we have yet to find. It is what powers the wheel on the weaver's spindle. Spirit is the web, and it is the weaver. Spirit is the thread, and it is the fiber. It is the element that, in perfect combination with itself, creates the greater weaving of life.

Spirit is indivisible, yet maintains separate parts of itself. It is that rare element present in all matter of energies. It is the universal common denominator. All things expand from and are reduced to spirit.

Spirit is eternity in the now. It is the element of the place we find when we are able to "be here now."

Spirit is the void filled with all that was, all that is, all that can be, or all that will be. It is the element of the silent emptiness and the peace that supasses all understanding. It is secular, yet it is the foundation of all religion. It is pure philosophy, unencumbered by doctrine; it is devotion without dogma. Spirit is the element of the living creed. It is the mystical church, devoid of hierarchy and greed.

Spirit is the element of redemption that laughs in the face of original sin. It is the truth, unbound, unstructured, and resistant to all attempts to regulate its distribution.

Spirit is the element of universality. It is being at one with the cosmos. It is complete attunement experienced purely by each, by all.

Spirit is the element of realization. It reaches through all aspects of our Self, bringing us to discover new dimensions of the Self. It forms the bridges that enable us to cross the wide chasms of uncertainty we encounter on our journey of becoming whole. It is the element of eternal curiosity.

Spirit is the element with which we may chart our course to the stars. It is unlimited expansion beyond the confines of our convenient constructs. It is the element of multidimensional explorations launched forth from mundane experience, as well as from mystical ecstasy.

Spirit is expressed with the most elaborate ritual and regalia, yet it requires none. It is equally present in the grand celebrations exalting divinity and the gentle ceremonies of everyday devotion. It is the element of deification. It reflects the greater gifts as gods.

Spirit is the element with which we sanctify the simple goodness of humankind and the glories of Nature. It teaches us to house the divine in all that life brings to us. It annuls judgments by revealing the ultimate perfection.

Spirit is the element of love—pure, beautiful, strong, and ruthlessly compassionate love. It is the element of enlightened love. It is always glowing gently to guide our personal actions, or blazing forth like a comet to change the course of civilization, alter history, and realign the path of our planet.

Spirit is the element within all elements, the space between the spaces, and the tissue of events enveloping our existence. It is the catalyzing element of all creation. It is the foundation of all life forms, regardless of their dimensional manifestations.

Spirit animates all things relatively. It reveals the hidden life force in that which appears inanimate, and reawakens the inherent consciousness in that which seems unaware.

The element of spirit brings us the sacred gift of connection to a higher form of shared consciousness and universal awareness. Spirit is the element of evolved power—personal, cultural, and universal.

The power of spirit expands in proportion to our awareness of its presence and to our acceptance of its gifts. What we see as the presence of spirit made manifest in something or some force, is, in truth, a pure reflection of spirit present within our Self.

Spirit is the transcendent, transpersonal mirror. It is a mirror that reflects only that which we are clearly conscious of and completely accept. It shows us reflections of our Self in all aspects of Nature, all realms of reality, and all dimensions of the mind—personal, cultural, universal.

Spirit also presents all of life to us in the form of a magickal mirror. It empowers us to step through the looking glass to find the purest reflection of Self. It also will require us to gaze into the great smoking mirror many times before our reflection begins to emerge, cleared by our willingness to acknowledge and accept responsibility for our Self.

Spirit brings us face to face with the highest aspects of our Self. It provides us with the power to transform in accordance with our potential, and to manifest the gifts of spirit in the clear reflection of our lives.

Spirit is the element of tolerant transmutation. It patiently disperses the shadows of resistance and rebellion that we cast to block the light of truth. It forgives us for being human, with all the frailties that condition encompasses. It loves us purely and accepts us completely in all our humanity. It teaches us to love, accept, forgive, and be tolerant of all that is human, within our Self and within others.

Spirit also teaches us to transcend our limitations with tolerance and love. It enables us to transform vulnerability into possibility, confusion into evolution. Spirit is the element of universal change, carefully seeded in the willing transformation of each human being.

Spirit is the element of divine detachment. It is the observer that guides our journey along a crystalline path into light. It will allow us to get lost from time to time, until we learn to look for the light in all things, all places, and all dimensions. However, it always leaves the light on for us so we can find our way home.

Spirit is the energizer of the soul.
Without it humankind is merely a husk.
—Stardragon

Spirit: Basic Breathing Exercise

 It is time to take a quiet moment to evoke the element of spirit, and personally acknowledge its ever-present power in your life. The key here is to touch what is ultimately intangible, and to sense what is imperceptible in any but the most expanded dimensions of your life experience.

Breathe gently. Find your natural rhythm and focus your awareness inward. Find that quiet place within.

As you breathe, pay close attention to the gentle pauses between each inhalation and each exhalation. Notice that quiet space. Feel the stillness and strength of spirit within.

For a few moments, let your breath breathe for you. Observe its natural rhythm with quiet, centered detachment. Know that spirit moves through you as naturally as your breath does, filling your total being with light and life.

Consider that all elements are present in spirit, just as spirit is reflected in each individual element. Amplify the aspects of each other element by evoking the element of spirit from within your Self.

Breathe rapidly now, the breath of fire. Breathe in and out through your mouth for a few moments. Focus on the strength of spirit energizing the strength of fire reflected within your Self. Feel the heat of life force activate and amplify your positive sense of Self.

Empower your Self physically with spirit and fire. Expand your Self with devotion and self-determination. Transcend your self-imposed limitations and be all that you can be.

Breathe more slowly now. Inhale through your nose. Exhale through your mouth. Focus on the sacred transmutational healing of spirit deep within your Self. Feel the soothing power of water flowing through you just as your breath dies. Feel the flow of gentle healing amplify your self-attunement.

Empower your Self emotionally with spirit and water. Experience your sacred right to inner knowing and self-healing. Transcend your self-imposed emotional obstacles, and receive fully the transformational power of healing light and love.

Breathe with a measured pace now, until you feel calm, grounded, and centered within your Self. Focus on the supportive connection of spirit and earth within your Self. Feel the structures of your Self and your life amplified by your connection to the supportive power of spirit.

Empower your Self with the sacred energy of spirit and your own self-determination. Transcend any self-imposed structures which bind your progression into the light. Redesign your life to connect with that which is divine.

Breathe with focused awareness. Allow each breath to sharpen your perception and stimulate your thought processes. Continue conscious breathing until you feel focused and alert.

Feel the creative energies of the air element awakening the capacities of your brain and mind. Feel your awareness increase as you amplify your access to the expanded dimensions of your mind.

Allow the element of spirit to increase your access to the source of inspiration within your Self. Empower your mental processes with air and spirit. Experience the fully awakened aspects of your brain and mind. Transcend your doubts and confused, self-created thoughts. Experience fully the power of clear mind and focused awareness.

Once again, let your breath breathe for you. Focus on bringing all aspects of your Self into full awareness of the present moment.

Notice the sensations of your body at this moment. Briefly center all your consciousness on the physical. Come completely into your body, and activate your strength and sense of Self.

Shift your awareness to the state of your emotions. Observe, with compassionate detachment, the flow of your feelings. Acknowledge your emotions and breathe through them as they pass through your consciousness.

Begin to take measure of your Self in this present moment. Notice how you have structured your environment at this time. Deepen your connection to the activity you are engaging in at this moment.

Determine your chosen part in the restructuring of your personal power. Breathe and deepen your experience of the moment.

Focus now on the thought processes moving through your mind. Breathe and still the flow of extraneous thoughts and sensations. Focus your awareness sharply, and allow your perceptive skills to deepen your personal experience of Self.

Breathe gently now and feel the interwoven elements of your Self amplified by the power of spirit.

Become fully aware of your Self at this moment in time. Focus only on sensations, emotions, and thoughts of your Self in this, the present moment. Observe your Self as an integral part of the environment in which you exist now.

Accept your Self as a conscious, integral part of your own life experience and of all life.

Personal Journey Account

I close this chapter with a personal account of a ceremonial journey. This account represents the experience of an actual ritual of protection and empowerment that was made with the elements of fire and spirit primarily. This experience came from a community healing and protection ceremony that was shared by many. Some of us worked alone, others worked within their own groups.

As you read this account, see if you can determine which elements are utilized at different times during the ceremony. Remember that a ceremony is far more free-flowing than a ritual. Whereas a ritual will often spell out what is happening, a ceremony instead will utilize a subtle, unstructured flow of energies.

Remember the aspects you have already learned about each element, and you will recognize their energies in this ceremony.

Spirit Fire Crystal

I hold a crystal of pure light and spirit. So intense is the laser energy of this stone that Mother Nature forms it only within the watery depths of underground streams. Once removed from these depths, the crystal becomes a sword. Its prism structures are sharp as steel blades. They swing their double-edged forces in an erratic pattern that emerges as its powers are put into play.

It is a full moon night, clear and cool. A strong breeze from the ocean lifts the mosses clinging to the great trees I see silhouetted against the sky. I find a place where the full force of this reflected light comes blasting through the branches of an old live oak.

I seek the highest protection of the light. I seek spirit through fire. There are several of us simultaneously engaging in this quest—each of us solitarily, within our own light, within our own space.

In the mundane present, the nuns of a nearby convent undertakes prayers for our shared purposes. We protect the community in which we live as we did in ages past, when the abbeys rang with chants to grant courage and holy protection to our deeds of service. We search for a laser-pure injection of highest light to create an impenetrable force field of love, light, and protection for the good of all.

I reach into the sky with my left hand. I am a vessel of transmutation, a conduit of the light. I open to the purposes of my service. The crystal sparkles with fiery lights, golden and warm, which it reflects from the moon.

Behind me, candles on the porch merge into one misty flame. I call forth the most sacred keeper of my own spirit. In respect for the holy sisters who have helped our cause and aided us in our deeds, then, as now, I use their names for Her, along with my own. I lift the crystal higher.

> *By the blessed flame of St. Bridget, I call for the protection*
> *of the highest light of spirit and truth.*

> *By the sacred fire of the ninth eternal flame, I open to this*
> *force for the good of all.*

I feel the power of shared purpose with each bright ray of light that sends its fiery beams through me.

I lift the crystal with both hands now and make the sign of the cross. I do this wordlessly, without the confines of definition. Then I express the prose, now transposed, with the rhyme retained. I speak the words, some changed, with the purity, wisdom, and power intact.

> *Hail Mary, full of grace.*
> *Blessed art thou amongst women,*
> *And blessed is the fruit of thy womb,*
> *The Christ.*
> *Holy Mary, Mother of gods,*
> *Pray for us now*
> *And at the hour of our transformation.*

I bring the crystal to my forehead. It sends a laser beam of light vision into all the shadowy corners of my mind. I speak the ancient words in true accord with all purposes of the light.

> *Bless me Mother, for I am your child.*

> *Bless my eyes*
> *that they may see clearly the path you set before me.*

Bless my lips
  that I may speak in true accord with your will.
Bless my breasts
  that I may know the faithful service of your work.
Bless my center of Self
  that I may find the strength to meet my tasks.
Bless my feet
  that I may walk in a more balanced connection to all life.
Bless me Mother, for I am your child.

Called forth on a moonlit night of crystal and fire, time and again, the sign of the cross and the ancient blessing of the Goddess ring out until they form a pure rhythm resounding clearly in tones of light and beauty.

Finally, the moon banks its fire behind the cool mists drifting in from the ocean, bringing water over fire. I place my laser crystal in the cool waters of gathered rain to rest. As the moon begins to set, I feel the laser light beam become first a wider band, then a shower of crystalline sparks, shooting stars blazing into the atmosphere we had requested.

I feel the winds sweep the great old trees, causing them to cast moonlight in lacy patterns on the ground. I watch the patterns dance for a time, and, for a time, I dance with them. Then, in gratitude for what I have experienced, and in honor of the light, I leave the candles burning with a joyful, merry glow of shared and reflected light.

Fire:
The Warriors

Honoring the Element of Fire

Fire was a source of great mystery to the ancients. This honored element provided heat to keep the tribes alive during the bitter winter. It kept the fierce predatory animals at bay during the long, dangerous nights in the forests, caves, and villages. Fire brought light to the lodges, and allowed the ancient Celts to craft the tools, weapons, and clothing after the Sun had set. It made edible the meat brought by the hunters, and transformed into bread the pastes made from grain and water.

Fire was the first magick of the ancients. It was the senior element, often sent directly from the heavens in bolts of lightning. It could consume the great forests and sweep through the grasslands, racing with the magickal winds that accompanied it. It made nighttime into day, and transformed the green growth into a wasteland.

Fire was the creator and the destroyer, the provider and the conqueror. It was the ultimate hunter, the inexorable warrior. It thrived on friction; it awakened from wooden sticks rubbed together properly and burst forth in sparks from the sacred stones, the magick gift of the gods—the flint.

Fire was the first ally of the Celts. It transformed the very ores of the Earth into indestructible tools and weapons. It was the alchemist force for the magick of bronze and later steel. It awakened the secrets in the stones. It forged the weapons that made the Celts unconquerable in battle. Fire was the force of victory.

As the Celts evolved, they developed greater skills involving the use of fire. Fire, which had been regarded with awe and fear as an inexplicable, mysterious element, came to represent all the forces and gifts it brought to humankind. It became the symbol of faith, strength, courage, and protection. These powers were manifested by the red force of the inner flame, the life force within humankind. The black forces, the smoke and ashes of fire, were the destroyers of fear, weakness, doubt, and vulnerability. These dark shadows were dispelled by the powers of the inner fire, just as they are now. Fire cauterized all wounds, physical and metaphysical, seen and unseen. The inner flame challenged the Self to become strong and fearless. It brought tests of faith and trials of courage. It brought power to rituals of magick and honor to celebrations of victory. It awakened sensation. It awakened the true sense of Self. Fire was the catalyst of self-creation. So it was then. So it is now.

Activating Fire in Imagery

Active imagery with the element of fire is ideally accomplished in the presence of a blazing bonfire or before the warm crackling flames in the fireplace. Fire is also clearly felt in the driving force of a high noon summer sun or the gentle insistence of a candle flame. Fire, like all elements of Nature, reflects most powerfully in its literal form. Yet, like all elements, it also reflects within the consciousness of humankind. The force of fire can be felt in our dreams, our visions, and our journeys into the realms of consciousness.

Fire reflects itself in our images of its power quite actively. Fire journeys are sensational, physical, and dramatic. Fire imagery brings us tests of inner courage and assurances of our strength. The inner fire is the force that brings us the sensation of our Self as powerful, vital, and alive. As we journey into the image of fire, we feel the inner rhythm of our life force. We learn to dance with joy to the inner rhythms of our Self. With fire as an ally on our inner journeys, we find the faith with which to transform ourselves into the sacred, spiritual warrior we wish to be. With fire, rage transforms into resolve, weakness gives way to willpower, cowardice becomes courage, fear fades in the light of faith, and insecurities are transmuted into strength.

Fire is the element of the inner flame of self-esteem. It is the inner element that enables you to choose your path, to evoke visions of your desires. It is the inner force that gives you the strength of body, the courage of mind, and the faith of spirit with which you may achieve your goals.

Fire is the element of Self with which you fashion the spear and track your quarry. It brings a balanced shaft of strength to your image of your Self, your self-esteem. This inner flame sharpens the spear point of your senses and ensures your aim. Your inner fire gives you the will and the skill with which you may truly hit the mark.

Fire is the element of Self that places the sword of power into your hands. Your inner flame forges the blade and empowers your purposes. Strengthened by the light and force of truth, your inner fire brings you the sacred swords: Caliburn, Excalibur, and Solias (the sword of light).

Fire also brings us the less flamboyant, yet foundationally stronger power of kinship, love, and joy. Empower yourself with this imagery exercise. Extend and expand your image to greater dimensions for the personal relationships in your life. Make the blessings be real for all.

Blessings in the Flame: An Imagery Exercise for Kinship

Imagine that you are in a little cottage, sitting on the hearth in front of a gentle fire. Beside you, a cat lies curled up, purring with contentment. You warm yourself next to the fire for a time and muse on the many pleasures and contentments in your life.

You call to mind the memories of friends and family who have brought you joy and made you feel loved throughout the years. You feel the energy of their love as surely as you feel the heat of the fire. You call forth images of their faces, and sensations of their strength and yours.

As you see them there, you toss fragrant herbs into the flames, perhaps cinnamon, lavender, bay leaves, and cloves. As the herbs burn, the flames brighten and flicker merrily.

With joy in your heart, you celebrate the people who have brought you the blessings of their love. With love in your heart, you send forth blessings of your own. With pleasure and contentment, you imagine your blessings rising up into spirit, empowered by the strength of your love. As the fires cool, you know, with the faith of pure acceptance, that your blessings have been received.

ᕙᔕᕉᐁᕚ

Fire brings us the ability to have a more powerful sense of self-esteem and personal confidence in our fully activated, unique, and special potentials. Try this imagery to celebrate your personal strength. Expand and adapt to your own specific needs.

Shadows on the Stones:
An Imagery Exercise for Self-Empowerment

Imagine yourself on a dark, starry night, dancing around a roaring fire amidst a circle of standing stones. The air is cool against the stones, but warm near the flames. You dance to the rhythms of a distant, inner drum. You dance in circles out from the fire, and weave your steps in and out around the standing stones.

You bask in the warm sensation of your own strength. You celebrate the life forces that created you, the essential, independent dancer. You dance your own dance, free and unbound by any restrictions. You find your own rhythm.

Dancing closer to the flames, you feel the power of its heat. You feel the power of your inner courage. The light from the flames casts your shadows onto the faces of the great standing stones. As you dance, you create shadows of your Self, empowered only by the energy and shape of your movements. Imagine, now, a shadow that is frightening, a shape projected on the stones in your own image. See it lurking there, unable to define itself alone. It is at the mercy of your movement, controlled by the direction of your dance.

Shift quickly to the stance of a great warrior. Show your strengths. Show yourself the shape, the feel, the sensation of your power. This, too, can be a shadow. Its form is determined at your own discretion. Choose the shape of your Self. Choose the projection of your power.

Dance for a time in this place of inner vision. Dance around these sacred flames. Dance in the light of your inner fire. Feel the rhythm, the heat of your power. Shift the shapes of your shadows projected on the stone faces surrounding you. Shift the shape of your shadows as easily as you shift the steps, the movements, and the rhythm of your dance. Define the shape of your strength. Find faith in your Self. Dance and celebrate your unique Self.

Fire enables us to face the inner fears and blocks that prevent us from reaching our power and being all that we can. There are times we must bring our fears out from within ourselves, and allow them to take shape in our active imagery. In that dimension of conscious mind we are able to do battle with our fears. We may be surprised to find that these fears are no more than shadowy reflections waiting to be transformed by our strength, faith, and confidence. After all, what happens when light shines on a shadow?

Personal Journey Account

This journey was made with the intent to "dance with shadows," or deal with aspects of my Self. These aspects were causing me to cling to the role of healing rescuer rather than have the confidence and faith to "change that which can be changed, accept that which can't, and have the wisdom to know the difference."

Inspired by the music of Peter Gabriel's album "Security," I had already determined that the image I created would contain a shadow with a spear, and of course, a fire.

After those guidelines had been set, I entered a state of focused consciousness, and reflected upon the sensations I had in regard to the shape of my shadow and my addiction to being the rescuer.

As the image emerged in my mind, I sought to hold the sensations as well as deepen the experience. All active imagery and shamanic journeys require a measure of self-involvement that goes well beyond intellectualizing the experience. With fire, which is particularly physical, this is always true.

Active, experiential imagery involves your body, mind, and spirit in alliance with a personal willingness to open to the deepest dimensions of your Self. Fire is the element that teaches this most effectively. Thus, we begin with fire.

The Shadow with a Spear

I walk across the barren wasteland of my own weaknesses. The hot Sun of high noon casts shadows of doubt and fear at my feet. I tread cautiously. Each step on the sharp rocks of reality reminds me of yet another point of vulnerability.

I have come to quest for courage, to find the strength of will forged by the fires of faith and tempered with the pure protection of truth.

The ground before me shimmers, a veil of great white heat rising up to meet a blue and golden sky. I seek the burial cairn of a long dead warrior. Ashes swept away so long ago now return and reform for me; they connect me to that warrior spirit, that source of strength and self-assurance.

I wait for the sunset and beyond it, the coming of night. The Sun hangs interminably above the western horizon, refusing to yield to the darkness. While the last rays of day duel with the gathering clouds of night, I prepare a circle of fires: four flames at the cardinal points and one center fire for spirit. I gather sticks and branches to keep the fires fueled throughout the night of darkness and shadows.

As the light shifts its focus beyond the curve of the Earth, I feel the eternity of its purpose. I set it free of the tethers of my personal fears. The light fades from the skies with promises of eternal returns and warm, secure mornings after the cold night has passed.

I gather scrub brush and dry grass. The supply of fuel seems very meager to me just now. I search within for the faith that it will be enough. I remember, and in that remembrance, I find resolve.

I have chosen—freely—to face the shadows of my Self. I will stop the arrows from flying by taking them directly into my heart. I will bleed, but I will not die. Instead, I will transform, forged anew. I remember that this is truth, and I find faith.

Darkness gathers with an ominous insistence. Outside my circle of fires are frightful presences, projected there by the power of my personal fears. They taunt me from the shadows, reminding me of my mortality, my vulnerability, my weakness, my humanity.

I feed my fires with dry twigs, willing them to be adequate. I am unwilling to use my larger branches, now held in reserve for the coldness of the deep night yet to come.

For a time, there is quiet in the shadows. It is an uneasy calm, and I must prepare for its retreat. I strip a long, strong branch of all its spreading foliage. I feed only these to the flames of my center fire.

In the light that my center fire provides for me I find a sharp piece of stone, suitable for crafting a spear point. With a few blows on its surface with another stone, I shear the natural edge and create a sharper, more penetrating point. I create a weapon.

I tear the leather laces out of my boots and bind my spear point to the stripped branch. I pull off my boots to feel the ground beneath my feet more purely. It is strong ground, despite its many scars. It is battleground. I feel its power pulsing through me as I raise my spear and signal my readiness to do battle.

From the darkness, my shadow steps into the light. I see its form shifting shape just beyond the boundaries of my fires. I know that it cannot cross the barriers of my faith or enter the circle of my courage. I steady myself, and the flames grow stronger. I feed the center fire with stronger branches, and the flame circle blazes into the night sky.

My shadow shows itself clearly, reflected in the fires of truth. It also carries a spear, one of similar fashion to my own. I raise my spear in salute. My shadow brandishes a reply in kind and waits. I stamp the shaft end of my spear significantly on the ground. I hold my spear point skyward, out from my body. I lean on its strength for steadiness and support. I will not attack or defend. I will simply hold the line to the best of my abilities.

The voice of my shadow hisses across the fires I have set.

"You are afraid to fight me."

The branches in my center fire crackle, sending sparks flying into the night sky.

"Why should I fight that which I love?" I reply, sending a force of light outward with my words.

Wind sweeps the fire circle into the grasses surrounding me. The circle widens and steadies itself.

"Why have you summoned me?" my shadow asks disarmingly. "Why do you call forth the very forces that can defeat you?"

We stare at one another, my shadow and I, across the barriers of flame. A light breeze flickers through my center fire, and I speak to my shadow directly.

"I call you forth not to do battle, but to forge an alliance of strength that will be undefeatable."

My shadow makes a derisive sniff. "You are still afraid to do battle with me. You would rather hide behind the skirts of your mother love than take me on directly," it sneers through the smoke.

My circle fires grow fainter. I have only enough fuel to maintain one flame throughout this night. I stand behind my center fire and invite my shadow to cross the protective perimeter I have established.

My shadow smiles, anticipating victory at my expense, and thrusts the spear point of its voice through my barriers.

"You will never defeat me," my shadow pricks into my consciousness. "You will never defeat any shadow of your Self so long as you are afraid of your own aggression. You are a hawk afraid to hunt, a warrior in fear of your own weapons. You are doomed to be a predator ensnared by its own prey!"

My shadow moves in closer, circling, skirting the light cast by my center fire. I can see the many faces of my shadow as it seeks to take me by surprise, to thrust its poison point into into my back or my soul.

I circle with my shadow, turning to keep us face to face. It is a dangerous dance, with an unpredictable rhythm. I trust my feet, connected to the bare bones of the Earth, to keep the pace and hold my balance.

I take a stand and hold my position. My shadow ceases its circling and stands directly before me. I bind it with the force of my faith and the strength of my words.

"None can prey upon the pure in heart. None can hurt where hurt is not accepted. None can be victorious over the weapons of truth and wisdom. None can conquer the pure power of mother love. Love conquers all."

My shadow scurries into the darkness. I cannot see it, but I hear it scratching at the edges of the light. I feed the last of my fuel to the center fire and wait.

The voice of my shadow sneaks closer to the core of my flame.

"Mother love," it spits at me. "Woman's weapons," it sneers. "You wear your womanhood like a warm, cozy shawl, covering the aggression of your nature."

My shadow moves into view once more, wearing many familiar faces. It smiles at me, both smug and insidious.

"It is a warm, comfortable shawl, is it not? Yet no more protection against me than the thin cloak you wear against the coming of the cold, dark time of night."

I reach to unclasp my soft, comfortable cloak. I remove it from my body and tear it into many long fragments of material. I cast all but one ribbon of cloth into the center fire. I do this so that it may fuel my purpose with the very threads that threaten to weave me into my warm, false securities. The remaining ribbon, no more than a fragment of my cloak, I tie around my spear. It is scarlet in hue, like fresh blood. Its strands are of a strong fiber. They blow in the night breeze like a banner. The red hue burns brightly in the firelight.

I turn to face my shadow with nothing to armor me but a chain mail woven of conscious faith and fearless strength.

My shadow pierces with a small, needle-sharp point aimed surely at my weakest spot. I feel it enter just beneath my heart as my shadow speaks, whispering close to my face.

"Why, oh you of great mother love, why don't you do more to help all your children? Can't you hear them crying out for their causes and their needs? How can you turn away and still say that you care, mother love?"

I search in the flames to find a vision to inspire my failing strength. I find an eagle there, with great golden wings. I watch as it flies into the darkest point of night. The breeze shifts its direction and blows gently into my soul, bringing music to my spirit. I echo its sound and its melody across this barren landscape, blessing its creator. I sing out with the forces of fire and wind to back me up.

> *Though you may disappear,*
> *You are not forgotten here;*
> *And I will say to you,*
> *I will do what I can do.*

Visions of St. Peter and the sound of Gabriel's horn vibrate into the darkness, bringing light.

My shadow attempts to conquer me once more. It moves in close enough for me to feel its breath. It seeks to inhale the very air I breathe. I pull in the fading warmth of my center fire. It is spare now in its energy. There is nothing more to feed this flame, I fear.

Then I feel the strong shaft of my spear, and I realize the purpose of its creation.

I break my spear across my knee and cast the pieces into the center fire. As the shaft burns brightly, I stare my shadow directly in the face—and I laugh. I laugh with the pure joy of love's triumph.

"I shall not be tempted to strike at you. You have brought me the grace of opportunity and with it the gratitude of wisdom well earned," I call out across the center fire. Its flames are fierce and proud now. I steady my gaze and call forth the faces of all my shadows. The faces of my failures and those of my successes are one and the same in the pure light of truth.

I shout with the victory of spirit and with the strength of love, conqueror of all shadows.

"I forgive you," I open my arms wide to welcome my shadow. "I forgive myself for misunderstanding, and for being misunderstood. I have done, and I will do, all that I can do."

From the center fire there emerges a sword of great magnificence. It is suspended in the flames, hilt skyward. Its double-edged blade gleams brilliantly with a power that transmutes all darkness into light.

My shadow wisps away, no more than the dark smoke from a purification fire. Far beneath my feet I feel the Sun begin its journey homeward, bringing the light as it comes. The darkest hour of midnight has passed.

I am alone at the center fire, gazing at the sword of flame. It illuminates my vision and brings me the power of purpose. I must learn how to receive that power, for I must journey farther during this night or during another yet to come.

Fire brings us the power to see clearly the reflections of our Self and the patterns of our life. Fire burns away the illusions that prevent our full recognition and acceptance of our Self. Try the following imagery exercise to gain true perspective about your Self and to project new images of strength into your life. Program power by first accepting your weaknesses, then by activating your strength. Don't be afraid of your weaknesses and fears; this only feeds them. Fears and weakness grow fat on denial. Accept them and adapt.

The Great Smoking Mirror: An Imagery Exercise for Gaining Personal Perspective

Imagine that you are in a dark, ancient temple. You stand before an altar made of stone. Its surfaces are covered with intricate carvings of serpents intertwining themselves in symbolic knots. Upon the altar are nine candles and a statue of a hawk in flight. Behind the altar is a mirror made of polished bronze, its surface reflecting through the smoke from the candle flames.

As you gaze through the smoke, you find mysterious images emerging in the mirror. Images of your tests and trials are depicted there. You see obstacles you have overcome and battles you have won. You find images of fears you have conquered and limitations you have already released. You find them there as they truly are now, nothing more than shadowy reflections, ashes and smoke.

As you see the reflections of your tests and your trials, you realize, with a sense of triumph, how very strong you truly are. As you sense the victory you have achieved over your vulnerabilities, you find that the image has cleared. The smoke fades away, and the bright candle flames reflect clearly in the polished surface—an image of your Self, strong and sure. Tested, tried and true, you are triumphant.

Fire is also the element of rage and frustrating anger. Activating imagery to "play out" anger is an effective, safe technique. Acting out anger in imagery prevents the build-up of unnecessary negativity and provides the release you need. Do as you will inside your mind. This will help you think more clearly when you need to.

Personal Journal Account

This account represents a journey into my own "red rage."

Nemesis

I drop into the inner blood fire to reject an unwarranted poisonous invasion. I enter the red rage to protect the highest purposes of my self-preservation, and, in turn, those of my ken.

I call forth a vision of justice, the great Lady of Liberty. Instead, Nemesis races through my vision in a golden chariot drawn by lionesses. I feel their tawny fur brush against me as they passed. I hear the rumble of the chariot's wheels and feel a blade pierce my core. I bleed in torrents of rage, bright, clear and red. The red rage of legends long-told courses through my blood and enteres into the ancient codes of my bones.

I emerge in an image of my Self, one long, deeply encoded, now breaking forth from the thin shells of civilized forbearance.

I ride a great, red war horse at battle speed. I feel its ruddy mane lashing my left hand as I hold the woven leather reins. In my right hand I hold a double-edged broad sword. Ahead of me I see Nemesis in her chariot. Her golden hair gleams in a blaze of light, leaving a trail of its power along the paths it traveled. Her robes are white, and her cape flies like golden wings behind her. She wears bracelets of bronze, serpents coiling around her arms.

In the auric trails of her light I see my Self as the reflected repository of my barbaric ancestry. I see the shape of my purest, most righteous rage, and sense the strength of my deepest resolve. I resolve to follow Nemesis for a time to hone my blade.

As I attempt to move toward her, I am astounded to feel a binding wound grasp at me to hold me from my purpose. I reach deeper into the red rage of my ancestors.

I feel the sweat dripping from the horse's neck onto my hands. My fingers are cracked and bleeding. The salty sweat of the horse stings my fresh cuts, yet still I hold on.

I ride this great red horse into a battle to regain my strength and resume my purpose. I see that I am without armor, riding bare-breasted into battle. My hair is unbound and free to create its own fires. Massive dogs like great red wolves run beside my steed. They snarl and snap in competition for the blood that drips from the heads of my one-time enemies, now tied securely to my saddle.

I feel the full power of this image, the ruthless efficiency of it, and the ultimate compassion of its purpose. I feel it deep in the protective fires of my spirit. As I experience it fully, I feel the binding claws loosen their grasp. Startled at this, my most ancient aspect, I feel the spear point slip out as what held it there loses its grip. I feel clear fire flow up my spine, energizing the center of my courage. I turn quickly and swing my sword behind me. I swing truly so that the vanity of this strife might never again achieve a hold on me in any way.

In the periphery of my vision I see this greed-driven strife fall to the ground beneath my horse's feet. Before it falls, though, I see its head separate neatly from its shoulders, no longer able to send bindings from the mind into the body.

I wheel my horse around and ride back to gaze in contemplative regard at the remains of my invader. The dogs wait anxiously for my signal. I consider the merit of this head as a trophy; however, with deeper thought, I realize that it was unworthy to share the tribute of being called a true foe. With a wave of my hand, the dogs feast.

My fires burn cooler now. I turn to follow Nemesis.

These images, exercises, and journey accounts can be easily adapted into ceremonies and rituals of your own creation. Use my formats to create your own forms. Create the shape of your own power. Adapt to reflect the imagery in symbolic form. A bright source of light (such as several candles) and a blank wall can become the circle of standing stones and the center fire for a ceremonial shadow dance. A column candle or votive onto which you have poured an herbal oil (such as one with a spicy fragrance) can be placed in front of a mirror in an otherwise darkened room to create a temple mirror reflecting your triumphs and your truths of Self. A gentle fire in your own fireplace or a simple candle of any kind is enough to create a ceremony of blessing, honoring those you love.

Remember, it is the force of your conscious intent that creates the transformations in your life. All that you think, feel, say, or do are no more or less than reflections of your consciousness. What you feel or see in your life reflects the sensations of your inner Self in relationship to the world. If your relationship to the world is strong, positive, and filled with faith, it is truly a reflection of your Self. Develop a positive relationship with your Self, and it will reflect out from you. Envelop your Self with courage and faith, and find the warm protection of self-assurance.

Evoking the Allies of the Element Fire

 Consider the aspects of the element fire—strength, protection, guardianship, force of will, security, and kinship. Consider your experience of this element—confidence, self-esteem, power.

Within your mind, carefully structure the images you have created to describe the forms, shapes, and details of two figures emerging from the realm of the element of fire. They may be as mystical or symbolic as you choose. They are your images of the spirits of fire, the keepers of the flame.

They may be human or not, as you choose. They are your personal inner guardians, a reflection of your deepest inner strength. Call them forth to forge an alliance of personal power. Whenever you need them, they are there.

Amplify your vision, including as many aspects as you can to bring these figures into detailed focus. Note all that you see, hear, feel, smell, taste, or touch within your image. Record your reactions to each contact you have with your allies from the element of fire. Expand your alliance each time you evoke these friends.

Personal Journey Account

This account represents the image I activated by using techniques such as those described in the exercise "Evoking the Allies of the Element Fire." Sometimes it requires several attempts to create an in-depth image of an element; other times the image comes in fast and clear. For me, fire images came quickly.

This journey was made to actively work with imagery that had appeared on other occasions. Evoking the allies of the fire brought forth my personifications of what that element symbolizes. This is an internal process, an internal projection reflecting in active imagination. Just how three-dimensional these journeys become depends on one's own style.

Guardians of the Flame

I gaze into a roaring fire and behold the sword of flame therein. I cannot reach it from where I stand. Instead, I must enter into its own dimension.

Flames of memory pass through my mind—power rebuked, power persecuted, power rewon, power exalted. I must grasp the hilt of this sword of fire, or I shall feel its blade deep within me. It is the blade of final fear. It is the fear of accepting, purely, the gift of faith, the power of courage, and the support of strength.

I call forth the force behind the flames, the elemental energy of the experience that is fire. I open to the full force of its power and vow to honor the gifts it brings me.

Then, blazing forth from my inner vision, there emerge two fine warriors—allies from the realm of flame. They are a man and a woman, a sacred pair, each in sturdy reflection of the other's aspects, both male and female.

They wear cloaks of red, black, and orange, woven from large strong threads. The weave is tight, like chain mail, I think, yet not as such. The texture of the cloth is nubby and rough. These are battle cloaks, woven for power and protection, and devoid of anything purely decorative. Only the clasps holding the cloaks across their shoulders could be mistaken as decorative. This thought, it appears quite clearly, would be most foolish, for the clasps are talismanic.

These forceful talismanic clasps are wrought of bronze, set with fiery carnelians and smoky quartz. They are fashioned in the shape of

115

huge Maltese crosses. I feel the force of their energy flowing in equilateral streams from the fiery center stone. The power they produce spins outward in a centrifugal circle of energy forming wheels of light.

Beneath their cloaks, these guardians of the flame wear golden breastplates. There is a rich, rosy light gleaming from their polished armor. It reflects in their amber eyes and warm, sun-bronzed skin. Both the man and the woman have their thick, fiery hair neatly plaited and pulled away from their faces, perhaps in preparation for battle, or to provide a clear view for guardianship. The woman wears a multitude of braids bound together with a leather cord. They stream down her back in rivers of red-gold. The man has braids of a bronze hue brushing down either side of his face. The rest of his hair is swept back to expose a clear, strong forehead. It is a face that reflects, unlined, the acceptance of power and purpose. It is an expression that matches that of the woman's face. I note, though, that her eyes seem to flash this fire with a bit more resolve—or is it rage?

In looking closely at her eyes, I see suddenly that the power of the female predator relies on a deeper ferocity of spirit. I wonder at this. Perhaps it is to compensate for the physical dimensions of her size; perhaps it is to prevent the possibility of persecution for and to ensure the protection of her special power. The woman's power burns brightly with fierce, new flames of remembered strengths and ancient faiths.

I note that the male of this elemental image is more calmly assertive of his power. He is almost tender, the gentle warrior, confident, and accustomed to his strength.

The guardians of the flame, these fine warriors of fierce spirit and tender mercies, these protectors of purest intention, reach forth from the flames in clear alliance with my Self. I take their hands and step into the eternal, inner flame.

I dance in the rhythm of the heat, still holding fast to my guardians of the flame. I'm enraptured at the affinity I feel for this element I had so long hidden or tried to hide from. I rejoice in the sensation of strength now remembered, regained, and retained.

I loosen my grasp on the guardians of fire and reach deeper within my Self to find that faith is holding me securely. The sword of fire, faith, and trust still hangs suspended in the flames awaiting the acceptance of my courage. I look to the guardians to affirm this courage for me, within me. I turn to see myself reflected in the rosy-golden breastplates of their armor and in the gleaming bronze of their Maltese crosses. I accept this reflection for the purity of its purpose. I accept the fire of my Self.

I turn slowly, moving ever more deeply into the hot center of the flame—blue of valor, truth, and honor; red of courage, faith, and blood; orange of strength, vitality, and health; yellow of pointed focus, the tip of the flame. I immerse myself in the heat of these fiery hues.

After a time, untold, I reach with both hands and grasp the sword of fire firmly by the hilt.

Mythic Figures of Fire

Though none of our Celtic, mythic ken can be said to reflect this one element, there are several whose images seem to emerge most clearly from the flames. That is to say that fire best describes the element of their image and their messages for us, told still in the myths that keep them alive in our consciousness.

It is my hope that the sensations you receive in activating your Celtic consciousness will fuel your desires to explore Celtic mythology further. To that end, I have provided a list of bibliographic sources at the end of this book; it remains for you to seek them out. When you do, I expect you will find a deeper connection to your Celtic heritage and a stronger sense of your Self, as well. It is my hope that these brief introductions will deepen your active connection to the figures you find in these myths and sharpen your image of your Self as a reflection of the elements they represent.

Cuchulain

Cuchulain (pronounced Coohullahn) was the greatest hero of the heroic cycle of Irish mythology. His spiritual father was Lugh, the supreme Lord of Light. His mythic role was that of the self-chosen warrior protector who wills himself to be the pure hero. His exploits led him to be chosen as the undisputed champion of all Ireland, and his courage made him the envy of all the great warriors, including the famed knights of the Red Branch.

His undoing, however, came from the same source as that from which his fierce strength was derived. Cuchulain was renowned for entering into a state of pure battle frenzy called the red rage. In this red rage, he slew his closest friend and foster brother, Laeg, and was himself ultimately slain.

Imagery application—Create and activate an imagery with Cuchulain when great courage and strength is needed. Also activate this imagery when inhibitions or prohibitions about expressing anger prevent you from taking positive, responsible guardianship in your own life.

Maeve

Mauve was the legendary queen of Connaught whose unquenchable desire to obtain the finest bull in all Ireland led her to make war upon Ulster. Ulster was defended by none other than our epic hero, Cuchulain. While the Ulstermen were in an enchanted sleep, placed there by a druid in the service of Maeve, Cuchulain defended Ulster alone and held the forces of Maeve at bay.

Before we judge Maeve too harshly, we must remember the role of the queens in ancient Ireland and other Celtic lands. The amount of power to which a queen such as Maeve was entitled was determined greatly by the value of her collected possessions, of her dowry, or both. Maeve had to obtain the Brown Bull of Cooley to maintain her power of rule over Connaught, and to prevent neighboring kingdoms from attempting to force her and her people into subjugation by another leader. Had Maeve been less than inflamed with her need to protect her lands and her rule, then Connaught would have fallen under the powers of Ulster or another region.

Perhaps we are best reminded to view Maeve as she was then in that era of blood and sword. Perhaps she represents the essential Celtic warrior queen who struck first, rather than be struck as her British counterparts, such as Boadecia and Cartimantua were. They, too, reflect the element of fire quite clearly, and, I might add, are a matter of historic as well as mythic record.

The warrior queens, like their balances, the warrior kings and the champion knights, all reflect the fierce qualities of fire that protected the lands and the people in ancient times, or forged nations around the world in times much closer to the present.

Imagery application—Activate imagery with Maeve when it is necessary to establish and maintain boundaries in your life. Also activate it when your strength is being depleted, or when someone or something unfairly takes advantage of your vulnerabilities.

Scathach

Scathach was another fiery figure in Celtic myth and represents the inexorable warrior. Scathach ran a school for warriors on a remote island which was perilous to reach. Her methods were brutal, but those who survived her course became warriors of great fame. Chief among her pupils was none other than Cuchulain himself. Had Scathach been able to teach Cuchulain to tone down his red rage, he might have avoided his fate and not had to come face to face with our next fiery figure.

Imagery application—Activate Scathach when you need the will power to meet challenges and changes in your life. Also use Scathach when you need an inner trainer to bring yourself to peak condition and performance.

Morrigan

Another Triple Goddess, Morrigan's two other aspects were Badb and Macha. She is more properly referred to as the Morrigan, the goddess of battle, strife, blood, and panic. Her appearance on the battlefields was symbolized by either two or three ravens. Her cries heated the blood of the warriors and led them to victory or death, each being of equal value in the ancient view of the Celts. Death in battle assured entrance to the finest realms of the Otherworld, so long as the warrior fought bravely and, later, with chivalry.

This theme echoes in the Nordic concept of *Valhalla*, the sacred realm of warriors who died in battle. The Morrigan was also renowned for her ability to shift shapes and transform into whatever creature would serve her purpose most effectively. The Morrigan represents the force of will required to do what must be done.

The Morrigan is often equated with Morgan le Fey of later Arthurian myth, but I feel this is not quite fitting. Though Morgan le Fey did what had to be done, in my opinion, her connection to Avalon would have prevented her from having the same consuming fire the Morrigan represents.

Imagery application—Activate imagery using the Morrigan when a threatening situation in your life must be changed. Also use it when strong, assertive positions are required, and you want to make a stand.

Fire emerges as the catalyzing force for many figures in Celtic myth and history. Wherever there is the element of quest, there is fire. Wherever there is unselfish sacrifice, there is fire. Wherever there are great deeds of courage and heroic acts of bravery above and beyond the call of duty, there is fire.

Fire is the element of gallantry in Celtic myth and history. At its best, fire is nobly reflected in Celtia. At its worst, it finds its reflection in destruction and all-consuming greed. These, too, are recorded in Celtic myth, and, alas, in Celtic history, as well. The red rage of Cuchulain is a symbolic lesson for the Celts, one to which we need to pay heed even now. Indeed, perhaps especially now, as the spears we cast and the swords we swing have grown in power. Now we must learn to trade swords of blood for swords of light. Therein lies true power.

Keynote for Fire

Balance the fleeting urge to conquer (which fire can catalyze) by using faith in the power of pure, "ruthlessly compassionate" love.

Water:
The Priestly Ones

Honoring the Element of Water

Water was the essential element of life for the ancients, the vital element of survival. It brought life to the land and life to humankind. Without it, all life ceased to exist. Water was a gift of Nature in the form of rain that filled the lakes and sacred pools, and provided sustenence for the continued growth of the plants. The sources of water caused the Celts to cease their wanderings and begin to settle into villages. Water allowed them to develop methods of agriculture; it nurtured the crops that fed the people. Water was the element that could draw forth sustenance for the entire tribe, creating nourishing broths where there had only been scraps of meat, bone, and marrow. It transformed grains and fruits into elixirs and medicines that both enhanced and healed the people.

Water was the mysterious element that transformed itself into solid structures of ice in the cold, dark times of winter, then shifted its shape in the spring once more. It swelled the rivers and streams as the Sun thawed the frosty ice caps on the mountains. It could force the rivers to rise above their banks and flood the lands all around. It could trickle gently over rocks in a quiet stream or sweep down in white, churning forces to tear the great trees from their roots.

Water was the magickal healing element that bubbled up from the ground where it was least expected. It sprang forth from the Earth as a sign from Nature, bringing the healing gift of life. It arrived unannounced on the land in sacred pools and springs. It filled the wells even when the rains did not fall upon the land.

Water was the element of the great oceans, the mighty seas that the Celts crossed to find new homelands. It was also the realm in which fearsome sea serpents dwelled, ready to catch the unwary or unskilled travelers drifting on its surface. Water required great respect, caution, and even sacrifice, before its vast realms were entered.

Water also provided sustenance in the form of fishes, mussels, clams, and salt. At the edge of the great seas, water flowed in and out, its tides mysteriously connected with the phases of the moon.

Water was to be honored and accepted, never conquered or controlled. It was the magickal element, controlled only by the gods. Even as the knowledge of irrigation and the construction of wells and dams began, water remained ultimately supplied and maintained at the whim of Nature.

As water became more thoroughly understood in its natural role, its symbolic role grew. Water was the symbol of purity, healing, and transformation. It was the element of the inner Self. The waters of life dwelled within the body of humankind, creating itself as the essential element of life, the magickal connection to the mysterious source of all life. It was the element of the cauldron of transformation and wisdom.

Water was the element of inner life, reflecting as emotions, feelings, and transformations of health. It allowed the functions of the body to flow properly. It cooled the fevers of the body, and when expressed in tears, soothed the spirit as well. It cleared the toxins from the body and brought healing to the spirit.

Water became the holy element blessed by the priests and priestesses, life and spirit symbolized in one element.

Water became the mystical element of the holy communion with the divine. It became the element of the Grail, the element of communion with the source of life.

Attuning with Water in Imagery

Attunement with the element of water is ideally accomplished beside a beautiful lake, on the banks of a mighty river, or at the seashore. Its elemental power is felt in the driving rain or in the quiet mists of a rising fog. Its gentle powers shine in the dew drops glistening in the morning sunlight. Its powers of transformation pierce the sky with sheets of ice, sleet, hail, and snow. Its quiet magick sparkles in the crystal icicles that form on the boughs of the winter trees and the corners of the roof.

Water reminds us to have patience during the cold times of our self-transformation, when all seems silent and frozen. With every drop that falls from icicles melted by the warmth of the sunlight, we are reminded of our powerful abilities of self-transformation. Water reminds us that the warmth of our feelings and the heat of our emotions can transform the coldest, most icy barriers we have created. It reminds us of the tidal nature of our emotional cycles. It attunes us to the inner flow of our Self and the eternally changing tides of our feelings. Water attunes us to the inner transformations of our Self, the clearing forces of our body, the tidal changes of our minds, and the sacred communion of our Selves in connection to what is divine.

Our attunement with water brings us to the magick of our Selves. We become the cauldrons of our own transformations. We learn to listen to the flow within. With a sacred attunement to what flows within our Selves, we learn to seek the source of our lives. We learn to recognize what is mystical, holy, and divine flowing from within our inner knowing. With an attunement to water, we learn to seek the Grail, and we find it within our Selves. In so doing, we are transformed by wisdom and healed from within. Thus are the images and our journeys into water.

Water also brings us the power to use our inner knowledge, and to reflect this wisdom in our life for self-healing and emotional well-being. Water imageries, like the element itself, are often quite emotional. Like water and emotions, journeys into this element are sometimes beautiful and flowing, sometimes storming and blowing, and sometimes simply babbling. However they reveal themselves, water journeys are always transformative and healing.

These three imagery exercises can be used to bring personal attunement, emotional wellness, and the powers of intuition into your life. Use them and the journey accounts that follow as I have suggested, then adapt and personalize them to suit yourself. Your own active imageries and ceremonies can be as elaborate or as simple as you need. As always, take time to note the special images that emerge within your mind.

The Sacred Pool: An Imagery Exercise for Releasing and Clearing

Imagine that you are sitting beside a deep pool of dark blue water surrounded by soft, lacy ferns. On the surface of the pool, lavender water lilies float amidst bright green, heart-shaped leaves. Here and there, iridescent dragonflies dart over the waters, their tiny wings reflecting in the sunlight.

You have brought a wooden bowl, which you dip into the pool and fill with the cool, pure water. As you do so, the surface of the water shifts and swirls, causing the water lilies to dance in delight. You cup your hands and fill them with water from your bowl. You hold your hands high, prayerfully honoring the beauty surrounding you. You gently splash your face with the crystal-clear water. The coolness brings a sense of refreshment deep within your Self. As the water trickles down your face and neck, you feel it wash away the worries, the sadness, the pains, and the problems that have expressed themselves on your face.

You continue this little ceremony, each time clearing away more and more of the feelings that have lined your face and brought you frowns. As the Sun dries the water on your face, you find that you are smiling once again.

The Healing Rain:
An Imagery Exercise for Emotional
Expression and Self-Healing

Imagine that you are alone in a mountain meadow on a warm summer day. Above you, soft rain clouds drift across a deep blue sky. A gentle breeze signals the onset of rain.

The drops fall slowly from the sky. You can see them as they splash against the rocks and bend the blades of grass. You can hear them pattering purposefully on the bright petals of the mountain wildflowers. You open your mouth and feel the quick splash of raindrops on your tongue and against your cheeks. They make you laugh with joy at the delightful feel of their cool contact with your body. They splash into your eyes and flow across your forehead.

The raindrops fall faster now, with an insistent rhythm. On impulse, you strip the clothes from your body and dance in this gentle, healing summer rain. All of Nature seems to dance with you. The flowers and the grasses sway to and fro in tune with the rhythm of the raindrops falling on the ground.

You dance to celebrate your feelings of joy at being healthy, clear, and vitally connected to the nature of your Self. You improvise your dance as an expression of your healing emotions. You dance to express gladness and delight. You dance to express your Self.

The rain softens and ceases, and the Sun emerges from behind a silvery white cloud. Then, as the rays of the Sun reflect through the veils of the sky, you dance to celebrate the rainbow that appears across the horizon. You rest and reflect on the many colors of the rainbow. As you do so, you recognize the many aspects of your Self that reflect moods and feelings like the banded hues of the rainbow. Resting there in the warm sunlit meadow, you accept your wholeness, the full spectrum of your inner being as it reflects in many tones of emotions, many shades of feelings, many forms, light and dark, forming a single, beautiful reflection of your Self.

The Silent Storm: An Imagery Exercise for Finding Much-Needed Inner Wisdom and Solutions to Deep Problems

 Imagine that during a raging storm, you are seeking shelter under an outcropping of rocks that juts forth from high steep cliffs at the edge of the sea.

As the gale-force winds drive the rain between the stones, you feel the depths of your despair. You feel cold, uncertain, and alone. As the winds howl and the waves crash against the cliffs, you cry out for help. You do not know which way to go. You do not know which path will lead you home to safety and calm comfort. You remember all the storms you have weathered before, but they seem to be nothing more than insignificant tempests compared to the storm you face now. Your tears blend with the salty spray sweeping in from the sea.

In anguish, you reach within your Self to find the answers, the solution for the situation you are in now. Deep within, you hear the voice of reason counseling calm, patience, and comfort. You reach ever deeper within your Self, seeking that inner voice of wisdom. As you do so, the wind ceases its furious onslaught, the waves smooth out, and the rain sweeps out across the sea. All is quiet, peaceful, and calm as you find the wisdom within your Self.

In the tranquil moments that follow the terrible storm, you hear that wise inner voice. You hear the wisdom within, and you know what you must do. You listen and find new direction. With relief and renewed purpose, you find the path that leads you home.

∞∾↺∾

These images, exercises, and journey accounts may also be adapted for personal rituals of self-healing and celebrations of self-transformation. A simple bath with fragrant herbs can become a sacred pool in which you immerse yourself with the conscious intent to catalyst self-healing. A dance in the rain is most delightful, but a warm shower can be a ritual of release and renewal, and work miracles. Followed by quiet times of rest and reflection, they can lead you to that sacred realm of inner knowing.

Times of trauma, chaos, and upheaval can be weathered in the shelter of your deep, inner Self. Though these times of stormy emotions cannot be controlled, their damaging effects can be much diminished by the guidance you receive from your inner wisdom. As you learn to face head-on any stormy emotions that arise in your life, you will find that they pass far more quickly when you let them flow through you without fear.

Sometimes water imagery can become quite extensive, deep, and flowing, due to the essential nature of the element itself. When this happens, try to flow with the healing qualities of the element and receive from the wisdom within. It is no mistake that two of the deepest mystical symbols, the Grail and the cauldron, are associated with the element of water.

Personal Journey Account

This journey is another example of how mysterious the realms of consciousness can be when we actively reach into them. My intention was to focus on an image of the Crone and on the cauldron of transformation, and devise a deep personal healing and release. I called forth an image of Loch Gur in County Limerick, Ireland, a place I had found to be profoundly powerful.

After that image came, the rest emerged unbidden. This journey reveals some ancient mythic interpretations as well. By working with the images that emerged, I was able to bring much more depth to my inner experience.

Only one expectation is suggested when making these deep journeys on your own. Expect the unexpected—or, perhaps, be ready for what you really expect.

The Cauldron of Transformation

I am aware of nothing, and yet I feel able to perceive everything. I am in the void. I realize that I am quite alone at this moment. My gentle guide, Manannan, Lord of the Waves, has gone now. Having cast his magick cloak over me, he left me garbed in a silken gown of self-transformation. I wait in the silence and darkness of this place of anticipation and anxiety.

I wonder if this is how waiting to be born feels. An ancient yearning wells up inside me. I feel a pull stronger than any current I have yet encountered. Emotions flood my senses, and I cry out in the darkness. "Mother, where are you? Can you hear me? Can you feel me? Do you even know I'm here at all? Mother, Mother, Mama! Come to me, please!"

A violent force propels me forward. I tumble about wildly in the darkness for awhile, then the movement ceases as suddenly as it had begun. I can see light clearly above my head. It reaches down through the waters around me, revealing a smooth sandy surface just beneath my feet. I stand up, slowly realizing, with a sense of chagrin, that I am actually in rather shallow water. Little waves lap around my knees to confirm this. I feel delightfully silly as I survey my surroundings.

I am in what appears to be a small, natural harbor. There are several small, hide-covered boats anchored close to the shoreline. They seem to be woven together with leather and wood. Farther away, at the mouth of this harbor, a longship floats majestically on the waters. I can see its dragon prow silhouetted against a midnight-blue sky filled with stars.

A razor-sharp crescent moon gleams above me, its points up. I think it resembles a dark crystal ball resting on a stand made of fine silver, delicately crafted, and thinner than a cat's ear. For a time, I am lost in that dark orb upon the crescent moon.

I jump at the sound of a large metal gate opening behind me. My movement sets the little boats rocking. I hear a wave slap the hull of the longship. A voice crackles through the night, stirring me to action.

"Are you planning to wait for a lower tide before you come inside?"

The voice is stern, biting, but not sarcastic. It is the voice of an elderly woman, one who is not just a grandmother, but a great-grandmother. The voice is completely devoid of warmth, yet not cold. It is clear of emotion, yet filled with wisdom. It is a good voice, even if it does scare me a little.

When I turn to face the source of this voice, I see a bony old woman standing beside an open gate. It is an iron gate at the top of a steep stairway leading up to a large stone castle-fort. I can see the outline of its rounded shape blocking the sky from my view. Here and there a window glows with light, indicating the presence of fire within.

I feel very cold as I make my way through the water toward the castle-fort. It would be easier to swim in, I'm certain. Still, trudging through this water gives me time to collect myself.

I am not altogether sure how I feel about this, in any case. I had called out for my mother; I had not expected a hag. I had felt the womb joy of anticipating rebirth; I had not expected a rough old pile of rocks thrown together, gods know how or when. I had not expected a craggy old castle-fort and a haggy old woman.

I make my way out of the water and onto the rough, stone step. I climb halfway up the stairway before stopping to sit and rest.

I am a sodden mess, an old wash rag someone neglected to wring out. My lovely silken gown hangs on me like a fishing net. It is heavy, and I want to take it off. I squeeze the hem and send water dripping down the steps.

"Best leave that wet rag here."

This is more of a command than a suggestion. I wait for promises of dry, warm clothes and soft blankets, but none come. My gown is very uncomfortable now, but I have become used to the way it feels on me. I wonder about this need I have to keep it on. I attempt to diffuse the issue with a retort.

"Which wet rag do you mean, Crone Grandmother?" I ask her. "Are you referring to me or to what I'm wearing?"

She hobbles down the steps toward me. I can see her cheekbones sharply projecting from her sunken face. Her eyes are dark and shrewd as they appraise me. Her garments are moldy and old, once black, now gray. As she walks, matted hair falls forward in strands of tarnished silver from inside the hood of her cape. She is bent over with age, yet her strength is bone deep. She pokes a sharp, twisted finger in the center of my chest.

"One and the same, my girl, one and the same." She jabs her finger again to bring home her point. "You've become used to the discomfort that you've wrapped around yourself. You don't feel natural without wearing it."

I think of how lovely my gown had once been. I think of how it had moved, as if it had been woven on me. Now it hangs in dull knots, its fine threads transformed into frayed ropes covered with slime and seaweed. Was this what I had claimed to be my second skin—or even my first?

129

"How can what seems so fine become so foul?" I moan, pulling the heavy garment away from my shoulders. As I stand up to struggle with one of the knots, the garment falls around my ankles in a damp, smelly heap. I try to kick it off of my feet, but it will not budge.

I cannot figure out what to do. I look at the crone for a clue. I do not expect pity, but I would be grateful for advice, at least right now. I know not to ask for help too quickly. I suppress a desire to scream when I speak.

"What lesson would you have me learn from this, Crone?" I shiver and strive to remain calm, standing there cold and naked under a tangle of rotten ropes.

The crone speaks with a compassion that is not tender, but ruthlessly productive.

"'Tis not the weave of the garment nor the threads themselves, that create the problems. 'Tis the weaver of the fabric and the substance from which the fiber is formed. If the fiber is made of material that absorbs all that it encounters, then the threads will soon become swollen and glutted. The cloth will weaken from the strain of carrying around a load that it was not intended to bear."

She pauses to see if I have understood her properly.

"And the weaver, Crone Grandmother?" I feel the threads of rope at my feet. They are pulpy and soft.

"The weaver must first learn the nature of the fiber. The weaver must know this before the threads are spun, before the fabric is woven, and before the cloth is cut into a pattern and sewn together."

The crone pokes her finger at me once more. "The weaver must know the weaver," she tells me. "You must know yourself. You must become familiar with the fibers, and know the purpose and the patterns with which you choose to weave the threads of your life. You must know and accept the cloth from which you are cut. Finally, you must know when to scrap what you have created and begin anew."

I look at the fragments of fabric clinging to the rough fibers of the ropes.

"How do I start anew, Grandmother?" I begin trying to loosen the wet strands around my feet. I wish briefly that I had a sword or battle axe. I realize that these would only end up cutting me, as well as my bindings. Still, I wish for a sword.

"This is such a futile process," I gasp, struggling to shift the ropes. "And what can be done to keep it from happening again, even if I do free myself from this mess right now?"

The crone actually seems pleased. A flicker of satisfaction crosses her stern face. "That is the question I was waiting to hear you ask." She turns to climb the stairs. "I'll show you the answer as soon as you come inside."

The crone reaches the top of the stairs and passes through the gateway. She pauses at the doorway of the castle-fort and calls down to me.

"You'll never cut those away with anger, my girl. They'll only cling tighter." The crone enters the castle-fort muttering something about too much fire and hot water.

Fire and hot water sound like wonderful enticements to me, even if that wasn't how the crone had meant them. It is time to have done with these sodden bindings. I am anxious to follow the crone inside and hear her wisdom.

"I know that I cannot tangle myself further with anger and frustration. I cannot feel resentment for the ropes that hold me fast." Perhaps the crone can't hear me, or isn't listening.

"I can only accept responsibility for what I have created and accept the need to learn new ways of being. I can only free myself by becoming detached from these bindings. I can only be grateful ...." I stop short at the sight of the crone leaning against the doorway of the castle-fort.

"When you're through preaching to yourself, you can step out of that mess and come inside. I have something to show you," she says, singularly unimpressed with my efforts. "Just step out of it and walk away. If you want to, it's easy."

I discover this is true. "Damn," I say, moving clear of the ropes and making my way up the stairs. Something makes me pause to glance back at the bindings I have left behind. I watch as they melt into a pool of water that begins to trickle down the stairs and into the harbor, merging with its own element for transmutation. I watch for a moment, then turn to rush up the stairs and into the castle-fort.

I find the crone in a large, round chamber at the center of the castle-fort. A fire burns low in a pit located in the center of this room. Over the fire hangs a huge, black cauldron. It is suspended from strong iron stands imbedded in the rock floor of the chamber. Crystal vials, stone jars, and primitive woven baskets cover the tops of several stone-carved tables. Dried herbs hang from rafter beams, and an ancient loom gathers dust in the shadows.

I move close to the fire, seeking its familiar warmth. The cauldron is certainly large enough to bathe in. It would be a warm bath, as well, I expect, judging the heat of the fire. The crone stirs some fragrant herbs into the cauldron. I catch the scent of lavender as the steam rises. I peek into the cauldron and find a crystalline blue-violet liquid inside.

"It's beautiful," I exclaim. "I just want to immerse myself in it."

"Imagine what would have happened if you had entered these crystal waters wearing those rotten ropes?"

The crone waits for my answer.

"But I couldn't do that, could I? I can't even imagine it," I reply.

"'Tis precisely so," she tells me. It would be completely impossible. That is why so many fail to find the cauldron. They have allowed themselves to absorb all manner of poisons and rarely let themselves release any of it at all."

"Without the release, there can be no renewal," I add thoughtfully.

The crone nods in agreement and speaks again. "It is not purity that is required to enter the waters of the cauldron. It is clarity. It is a true willingness to transform one's Self that leads to the healing powers of the cauldron—or of the Grail."

The crone tosses some more lavender buds into the cauldron. She stirs these into the water for a time, then skims them off the surface, leaving it crystalline clear. She motions for me to climb inside the cauldron, and I do so without hesitation. It is only after I enter the warm healing waters that I pause to consider this action.

"Now that I'm in here," I call from the cauldron, "shall I ever get back out? Shall I become someone's supper, I wonder?"

The crone makes her way to the cauldron with two small bowls in her hands. "Not yet, my pretty!" she says, mocking my jest. "And not without some salt."

She pours salt crystals into the waters of the cauldron. I feel them settle around my body. The salt crystals pull me deeper into the warmth of the waters. I notice that the crone's face seems softer now, almost maternal. I have no chance to bid her farewell as I slip into the depths of the cauldron.

At first, I am aware only of warmth and light, then a gentle sensation of being rocked, quietly rocked by some deep, nurturing power. It begins to blot out everything else in my consciousness. In that warmth and motion, I realize the true nature of the womb.

Once again, I await rebirth, this time from within a place of warmth, light, and love. Such is the true nature of the womb. Such is the true nature of the cauldron. Such is the power of self-healing, and the wisdom of self-clarification.

I immerse myself in the nurturing warmth until all other thoughts, feelings, and sensations melt away. For a time, there is only the light and the love. I drift into the embrace of the inner mother and sleep.

I awaken to another time, another dimension of my Self. The cauldron and the castle-fort have faded from my imagery. The crone has gone, yet I feel her wisdom within. I know that I entered and reemerged from the depths of my Self. I know that, having once merged with the cauldron, I entered into a realm of my being which is eternally present, pure, and powerful.

Evoking the Allies of the Element Water

Consider the aspects of the element water—self-healing, release, renewal, transformational inner-knowing. Consider your experience of this element—emotional well-being, clarity, serenity.

Structure within your mind the images you've created to describe the forms, the shapes, and the details of two figures reflecting the realm of the element water. These may be as mystical or symbolic as you choose. These are your images of the spirit keepers of the divine flow. They are your personal inner priestly ones and healers.

Call them forth for emotional support and clear intuition. They are ever present, flowing from your inner knowing.

Amplify your vision to include as many aspects as you can to bring these figures into clear focus. Note all that you see, all that you hear, all that you feel and smell, all that you taste or touch, all that you sense within your image.

Carefully note and record your reactions to each contact you have with your own allies from the element of water.

Tap into the depths of water's sacred flow each time you evoke the holy allies of this element.

Personal Journey Account

This is a description of an image that began as evoking the allies of the element water, but as it emerged, it became an imagery involving personal, transformative choice, and expanded into a deeper, personal journey. As an image transforms into one of greater depth, it is your personal choice to structure it as you will or go with its own evolving flow. Both approaches have merit for personal empowerment.

The Magick Chalice

I stand in a small pavilion made of white stone and gray-veined marble. Through the arches of the pavilion I can see a stream of water flowing gently over a moss-covered dam made from river rocks. Upstream there is a quiet, dark pool with willow branches caressing its surface. Downstream the water moves swiftly, sweeping between soft, grassy banks. The stream makes its way around smooth boulders and gnarled roots. It runs clear and pure. In the shallows I can see minnows, tiny silvery flashes along a white sandy bottom. Beautiful rainbow-hued fish rest in quiet pools between the rocks.

There is a small stone bridge at mid-stream and a path leading up to the pavilion. I see two figures crossing the bridge, a man and a woman. They wear soft, water-colored ceremonial robes. The cloaks are clasped across their hearts with crescent-moon brooches wrought of silver, and set with milky translucent stones and pearls. The fabric seems to float about their bodies as they move toward me. Both the man and the woman have blue-black hair that falls in thick waves around their pale luminous faces. The woman's hair cascades down her back and brushes against her ankles with each step she takes.

She is carrying a silver chalice. She holds it carefully with both hands, her attention completely absorbed in bearing this chalice safely across the bridge. The man follows close behind her.

At the foot of the bridge she pauses. The man moves forward and reaches to support her arm as she steps onto the path leading up to the pavilion. They seem to float through the archways together, holding the silver cup. They move as one, intent on the chalice and its contents. I notice that the chalice is quite full. I can see that it contains a silvery-blue liquid.

The man and woman glide across the cool, white stone floors, and place the chalice on a marble pedestal in the center of the pavilion, directly in front of me. Although they do not speak, they convey their intentions clearly. They have come to offer me the opportunity to drink from their lovely silver chalice. It is a magickal cup that may never be emptied, no matter how many come to drink from it.

I consider the complexities that this magick chalice represents, then I am struck by the pure simplicity of its meaning. It is life, ever replenishing itself as it flows through the sacred vessel of our Selves. It is the eternal flow.

Looking into the silvery-blue liquid, I glimpse a clear stream flowing within. Its current is deep and compelling. It draws me inside my Self and makes me wonder if I am worthy to drink from such a stream.

In silent answer to my concerns, the man and the woman begin to drape me with marvelous robes. The robes are silky, fluid to the touch. They are made from finely woven threads in shades of indigo, lavender, pale gray, and cream. Freshwater pearls are sewn at every crossing of the threads. The robes are encrusted with these and other opalescent stones. The couple continues to adorn me with rare, beautiful jewels and opulent fabrics. They continue until I can scarcely stand on my own, holding up the weight of all these treasures. I plead for them to stop. I can hold no more.

They stand before me, calmly regarding me with their strange lavender eyes.

They offer me a choice, unspoken. Either continue to quest for what I can never mortally feel worthy of, or simply stop and accept what is true and worthy within. Either search outward for symbols of achievement, or return inward, homeward, to what is real and true. I must remember how to receive.

I realize that I cannot hold on to all these glittering external adornments and still drink from that silver chalice within.

I shrug the robes from my shoulders and cast the jewels into the clear, fast-moving stream.

I lift the chalice from its pedestal and drink.

Mythic Figures of Water

Manannan

Manannan was the mystical ruler of the sea, the Irish lord of the waves. Whitecaps were his white horses, which often signaled his arrival from the deep ocean that was his chosen realm. His Welsh counterpart was Manawyddan, whose realm included the many tiny islands along the west coast of Britain. Today, Manannan is still strongly associated with the Isle of Man.

Manannan was able to transform himself into human or animal shape, such as a handsome, seductive man or a sea creature. He possessed a magick cloak that could provide invisibility, healing, protection, or simply cause an experience best forgotten to be erased from memory. Manannan did this to cause both Cuchulain and Emer to forget the false desires and jealousy brought on them by our next mythic figure, Fand.

Imagery application — Attune with the imagery of Manannan when you need the transformative power of release. Also use this imagery to learn to flow with your own stream of consciousness. Learn not to structure each experience, each time. Let your images flow forth naturally, then begin to structure your use of them. Do this from time to time to allow your deepest consciousness to send new images into your inner vision.

Fand

Fand was the wife of Manannan and a goddess of the sea in her own right. Her seductive powers led her to become involved with the fiery hero, Cuchulain. As a reward for protecting her realm, she offered to become his mistress. Because her powers were worthy of any sea siren, this caused Fand to encounter Emer, the next figure, who reflects the emotional elements of water.

Imagery application — Evoke imagery of Fand when you need to control your emotional responses and be "charming."

Emer

Emer, the wife of Cuchulain, was called the Tara of Women in honor of her many beautiful, gentle qualities. When Cuchulain became entranced with Fand, Emer appeared with fifty of her maidens, armed and ready to reclaim her rights to this hero of all Ireland.

Instead of a battle, though, there ensued an emotional exchange. First Emer expressed herself clearly to Cuchulain, explaining that she would rather release him to Fand than cause him the despair of being bound emotionally to someone he no longer loved. Cuchulain, without consulting his inner wisdom, suggested that he could love both women. This immediately allied Fand and Emer against Cuchulain. What followed was a round of emotional expressions of high regard from Fand to Emer and from Emer to Fand.

Fand, it seems, had not been serious, but had merely been amusing herself with Cuchulain. Fand, in desperation, called for her husband Manannan to appear unseen to the others. When he appeared, Manannan passed his cloak between them so that Fand could make her escape, thus leaving Cuchulain and Emer alone with a new emotional connection to each other and no memory of what had passed.

Emer, as some myths tell us, must have had some memory of all this, for she had the druids create a potion guaranteed to make herself and Cuchulain forget all but their love for each other. We are left to speculate on the nature of this potion, but we can assume it was similar in content to the one given our next characters, Isolde and Tristan.

Imagery application — Create an image of Emer when you need to clearly understand your emotional needs. Also use Emer to determine what is or is not negotiable for your Self and your personal healing process. Use this to aid you in expressing your emotions with clarity. Emer represents an "inner council" member of great power.

Isolde

Isolde was an Irish beauty of high-born rank who was bartered to a foreign king (some say Wales, some say Cornwall) in order to solidify an alliance between their respective kingdoms. This king, Mark, was not a bad king, just an unfeeling one in regard to women (or so it seems).

Mark sent his foster son (sometimes said to be his nephew), Tristan, to fetch Isolde. Once Isolde and Tristan met, they knew that their true love lay with each other. Though Tristan made a noble effort to honor his sovereign lord, he was ultimately undone. This was due to a potion prepared for Isolde to share with King Mark upon her arrival at his kingdom. This potion was created by a druidess (ban drui) at Isolde's request so that she could bind herself to her future husband and he to her.

On the voyage across the Irish Sea, Isolde shared the potion with Tristan, and gave herself to him. What followed was a series of chases and escapes to avoid the wrath of Mark. What resulted was Isolde still bound by marriage to Mark but by the heart of her emotions to Tristan.

Tristan was banished forever and found comfort with another woman conveniently called Isolde. By the time the first Isolde located Tristan once more, he was in the process of releasing his spirit into the Otherworld.

This sad, emotional tale is echoed in several forms of Celtic mythology. The tale of Diedre of the Sorrows and Diarmuid (also called Naosi) is very similar. The Arthurian version places Guinevere in the emotional bind of loving two men, Arthur and Lancelot. They, in turn, are bound together by their loyalty to one another and their devotion to the Round Table.

Each version of this myth represents the deep transformational effects of our emotions. It also represents the effects that deep emotional ties can have on the course of history. Wherever there are tales of stormy love, unrequited love, and stolen love, there is water. Wherever there is a division caused between people or between the land and the people that results in an escape or a quest to reclaim what was lost, there is the element of water.

Imagery application — Attune with imagery of Isolde and the others who similarly reflect her element in order to develop a deeper trust of your own intuition. Also let these images enable you to pause and reflect within before your emotions sweep you into decisions you may wish you had not made so quickly. The images also provide a sense of serenity and patience while waiting for the tides of emotional relationships to ebb and flow.

The more magickal aspects of water reflect in the myths that tell of cauldrons of transformation. Examples of these include the Welsh myth of the cauldron of Bran the Blessed. The cauldron of Bran could restore life to once-dead warriors who were immersed in its contents. This cauldron was naturally quite coveted by the ever-battling Celts.

Cerridwen and Taliesin

Another cauldron of great mythic quality was the cauldron of Cerridwen, senior goddess of power and magick for the Welsh. This cauldron was instrumental in transforming Cerridwen's son from a hapless character into Taliesin, the great Welsh bardic druid.

This transformation was not without trial, however. Taliesin, much like Moses, was cast into the sea in a small boat (a coracle) and left to the mercy of the element water. With the ingredients accidentally obtained from Cerridwen's cauldron and transformative journey into the mystic realm of water, Taliesin became completely initiated into the realms of magick. Eventually, he was able to gain the full acknowledgment and empowerment of his mother, Cerridwen, though it involved a bit of trickery on the part of his uncle.

Cerridwen represents wisdom that must be earned through trial, transformation, and quests within. This wisdom often requires cleverness and a ration of self-trickery to obtain.

The quests for the Grail also reflect the more mystical qualities of water in its aspect as an element of communion with the divine.

Imagery application — Attune with Cerridwen and come face to face with the Crone Grandmother of all healing and transformation. Know this aspect as your truest inner teacher and most inexorable healing ally.

Attune with Taliesin to be an inner council teacher bringing the wisdom and the skill you need to navigate the stormy seas of self-transformation. Taliesin brings the added healing magick of wit, as he was also very much a bard.

Keynote for Water

Learn when to surf, when to swim, and when to "shoot the curl." Also learn how to paddle out and wait for the waves.

7

Earth:
The Clan Leaders

Honoring the Element of Earth

Earth is the element that some have claimed to be missing from the alchemy of the Celts. This, I feel, is a misunderstanding or an underestimation of the Celtic connection to the Earth itself.

For the Celts, at least initially, the element of earth and the planet Earth were one and the same. Their mystical connection to Nature provided the Celt with the element of earth. This connection continued to be the prime source of the earth element until the Celts ceased being basically a tribe of hunter gatherers and began to develop agricultural skills. After the Celts began to harvest the land and create settlements, the elemental power of earth became more clearly a part of their alchemy. From the farms and villages came the foundational structures on which great civilizations were formed. This was truly a reflection of the element of earth at work in the progressive development of the Celts. Earth was the keystone element of Celtic civilizations and nations. It was the unifying element of the tribal Celts.

Earth was the element reflected in the ancient Celtic henotheistic view revering the spirit of place. It was the element from which the tribal gods emerged, each a force of empowerment in unique relationship to the specific tribe. These tribal gods were of such manifest power to the Celts that they were celebrated as the true rulers of the tribes. So real were these deities that in later times Roman legions often confused them with the corporeal leaders of the Celtic warring tribes. This, for the Celts, would have been viewed as only natural, because that view reflected the element of earth in the Celts.

Earth led the Celts to form great clans, each with an independent, self-ruling structure. Later, these clans gathered under the leadership of the high kings and queens of Ireland, Scotland, England, Cornwall, Brittany, and Wales. Still later, these nations structured systems by which they could share the common wealth of the lands they occupied. Continuing into current times, the element of earth was reflected in the formation of groups of united nations. This, in itself, laid the foundation on which a global community began to be built. The element of earth was and still is reflected in the Celts' connection with all the peoples of the planet Earth.

Earth led the Celts to create intricate systems of laws specifying the rights of each member of the tribe and later the rights of the individual as inalienably free and independent. Earth was the foundational force that led to the creation of the Brehon laws and the sets of customs ordering and guiding the existence of the tribes. Earth was at work in the role of the *brehons* or druidic judges. These brehons acted as the first circuit riders, traveling through the lands and teaching, as well as exacting judgments. This early judicial system of the Celts clearly reflected the element of earth.

Earth was expressed in the foundation of the druidic schools of wisdom that featured elaborately structured programs of learning. Later, these gave way to the structures of religious monks and nuns. Still later, the rights of the independent Celts reemerged in the foundation of secular orders and secular nations, in which individuals had the right, the choice, and the freedom to worship in their own ways. This power of the earth element was clearly reflected in the individual's right to connect with that which is divine according to his or her own heart, mind, and spirit. It also harkens back to the ancient Celtic concept of tribal gods and connection to the power of the personal homeland, and to the powers of Mother Nature.

Connecting with Earth in Imagery

Connection with the element of earth is most powerful when accomplished in deep, primeval forests, in fertile mountain valleys, or amidst fields of golden grain. The element of earth is strong and pure in the high country where the wide, blue sky seems to be supported by the mountain tops. In the lowlands, the earth is more diffuse in its energy as it softens and spreads out to connect with the rivers and the oceans.

Earth is clearly present wherever the great trees make their own root connections to the bosom of Mother Nature. It holds dominion over the orchards and the groves. It interweaves its energies in the arbors and the vines, bringing the abiding power of growth and abundance to the production of fruit, vegetables, and flowers.

Earth is present in every growing thing on this planet, from the simple grasses to the majestic elder trees. The element of earth reflects its power in the rocky, barren ground, and represents its eternal force of life in each grain of sand and each tiny stone. The abundant strength of this element reveals itself with every step we take and every move we make. We are eternally supported by the foundational forces of earth.

When we connect with earth, we enter into a relationship with the essential structures of Nature and of self-nature. Journeys into the element earth provide us with a connection to our deepest roots, our source of Self, our parental heritage in symbolic as well as earthly form.

Journeys into the earth element can bring us face to face with the miracles of Nature and the mysteries of our Self. Earth journeys are sometimes slow, step by step, self-building, stone by stone. They may also be forceful and unexpected, such as earthquakes of realization, avalanches of new awareness, landslides into wisdom. Earth journeys, like the element itself, require a blend of discipline and devotion to the process of becoming wise, aware, and awakened to the powers of Self and Nature.

Journeys into the element of earth teach us the manifestation secrets of order, abundance, and practicality. They bring sacred wisdom out of the esoteric and into the everyday experience of our lives. Earth journeys make magick real. They bring us to the grounded, centered core of our Selves. From this place of collected wisdom we find the means and methods to transmute the chaos and impulses that create diversions on our paths to power. In earth we find the structures of our strength and the supportive magick with which we grow in wisdom and in truth.

Earth also brings us the ability to make objective decisions about the structures of our Self. It brings us the patience to plan, to plant, and to produce what we need. Try this imagery to begin measuring and managing your own growth.

Seed of Self:
An Imagery Exercise for Personal Growth

 Imagine for a moment that you are a seed, waiting in silent anticipation for your time to sprout forth from the soil that has supported you during your time of germination.

You are a unique seed. You have the special ability to actively participate in the processes of your own growth. You are an equal partner with the elements of your own creation. You have a valuable role in determining the structures by which you will develop. You have a voice in this process. You have a choice as to how you wish to shape yourself and how you want to structure your life. You are aware of the firm foundations from which you have emerged. You know which structures are solid and unchangeable. However, do you know which structures actually are changeable? Do you know which of the foundational aspects of your life are flexible enough to allow you to form according to your own design?

Consider these questions carefully, for the processes of your own growth have already begun. It is up to you to determine the results of this growth, and to design the supportive structures by which you shape your ultimate Self. You are eternally the seed of your Self, ever seeking the light to empower your growth.

Earth also teaches us to create our own systems of personal empowerment, and to make our own connection to the power of the planet. Earth connects us to Nature in a mutually empowering relationship. Try this imagery to reawaken your Earth connected memory. Use it to access the dimensions of the mind where sacred symbolic wisdom are stored.

Stone Sanctuary:
An Imagery Exercise for Strength

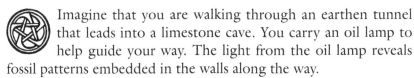 Imagine that you are walking through an earthen tunnel that leads into a limestone cave. You carry an oil lamp to help guide your way. The light from the oil lamp reveals fossil patterns embedded in the walls along the way.

Here and there, black smudges show that others have come this way before, perhaps in ancient days. There are no indications that this tunnel has been visited in recent times. You find that the passageway is clear and open. The limestone is pale and brightly reflects the light that you carry with you—and within you.

You find an opening leading to a small, quiet cavern, just large enough for you to stand up. This small cavern is rounded, smooth, and silent. You step through the opening and settle comfortably into this special place.

Lifting your oil lamp, you search the walls and ceilings for fossils, symbols, or signs that someone has been here before you. You search, but find nothing. Only the twinkle of lights reflecting off of the limestone is present in this quiet, pristine place. Slowly, you lower the flame of your lamp until the cave is comfortably darkened.

It is completely quiet in this, your private sanctuary of stone. You become aware of a strong, steady rhythm. Its sound vibrates off of the walls, amplifying itself with power. You wonder about the source of this sound, until you realize, with some amusement, that you are hearing the sound of your own heartbeat. You laugh out loud, and echoes of delight dance around inside your cave. After a few moments, the sound fades away, and all is silent once more.

You rest in the smooth comfort of your stone sanctuary, and reflect upon the strength and the steadiness of your heartbeat. You feel the steady strength of your Self as you rest there, centered and connected to the quiet rhythms of your self-nature.

All around you is a stillness and a silence of profound power and peace. You feel your Self merging with this stillness, becoming part of this power, entering into the silence, and finding the peace profound.

From deeper within the heart of Nature, you hear the steady rhythms of the Earth. You feel them inside your Self, strong, stable, and abiding rhythms of power. You feel the strength within. You feel supported completely by these peaceful abiding rhythms of the Earth, of Nature, of your Self.

In silent ceremony, you connect with the core of your Self. You connect with the structures inside your Self that bring you strength. In connecting to the heart of your Self, you find your deepest power waiting and abiding within; you find the foundation of patience and perseverance. You find that these have their origin in the profound power of peace that exists within the sanctuary of your Self.

You know, with sacred assurance, that this sanctuary is always there, abiding in peace, waiting for you to enter into its silent power and find your strengths.

Personal Journey Account

Earth also brings new meaning to symbolic messages. In the following journey, I became more deeply acquainted with the element of earth in a way that also reflected the truly balanced equality of both the male and female aspects of learning to craft and structure the aspects of Self.

This next journey, though brief, was both very deep and experientially effective. It resulted from my conscious attempts to work with the figure of the smith, most revered in Celtic myth, as well as in tribal life.

Smithcraft

I emerge in a busy village somewhere on the dimensional borders shared by Brythonic and Gaelic Celts. I pass through this village unnoticed, listening to the long-forgotten language of its people.

Tartans in a variety of different patterns show the blending of many clans in this place of commerce and trade.

I find the shop of the village blacksmith. I enter quietly and watch him at his work. His is the sacred art of creating strong metal from the simple elements of earth. His is the craft of forging this metal into material forms. He makes the weapons of war and the tools of peaceful harvest. I watch as he folds glowing metal upon itself, and pounds his own strength into its manifest form.

I watch him at his smithcraft, and I wonder at the source of his alchemy. In response to my unspoken question, he bids me to look beyond the fires of his forge and find the foundational core of earth.

Unexpectedly, I find Bridget, Goddess of Smithcraft, there, in an aspect I have felt but have not truly experienced until now. She stands beside the smith, matching his movements blow for blow, crafting metal into the shape she chooses.

I see her in this earthly aspect pounding out her craft, and I find a new sense of self-recognition. I find a new respect for the power behind the structures of any art, any craft, or any effort. It is a power that requires the catalyst of inspiration, the healing patience for transformation, and the structured will to create a new form that is both practical and progressive.

As I watch them, side by side, engaged in the active alchemy of smithcraft, I notice that they are working together to create an object of strength and beauty—a scabbard wrought of woven copper and bronze.

When the scabbard is complete, Bridget presents it to me with a meaningful, knowing expression on her face. At first I am confused about the significance of a scabbard without a sword. Then, remembering that I already have a sword, I am struck by the practical aspect of having a scabbard for such a double-edged sword.

I see the wisdom in providing a structure that protects the blade while, in turn, keeping itself protected. I see that the structures of civilization are a scabbard for the blades of our barbaric elements. The scabbard not only holds the blade, but connects it to the higher purposes of positive, evolutionary processes.

I see the scabbard as a reflection of the steady energy of the earth element as it emerged in the consciousness of the Celts.

As I accept this gift, I wonder, only briefly, what would happen if the blade became stuck in the scabbard. I wonder what would happen if the active forces of our inner creative energies were somehow bound into being stuck in one set form or another.

Then I realize the clear and present danger in all elements or all structures that impose their forms upon the energies of another, and I realize the danger inherent in having no structures at all.

I leave Bridget and the smith to their realm. As I return to the familiar structures of the present time and place, I am still musing on the wisdom of their gift and the lessons of their craft—and of their Craft.

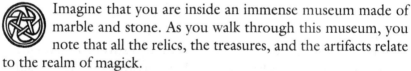

Earth also brings us the ability to input, associate, integrate, and output information. It provides us with the materials to build a storehouse of wisdom and an ordered, inner system for utilizing all knowledge.

Try this imagery exercise to examine what sorts of knowledge you have collected along the way in your life. Explore your Self as the keeper of sacred wisdom.

Museum of Magick: An Imagery Exercise for Information

Imagine that you are inside an immense museum made of marble and stone. As you walk through this museum, you note that all the relics, the treasures, and the artifacts relate to the realm of magick.

In one room you find ancient stone tablets with simple marks carved on their surfaces. These marks are no more than rudimentary lines and angles, yet you feel the complexity of their power. Even now, the magick with which these marks were made remains.

As you move through the next few rooms, you notice that these arcane artifacts become more complicated and elaborate. You see the magick regalia of wizards, wise women, and magicians from ages long past. In one corner the simple skins and hides of a shaman rest beside a white robe scrolled in gold and silver threads.

Throughout the museum there are books, some dusty and moldy, some crisp and new. On the walls are many charts, some of which show the seas inhabited by giant serpents. Several strange islands appear on ancient charts of oceans that are familiar to you. On the modern charts nearby, these islands no longer appear.

Further down the gallery hall, you find charts of the solar system, with laboriously wrought scripts describing the nature of each orb represented. Beside this chart, you find a photograph of the planet Earth taken from outer space. You find maps that mark the regions of the moon and lunar rocks brought back from voyages to its surface—so long ago, yet not so long it seems, relatively speaking.

At last you arrive in the final room. It is an atrium filled with beautiful green plants and trees. They bask in the light from the high windows in the walls and ceiling. All around this room are the artifacts of modern magick.

Wizards and wands in pewter and crystal, sets of runes, glass orbs in rainbow hues, laser lights and tuning rods, stereos, music and videos, tarot cards, computer games, synthesizers, and spirit drums all sit side by side with crystalline structures of an indeterminate age.

It is a wonderful merger of magick systems, a reflection of the present, a collection of the past, and a direction for the future.

In the midst of it all is the beautiful atrium with gnomes set in amongst the plants; waterfalls flowing over crystals; the rich smell of healthy growth; the sound of wind chimes; and spectrums dancing on the walls, reflections of the sunlight as it illuminates the ancient crystals with new energy.

As you start to leave this lovely place of magick, you notice a sign on the door at the far end of the hall. It is almost covered with sheets of plywood and plastic, but you make out the message just the same. It reads:

Pardon our mess.

Still under construction.

No completion date expected to be set.

These images of connection to the energies of earth can be adapted into more active forms. A quiet, comfortably darkened room can become the peaceful sanctuary. The soil on which you sit can determine the shape and the structure of your growth. The sense of complete silence might well require the white noise of environmental music if the modern world is too much with you (as it is with us all at times). However, the more you practice entering into the silence of your Self, the more you are able to do so, even amidst the distractions of daily life. That sanctuary is always waiting for you. No one can take it away from you.

An inventory of your own artifacts will reveal a great deal about the way you structure your growth, in both worldly and magickal ways. You might be surprised to find that these have melded into a modern blend just as the one depicted in the museum imagery. You might also find that you have changed your mind in regard to certain relics and regalia that once seemed to support your self-development and search for knowledge.

You may decide to change your path, which is as easy as changing your mind. You may decide to take new steps, in new directions, leading to a deeper connection with sacred wisdom. You can do that, you know. After all, magick is afoot—and it's also ahead.

❦

Earth is not the easiest element for me to access. On occasion I have felt as though I had to build these imageries brick by brick, laboring to let them come. Naturally, the way in which we work with an element reveals a lot about the aspects in our Selves represented by that element. It's tempting to stay with the elements that seem most familiar and that elicit the most easily accessed images. However, if we consciously activate all the elements, we find a more multidimensional Self emerging.

Evoking the Allies of the Element Earth

 Consider the aspects of the element earth—structure, wisdom, connection, leadership, and sacred symbols. Consider your experience of this element—ordered, successful, empowered, knowledgeable in action.

Structure within your mind the images you've created to describe the forms, the shapes, and the details of two figures representing the realm of the element earth. These may be as mystical or symbolic as you choose. They are your images of the spirit keepers of ordered wisdom and rational leadership. They are the patient, wise, and parental allies who teach us the mysteries of life. Call them forth to provide the supportive nurturance and structured patterns that help you govern your life.

Carefully amplify your vision to include as many aspects as you can to bring these figures into focus. Note all that you see, hear, feel, smell, taste, or touch within your image. Note and record your reactions to each contact you have with your own allies from the element of earth.

Examine the methods and the motives of your life when you evoke the allies of earth.

Find new meanings.

Personal Journey Account

The following account resulted from evoking the allies of the element earth, and has proved to be one of my most treasured connections. The imagery in this journey was very Scottish for me. I know some clans will be quite happy to hear that.

The Chieftain and the Clan Mother

I make my way through sturdy stalks of golden grain bursting forth in their readiness for harvest. I feel my bare feet against the warm ground as I walk across the furrows of this field. I smell the rich fullness of the ripe growth. I sense the deep satisfaction of a successful planting and the assurance of abundance promised and delivered by the powers of Nature.

I cross the fields and come to a group of apple trees. It is more a grove than an orchard. I note the deep, sacred connections to earth

151

in this place of abundant beauty. The apples on the tree are round and ripe. They hang heavy on the boughs in tones of red and gold. They shine like sacred jewels.

I choose an old, sturdy apple tree and spread my cape on the ground beneath its fruited branches. I pick an apple from the tree and bless the source of this bounty. A gentle breeze sweeps through the grove and the sweet smell of apples fills the air around me.

I take my dirk and make a transverse cut with its sharp, true blade. I pull the apple apart and reveal its seeds that form the sacred pattern of the five-point star. I place the pieces of apple on the ground as a gift to the element from which it emerges.

I sit upon my woven cloak and await the arrival of the allies from the realm of earth. I lean against the trunk of this abundant apple tree and drowse in the sunlight that slants through the boughs.

I awaken to another realm of awareness. There are two sturdy figures standing over me—a man and a woman of middle years in age. They have a parental bearing, with the confidence of respect well earned. They have been watching me as I drowse with sweet slumber in the warm apple grove.

They wear cloaks in a weave similar to the one on which I rest. It is a smooth, even weave made from strong, stiff threads. The fibers are sturdy, crafted of dense materials. The cloaks, and those wearing them, are of a more solid substance than most I've encountered in this realm.

The clasps holding their cloaks are five-pointed stars wrought of woven copper and set with deep violet crystals and green marble. I note that the colors of the cloaks reflect in the complexions of these allies from the realm of earth. Tones of forest green and earthy rust in their cloaks complement their deep russet hair and hazel-green eyes. Their faces are ruddy, with coppery freckles on weathered skin.

Their hair is tied back in neat, orderly fashion. It is, by nature, thick and unruly, a dense mass of tangled, wiry copper curls that would surely spring forth in wild disarray if not for the simple fiber cords holding it back. I wonder at the incongruity of this and reflect on what it represents. It is an untamed mass that no comb could pass through without losing a few of its teeth. Yet it is held, almost casually, in neat arrangement, bound by a simple structure designed to bring it under control. Their hair represents a wild raw energy, reined, but not tethered.

I begin to understand the unique, Celtic connection to the element of earth. It is an energy that finds its purest potential for freedom in the gentle, orderly adjustments of its civilized structures. It is a self-balanced wildness, natural and free. I love it. I acknowledge the source of its power and honor my connection to it.

At last I remember my manners. True to the courteous heritage of these, my ancestors, I invite them to join me. I pick three more apples from the tree and offer them for sharing.

As they sit down close beside me, I notice subtle threads of violet, gold, and white in the weave of their cloaks. These tell me of their station. They are the threads of a chieftain and clan mother.

They have brought me sustenance—food and drink to nourish me and the solid comfort of their presence to support my growth. They have also brought me a gift wrapped in natural linen. The chieftain lays it on the ground in front of me. With the eagerness of a child, I wish to open it right away. The clan mother signals me to wait and smiles with an indulgent tolerance at my studied attempts to restrain my natural impatience.

She slices the apples in equal parts and places them on another linen cloth. The chieftain empties a sack of nuts onto the cloth for us to share. He cracks these with ease in his strong hands and presents me with choice pieces of the rich nutmeat. The clan mother pours an herbal tea from a leather flask into small stone bowls.

For a time we feast in the comfortable, silent accord of kinship. As I sit between them, I feel the steady, abiding, abundant nourishment they have provided for me all along the way. They are the solid pillars that support the structures of my growth and the manifestations of my achievements.

We pass the afternoon together conversing in the mystical apple grove. We commune beneath the abundant fruited branches of my chosen tree. Tales of mythic kings, queens, and the marriages of great clans arranged to preserve the power of the land intermingle with family matters and the concerns of a mundane world.

As the Sun casts its last rays over the golden fields in the distance, the clan mother calls my attention to the unfolding of a sacred tradition. She bids me to watch carefully what happens amidst the grain. I turn to see the origin of our connection to the Earth in a vision of abundant beauty.

I see the golden rays of the Sun enter the ripening grain. I see the fields of grain reaching, opening to receive the pure energy of light.

I see the Sun transformed into a golden god, active, virile, and steady in his aspect. He is banked fire—the energy of the Sun as it warms the Earth.

I see the grains transformed into a goddess cloaked in green and gold. She is receptive, fertile, and secure in her own strength. She is awakened Earth; the abundance of her power reflects in the ripening grain. The fruit on the boughs show purely the nurturing labor she undergoes to produce sustenance for her children.

He is the generative force that activates and protects the planted seeds as they grow from within the womb of Mother Earth. He is the force that sacrifices its powers to ensure the fullness of the growth cycle and the abundance of the harvest.

Together, the Sun and the Earth connect to create the environment that sustains all growth. They are a royal pair ruling over the eternal cycles of growth and harvest. This golden god, lord of the light, and his sovereign lady, the goddess of Nature's rich green growth, dance together amidst the fields of grain and the fruited boughs. They dance to the ancient rhythms of the life forces. They dance in reflected lights celebrating the marriage of the Sun and the Earth.

As the dance fades into far memory, I remember the gift brought to me by the chieftain and the clan mother. I turn and see that they have gone. The gift, still wrapped in natural linen, lies under the apple bough. I open it slowly, reverently, and receive it with honor.

It is a shield crafted of hammered copper. There is a woven star painted in a rich green hue across its surface. In the pentagon-shaped center of this woven star is yet another golden symbol of power—a winged lion.

I wrap this shield carefully and accept the gift of its power within the center of my Self. I begin my journey home, carrying my new shield gratefully, close to the Earth.

Mythic Figures of Earth

The Dagda

The Dagda, the good god of Irish myth, represents a solidly aspected paternal figure. The Dagda was a craftsman who dressed in the garb of an artisan and carried a giant club. This giant club could either heal or destroy, depending on which end was used. The Dagda also had a magick cauldron that ensured that everyone who sought nourishment from its contents would go away satisfied. (In this aspect, the cauldron is more closely aligned with the cornucopia or horn of plenty.) The Dagda triumphed over the Fomorians when they challenged him to consume a giant's portion of food and drink from his own cauldron.

The Dagda was quite unique in his somewhat buffoonish qualities. These set him apart from his other refined de Dannan kin. However, his earthiness did not prevent him from mating with a variety of powerful and beautifully divine ladies symbolizing various aspects of the land.

The Dagda symbolizes an aspect we may call Father Nature. He is rough but solid, unpolished but powerful. It is also interesting that the nickname for "father" in many Celtic families is Dad or Dada. Dada is the correct pronunciation for Dagda.

The Dagda was also renowned for his great knowledge and in this aspect relates to the Nordic god Odin.

Imagery application — Connect with an image of the Dagda when you need to gain authority over situations in your life. This is a bit tricky because you are required to have authority over your Self first. Acquire this authority in an ordered, careful manner, using your strength and knowledge in a logical fashion. With the Dagda, we also learn to "walk softly and carry a big stick." The Dagda may also provide you with a paternal inner teacher, guiding toward abundant wisdom and growth.

Danu

Danu, in her aspect as mother of all the gods of Nature, reflects the deification of the tribal, clan mothers. Danu is her Irish name, as is Anu. She is also known as Don in the Brythonic Celtic myths. As Danu, she mated with Belenes, the god of Sun and light. This sacred marriage represents the Earth and the Sun in unison creating all of life.

As Don, she mated with Math. Math's elements were somewhat more connected to the Earth, yet he is in close connection to the activating powers of the Sun. Danu is of such antiquity that her aspect often seems difficult to define in mortal terms. Like Nature, her realms are so vast that they are beyond our complete understanding, but not beyond our reverence or our care. Any of the tribal goddesses or great queens who represented themselves ritually as the symbolic sovereignty of the land were in the direct service of Danu, Mother Nature herself.

Imagery application — Danu opens the deepest connections to your Celtic love of the land, and provides you with a maternal connection to the powers of Nature. Images of Danu change (as do that of another goddess symbolic of Nature, Bridget). With the element of earth, Danu emerges as the great sovereign Mother—the inner mother, nurturer, and gentle ruler within your Self that may grow to full power when connected with your personal image of Danu.

Mary, Queen of Scots

Since Mary, Queen of Scots, has become the legendary "clan mother" of Scotland and Scots throughout the world, it seems appropriate to include a version of her words here. These were said, I must add, while she still retained her head, but had just been forced to sign the documents which would deprive her of her ancestral throne. These lines are from "Mary, Queen of Scots," by Henry Glassford Bell, a true bard:

> *"My lords, my lords," the captive said,*
> *"Were I but once more free,*
> *With ten good knights on yonder shore*
> *to aid my cause and me,*
> *This parchment would I scatter wide,*
> *to every breeze that blows;*
> *And once more reign, a Stuart queen,*
> *o'er my remorseless foes."*

Imagery application — Use imagery of Mary, Queen of Scots to honor the noble sacrifice of all who spend their lives in service to the preservation of the lands and its heritage of power. Also use Mary and other great "sacrificed queens" to evoke nobility from within your nature. It's truly in you.

Nuada

Nuada (pronounced New-ah), was the de Dannan king who sacrificed himself for the protection of his people. Nuada is closely associated with a magick sword of light, a gift of the de Dannan, which allies him with the realm of fire as well. Yet his leadership and his protection of his people represent the most noble aspects of a chieftain, so I include Nuada here.

At the first battle of Moytura, when the de Dannan conquered Ireland, Nuada lost his hand (some say arm). Because the law of Tara required its king to be free of any disfigurement, Nuada had to forfeit his kingship.

The kingship fell to Breas, the beautiful but selfish son of a Fomorian father and a de Dannan mother. Breas was selected by the women of the Tuatha de Dannan, supposedly to form a stronger alliance between the two tribes. Since Breas' greatest claims to fame seem to have been his looks and his lack of regard for anyone else, he represents what is not to be looked at or for in a leader. Breas, along with the evil Fomorian wizard Balor and other chiefs of that tribe, began to plan a complete takeover of Ireland.

During this time Nuada had been under the care of Diancecht the Druid. With jealously guarded arts, Diancecht regrafted or restored Nuada's hand. Some say he fashioned a new one from silver. It was, at any rate, a magickal construction.

During the eventual battle with the Fomorians, Nuada was killed by the demon god Crom-Cruach, who had been released by the Fomorian wizard, Balor. Nuada went into battle with Crom-Cruach knowing that his defeat might mean that his spirit would be trapped forever by the wizard Balor. The battle proved to be fatal for Nuada. Upon realizing that even his sword of light was powerless against the evil of Balor and Crom-Cruach, Nuada chose to sacrifice himself to prevent the destruction of his people. Thus came the death of a noble leader and hero king. Nuada would have remained in the limbo of evil magick had it not been for our next leader king, Lugh.

Imagery application — Nuada provides us with a noble, self-sacrificing king. Imagery of Nuada will connect you with greater personal dimensions of leadership and power. Evoke imagery using Nuada as the wise warrior king. This balances knowledge and aggression within your Self, and helps you structure success in your life. Nuada also brings us the benefits of experience and the sacred systems of wisdom to guide us through times of upheaval and chaos.

Lugh

Lugh, the il dana, was master of all the arts and crafts of battle, poetry, smithcraft, and virtually every other skill that might be desirable in a Lord of Light. Lugh could be associated with any and all of the elements quite appropriately. The wealth of his knowledge and the strength of his leadership encouraged me to place him here in succession to the king he replaced, Nuada.

Lugh was de Dannan but also Fomorian; as such he represented the powers of darkness and light in perfect dynamic balance. Lugh was the grandson of the Fomorian wizard Balor and, as had been prophesied, killed his evil grandfather. This, too, is another example of the Celtic philosophy of dynamic polarities. Lugh as light, slew Balor as darkness, but they were related, and thus, mythically not separate.

Lugh's counterparts were Llew in the Welsh and Lugos in the continental Celtic myths. Lugh, as master of many arts, represents a leader among leaders, a shining one in a more human form.

Imagery application — Lugh is the enlightened one in our imagery, the unique brilliant creator of all our knowledge and skills. Use images of Lugh to develop your own skills and to master your chosen craft. Also use these images to inspire you to seek more knowledge, learn it well, and use it wisely. Lugh helps us maintain our own dynamic inner balance with grace and integrity. Use images of Lugh to help you manage the delicate balance in doing the right thing.

Wherever there are chieftains, kings, clan mothers, and queens serving their people with nobility and honor, there is the element of earth. Wherever there is great power or wisdom being demonstrated or spoken in unusually mystical fashion, there is the element of earth. Wherever there are ceremonial or ritual marriages to preserve the powers of the land or the tribes, there is the element of earth.

In this regard, one particularly ambitious chieftain king was Conchobar (Conor), who mated with four wives, each the daughters of the Dagda (some say). These four women are reputed to have represented four provinces in Ireland. Thus Conor made sure the security of Ireland was well preserved.

Th element of earth appears in Celtic myth as the talking heads of Bran the Blessed of Wales, whose wisdom (and head) was kept as a protection for the people. Cuchulain's head, when placed upon a stone, split the rock and merged into the stone itself, and thus was reclaimed by the sacred land. Historic legend tells us that the severed head of Mary, Queen of Scots, spoke for some few moments after her death. This is yet another example of history and myth interweaving in the tradition of the Celts.

Keynote for Earth

A strong relationship with the element of earth, formed by faith, will give you the constant companionship of patience to share in each step of your life journey.

8

Air:
The Bards

Honoring the Element of Air

For the Celts, the element of air was more than the breath of life. It was the essential element of the oral tradition. It was the element that preserved their past. It was the element the Celts used to celebrate their lives in myth, poetry, spoken wisdom, and song. Air provided the means by which the nature of the Celts could be transmitted into the future, in the most clear and compelling manner possible.

Air was the element of music for the Celts. It allowed them access to the sacred realms of the Muses. It brought inspiration and illumination directly from the White Goddess herself. It was the magickal element with which blessings and curses could be created. Air was the element of the *geasa*, the sacred taboos, and the satires, the means by which even kings and queens could be controlled with safety and impunity. Air could provide expressive reminders or excruciating ridicules to reveal the true nature of those being represented by the satirists.

Air was the element of scathing for the Celts. As such, its power as an elemental weapon was much revered. This reverence is still present in our modern admiration for comedy. Celts, then as now, have a particular fondness for parody, farce, and satire, as well as for slapstick, which truly scathes us all by showing us how silly we are by nature.

Air was the element of inspiration. It reminded the Celtic tribes of their honored heritage and their roles of responsibility. It reminded them of their gifts as well as their bindings.

Air was the element of sharpened awareness and perception. It enabled the Celts to think clearly, rather than simply react. It brought new skills into battle and new systems of learning to be shared. It is the element with which the Celts developed their finest ally—the power of intellect.

Air was the element of the resilient bards. During the times of persecution, when the mystical white-robed figures of the priestly druids were no longer seen in the sacred groves nor amongst the standing stones, their message was still carried in the folk memory of the people, and kept active by the bards, poets, storytellers, and troubadours.

Undoubtedly, these bards were unable to wear their traditional blue robes. They were also unable to carry, as they did in ancient days, the silver branch that signified their sacred connection to the Otherworld realms and their allegiance to the Muse of poetry. Nevertheless, their work was equally magick, if not more so. The bards kept the wisdom alive in folklore, songs, and faerie tales. This they did in any way they could manage, as traveling peddlers, old country wise men, grandmothers weaving tales beside the fire, jesters to the kings, or playwrights recording for all time, the old ways in new forms.

Air was the illuminating element that revealed itself in the poetry and myth of the once and future times. Air was the power of the bards.

Accessing Air in Imagery

Air is best accessed on a crisp morning in early spring, when life itself seems filled with the inspiration of Nature. This element is clearly felt in the dry lands where all thoughts find themselves faced with unlimited horizons. It is accessed as the precious breezes of the ocean reach far across the land to refresh our overheated brains in the midst of summer. In the teasing touch of fall, it reminds us of the ideas and concepts we forgot in the lazy atmosphere of summer. Air brings thoughts, inspiration, and messages of illumination into dark, cold winter nights.

When the night sky is so clear that the Milky Way becomes a pathway to the infinite, air is there. It brings words and sounds to express all that is perceived in Nature and in self-nature. Therefore, air is the element we find in the clear skies of Nature and in the clear minds of self-nature.

When we access the element of air clearly, our imageries sharpen in focus and expand to express our thoughts in new forms. Air journeys awaken our perceptions of our Selves and of all life around us. They bring us new awareness and new appreciation for the many dimensions of our minds. They develop skills that put us in a user-friendly relationship with our own brains.

Air journeys enable us to hear new melodies in our own minds. Air enables us to listen and receive new messages, even in the music that already seems well known, familiar, and even old. Air journeys give us a new view of the images we create for ourselves and in regard to others. Air journeys activate a greater potential for self-expression.

When we journey into the joyful element of air, we access the abilities that create new skills of communication. Air journeys communicate our images of how we think about our Selves and the world around us. Air journeys provide the sound stage on which we can compose new expressions of our thoughts and perceptions. Air journeys provide the inspirational messages and the illuminated medium with which we may present new acts, new plays of our lives—first in practice, then in dress rehearsal, and ultimately as command performances with four-star quality.

Air allows us access to the dimensions of our own consciousness wherein inspiration dwells. It invigorates our creative processes just as sunlight invigorates Nature. Try this imagery to awaken the Muse within.

February's Muse:
An Imagery Exercise for Creativity

Imagine that you are walking along a snow-covered path on a frosty morning at beginning of February. The snow is sparkling clean and forms a smooth white carpet across the land. The air seems filled with energy on this bright morning. Every breath you take fills your mind with inspiration.

You feel the ideas fairly bursting forth inside your brain. You feel the joy of creativity awakening with a new force, a new purpose. You are compelled to return home with a renewed energy for the projects you have begun. You return with a resolve to start the creation processes of ideas you have held dear for a long time. You resolve to act on the new concepts that have been emerging into your consciousness.

As you sit by a crackling fire, you feel its warm, dry air caressing you with confidence. You feel the inspiration of your own creativity. As you reach inside your mind for an image of this creative joy, you find your Muse is waiting with welcome thoughts and sacred melodies all your own.

The element of air helps us become acquainted with the unlimited capacities of our brain and mind potential. Use the next imagery to access your amazing brain power.

The Magnificent Soft Machine:
An Imagery Exercise for Mind Activation

Imagine that you are on a fantastic voyage into the realms of your consciousness through the pathways of your mind and into the regions of your brain.

Here within this magnificent soft machine that is your brain, you find the means by which all dimensions of your Self are motivated, monitored, and managed. Here you find the operational headquarters that controls the functions of both tangible and intangible forms of your physical, mental, and spiritual Self.

Here sensations are received and appropriate responses sent in return. Thoughts are drafted and submitted for your final approval of their design. Illumination from what you consider divine finds directions for the expression of its experience in the reflected image of your life.

Here, sitting at the control panel, carefully regulating the order of each synaptic step in your life, you find that your Self is ultimately in command.

&cm&

The element of air brings us the electric, creative flow that activates our brain and inspires us to express ourselves with the sharp focus and perceptive skills of a poet. Air enables us to amplify our thoughts and inner musings with the rhythmic power of the spoken word. These words come forth, carefully constructed, to create the effects we need with wit and wisdom. Air helps us access the best of our bardic Self within.

The following rhyming quatrain represents an ancient technique of empowering both the intent and the effect of the composer's work. This technique may be used to take mindful control over any given situation. It has the powerful benefit of humor, and humor outweighs even the heaviest and most oppressing of thoughts, words, and deeds.

Quick Wits and Wily Quatrains: An Exercise in Bardic Expression

The following extensive journey represents an experience of clear attunement with the air element. This element comes forth in a most conversational modality for many who work with it. I've come to refer to it as the "bardic frequency." The tempo for air journeys is often quite rhythmic and melodic. In fact, the rhymes sometimes seem to never stop coming and coming, drumming and drumming, strumming and strumming, humming and humming.

To follow this fast-paced account, recall the "conversations" with the inner wizard that you experienced earlier. Imagine them expanding to the dimensions of an active experiential journey.

Imagine that you are accessing and exercising your abilities as a poet of great respect. With the sacred rite of the bardic druid you will compose four-line rhymes. You will write quatrains that express, poetically, your perceptions about people, places, or even parts of your Self and elements of power.

To this end, I provide you with a few whimsical examples and a few that carry warnings. Practice creating a few of your own. It's amazing what you can do with a few bardic rhymes.

To Air
Air, you feisty little sprite,
You sleep all day and wake at night,
Bringing melodies sweet and light,
Sending songs of true delight.

To An Uncertain Idea
Teasing, tempting new conception,
Deviling me since your inception;
Do you taunt with sly deception,
Deserving naught but cold reception?

Tantalizing new conception,
Do you find your true inception
Dwells in light, pure, no deception,
Designating warm reception?

To A Trickster
Shall you see yourself deserving
Friendship worthy of preserving?
When, as far as I shall know,
Your actions more bespeak a foe.

Shall I be to you reserving
Judgments ill or kind deserving?
Thus my store of power grows,
Diminished not by tricksters' woes.

166

To A Mentor
Dragon of the morning star,
How I'm glad you're where you are.
Though I've traveled near and far,
No others were quite up to par.

An Affirmation
Fearful powers, forceful might
Lurking in the darkest night
Shall not conquer me with fright
For in me swells the Child of Light.

Personal Journey Account

This journey account began with my thoughts on how the images of Arthurian lore had shifted with each new era that came along. It was inspired by my own experiences and explorations of what I call the "Merlin Current." It also focused on my own perceptions concerning the way it might have been, had some of these mythic figures had the opportunity to speak their own minds. Naturally, the material presented in this prose represents the opinion of the management—namely, me.

The Merlin Current

"Wake up! Wake up! Wake up, I say!"

I am being prodded, rather unceremoniously, into a different dimension of consciousness.

I turn in my vision to face the wizard of myth and legend, the great Lord Merlin, archmage and friend of dragons. He stands at the foot of my bed prodding me in the side with his staff. It's the one with ram's horns on it, and it hurts. I wonder if I'm supposed to be amused by this particular approach.

"Go away," I tell him. "Go away before I forget how to sleep for lack of practice!"

I pull the covers over my head, seeking warmth and quiet. I feel the wizard jab at me again.

"Sleep is for mere mortals!" he exclaims. "Besides, there's work to be done."

With that said, he jerks the covers, and I find myself summarily rolled out of bed, awake and not amused.

I look up at him. He stands there in full wizard gear, looking infuriatingly unruffled and even somewhat smug. I come up swinging.

> *All right now, you lascivious old elf.*
> *You've got your way.*
> *Aren't you pleased with yourself?*
> *But none of your games now.*
> *No tricks, no stealth;*
> *Or I'll cork you in an old jar, and leave you there;*
> *Gathering dust on a shelf.*

"I love the sound of an Irish Witch in the morning!" the Merlin quips, and I have to laugh. I recover myself and respond:

> *It's a wise thing 'twas the Welsh you chose*
> *and not the ladies of Eire.*
> *If you had set your task for us, who knows?*
> *Your straits could still be quite dire.*
> *Of Ireland's weavings, the world does rave.*
> *They're a joy for all to see,*
> *And strong enough to bind a knave*
> *or a wizard in a tree.*
> *If Erin's daughters had woven your cave,*
> *then still in there you'd be.*
>
> *The Avalon ladies say you napped*
> *with one eye open, there's no doubt.*
> *And when 'twas done, you claimed to be trapped,*
> *with no way to get out.*
>
> *But the weavers know well, 'twas not the case.*
> *No wizard held for ransom,*
> *Yet rather a way to make a place to safely keep the wisdom.*

The Merlin is strangely quiet, pondering, lost in thought. I study the image he presents to me now. I have not seen him in quite this fashion. He seems younger than any other time I can recall. His hair and beard are still quite fair, with only a few touches of silver at the temples. His beard is neatly trimmed, short enough to show off a strong, Roman chin. I see with satisfaction that his ears are still decidedly elfin. His eyes are clear and blue as the skies. They match his robes to perfection. I like this aspect very much, but I do not understand it.

I decide to investigate this further, so I inquire:

> *What manner or what fashion*
> *does your appearance explain?*
> *What rhyme or reason do you ration?*
> *What purpose do you seek to gain?*
>
> *For though you are, in truth, quite dashing,*
> *you've never before made it so plain;*
> *Unless you have a chance to cash in*
> *what once seemed wise, now seems vain.*

The Merlin shifts his attention out of the realm of thought and memory. For a moment I can see the wise old man behind this younger man's piercing eyes. He seems amused by this questioning of his vanity. He hastens to express himself.

> *'Tis just so, for I am a swain,*
> *a fool, a troubadour.*
> *In my bardic blue, how can I restrain?*
> *my prideful purpose does me restore.*
> *I've come to court the Muse, it's plain,*
> *with no thought for place, nor time, nor more.*
> *I'm dressed to sing a sweet refrain*
> *to maidens fair, I do adore.*
> *And I've come to weave a glad quatrain*
> *for the Round Table,*
> *And chivalry, forevermore.*

The Merlin pounds his staff upon the floor three times three times. When the staff has struck the ninth time, a new journey begins.

We now make our way through a dark, drafty tunnel. The walls are gray stone, cool yet dry to the touch. Along the wall, at what seem to be long intervals, there are torches set in brackets illuminating our pathway. The Merlin fairly races along the path now, eager to reach our destination. He expounds upon some theories regarding the relationship of sound and imagery.

A gentle wind blows through the tunnel now. Electricity crackles in the air between us. I feel the current of communication strengthen its flow. Something serene moves into the energy that embraces us both while we stand together as friends. We share in self-recognition. A harmonic of new understanding sounds a tone clear and light and crystal.

The Merlin pulls a wand from inside his cloak. It is a beautiful piece of craftsmanship, simple and fine. Banded silver, I believe it is, set with stones of golden hue. He waves the wand around my face and taps me on both cheeks. He solemnly takes my measure. His expression is so serious and intense, I cannot resist teasing him.

> *Are you my fairy godmother, Merlin?*
> *If so I'm quite chagrined;*
> *For I don't have the magick*
> *to change the shape you're in!*

I can't help it; I start to giggle. The air is swirling around us in silly patterns. The Merlin is not amused, and he returns my teasing well.

> *How shall I fashion you now, my lady?*
> *As huntress, maiden, or maybe something a little shady?*
> *Maybe an empress you will make*
> *or a frightful dress-up witch.*
> *Perhaps you'll be a warrior queen*
> *or just a battle bitch!*

He waits until my gales of laughter have subsided and I am properly serious. I wonder at his purpose, but I look forward to adventures. I close my eyes and open my mind to a new image as the Merlin begins to recite:

> *Wind spirits gather quickly,*
> *Awaken from your reverie;*
> *For magick realms of wonder*
> *we are about to see.*
> *Come quickly and come free,*
> *For we create a new dream,*
> *a new reality.*
> *Come quickly to surround us,*
> *and most creative be.*
> *Come freely to astound us,*
> *with gifts of i-Mage-ry!*

I feel the touch of his wand on my forehead, illuminating the vision in my mind. I feel soft fabrics on my body where jeans and a sweatshirt had been. I do not open my eyes; I know that he hasn't finished. I feel his wand sweeping the outlines of my body as the Merlin recites once more:

> *Spirits of air, come in from near or far,*
> > *Come in and see the beauty dear,*
> > *and behold the fairest star.*
> *Air spirits enter here, I call,*
> *Arrive and say 'Ah-ha.'*
> *For once where there was another,*
> > *is now LADY DANA.*

He raps me on the head three times for good measure.

I open my eyes to my new inner image. I enter new dimensions of the element air.

I tap upon the ash wood door I find within my imagery. This door leads deeper into the realm of air. It swings open swiftly to reveal the realm of air within. I place my hand upon the Merlin's hand, and we enter into a new adventure. Another journey now begins. It promises to be one of true enlightenment.

As we step into the realm of air, the Merlin waves his magick wand once more. As a final touch to my ensemble, there is now a fine clasp to hold the airy gossamer garments around me. I see that the clasp is a pair of wings wrought of yellow gold and set with blue topaz and warm citrines.

"It appears to be less angelic than I would have chosen," I jest. "In fact, they look distinctly like pilot's wings to me. Am I the pilot of this flight?" I ask.

The Merlin replies, "Who else, if not you?"

"I am not always sure that I want to just be the pilot." I pose the issue craftily. "I may simply wish to co-pilot from time to time, or possibly even navigate."

The Merlin stops to consider this, and points his finger in my face. "I'll not be navigated by the likes of you," he says flatly. "But I promise that in the event of war, you may be the bombardier. I know that is what you really want to do most of the time anyway."

Upon practicing with my air imagery and accessing an even more expanded dimension relating to the element, I found that my images of the allies of air became the catalyst for expressing my ideas and inner visions. Take a moment to access these allies for yourself.

Evoking the Allies of the Element Air

 Consider the aspects of the element air—inspiration, perception, creativity, expanded brain and mind potential. Consider your experience of this element—focus, creative consciousness, awareness, illumination.

Structure within your mind the images that you've created to describe the forms, shapes, and details of two figures. These figures may be as mystical and symbolic as you choose. Call them forth to inspire the greatest potentials of creative, conscious mind. They are your inner poets, the inner catalysts of self-expression.

Tune in to the element of air and receive the rhythm, the music of clear thought and mindful consciousness.

Amplify your vision to include as many aspects as you can to bring your figures into focus. Carefully note all that you see, hear, feel, smell, taste, or touch within your images. Note and record your reactions to each contact you have with your own allies of the element air.

Open the windows of your mind and let inspiration flow freely.

Personal Journey Account

In this journey, I sought access to the Muse through the element air.

Courting the Muse

I clear my mind with an image of sky-blue light. I begin to breathe consciously now, measuring each cycle of breath. I sharpen my focus with a brilliant yellow that slowly softens to butter cream, then a warm, rich ivory. I call forth an image that has become a familiar key to the realm of air.

A massive door, made of pale ash looms before me in my vision. I find that the door is already slightly ajar. A warm spring breeze finds its way through the opening and tickles me on the forehead as it passes.

I touch the delicate carvings on the door and find the symbols I need. With only a slight touch from me, the ashwood door swings open, wide and full, to reveal a new landscape in my vision.

I find myself in a sunlit meadow on a most appealing spring day. It is a clearing, really, in the center of an open, airy forest. There is little underbrush in these woods, I note, as I observe the perimeter of my meadow.

There are already ferns in abundance within the wood. Their pale green fronds reflect a tender luminescence inside the circling forest. In the clearing there are wildflowers galore. Blue skies form a clear ceiling, and soft sweet grasses make a floor.

The melodies of bird songs move smoothly across the meadow. A gentle wind blows in from the trees and sweeps through the sweet grasses toward me. With the wind comes the strength of the forest—oak, ash, and pine—and my senses to restore.

I wait expectantly within the vision in my mind's eye. I listen as the bird song ceases and the breezes no longer blow. There is a moment of stillness and silent anticipation before a new sound is heard. It is a lyrical, haunting strain; a harp song weaves its way in from the wood. The music of the harp announces the arrival of allies from within the realm of air.

A sacred pair of twins steps into the meadow clearing—a brother and sister, each dressed in soft fabrics in shades of blue and white and yellow. Their garb is that of the bardic orders, in service to the Muse.

They are young and fair, eternally in the springtime of their lives. Their bardic blue robes reflect in sky-blue eyes and complement their pale, sunlit hair. Their faces are pale but glowing, like the clear pink blush of an English tea rose placed on a plate of fine white china.

At first they seem quite fragile until they begin to sing, expressing their joy in the sharing of their stories.

Their voices ring out clearly.

> *These melodies we do express; these stories we do share,*
> *enlivened by the bloom of youth and ample time to spare.*
> *We come to dance, to sing, to laugh.*

We come, in truth, by care—
to weave the rhymes, replete or spare,
of knights so bold and maidens fair,
and wizards caught in their own snare.

Mythic Figures of Air

Bridget

Bridget, the Triple Goddess of Poetry, Smithcraft, and Healing, represents the true Muse, the White Goddess of inspiration. She is the daughter of the Dagda and heiress to many of the qualities of Danu, mother of all the Celtic gods of Nature.

Bridget is an ancient goddess of the Gaelic Celts. She is also referred to as Brigantia by the Brythonic Celts. Her worship survived into modern times reflected in the perpetuation of her name, in new form, as St. Bridget. Some feel that the real person who became known as St. Bridget was originally a priestess of the old ways in reverent service to Bridget the Triune Goddess.

Regardless of the form she takes, her inspirational power remains the spiritual fire of creativity for all Celts. The nine fires of perpetual wisdom that celebrate Bridget continued to burn in Ireland until the invasion of the Normans. Now these flames burn within the creative hearts and minds of poets and warriors of spirit in modern times.

Imagery application — Gaining access to the elemental powers that Bridget represents can bring great inspiration to your life. Bridget, the shape-shifter goddess, can help you create new images for the way you live your life. Call forth images of Bridget in a young aspect (as Brigette) to bring creative zest into your work and your life. A more mature form (as Bridget) helps in the crafting or structuring aspects. The elder image for Bridget (as Lady Brede) taps onto deep healing and spiritual inspiration. For this profound power, you might try using imagery of a little old wise woman called Biddy.

The Bards

The bards who appear in Celtic myth all express the element of air. Of particular importance was Amergin, who crafted the conquest of Ireland for his people, the Milesians, a tribe of Gaelic Celts. When faced with a druidic wind sent by the de Dannan to confound the invading Milesians, Amergin invoked the higher power of the land itself. He sought connection through an acknowledgment of Ireland's true sovereignty as abundant Nature.

A section of this bardic invocation is found in Charles Squires' excellent work, *Celtic Myth and Legend* (London, Newcastle Publishing, 1975). Amergin speaks:

> *I invoke the land of Eriu!*
> *The shining, shining sea!*
> *The fertile, fertile hill!*
> *The wooded vale!*
> *The river abundant, abundant in water!*
> *The fishful, fishful lake!*

Note the emphasis on empowerment through repetition. Practice, practice, you will see.

Other bards of note are Taliesin, son of Cerridwen, whose transformational journey also associates him with water and the cauldron.

Ossian was the bard whose claim to fame included an extensive stay in the Otherworld realm, Tir na nog, the Land of Youth. Ossian's mother was transformed into a deer, and in that shape raised her son in the forest for many years before Finn, Ossian's father, found his boy while out hunting.

Angus Og, the bright, clever son of the Dagda, was renowned for his skills of love, as well as his bardic talents. William Butler Yeats (a bard in his own right) called Angus Og the "Master of Love." The harp on which Angus crafted his poetry and songs of passion is still a powerful symbol of connection to the Muse.

Ogma is also a son of the Dagda. His bardic skills led him to develop the famous druidic Ogham Script, an essential means of communication. Ogma is also associated with Ogmios, a strong, herculean god of wisdom and eloquence.

Imagery application — Access imaginative abilities beyond expectations with the "bardic frequency." Imagery using any of the bards can provide much clearer thinking, perceptive abilities, and focus. This in turn awakens greater dimensions of brain and mind capacities. Bardic imagery is most helpful to train your brain. It is also helpful to specify bardic imageries according to their associated qualities. For example, Amergin is a solar-type bard, most often representing wide, sweeping issues and actions. Taliesin, on the other hand, is more lunar, more often representing the personal inner world of transformations into power.

Wherever there is melody heard behind the words of myth, the tales of heroes, or the histories of the Celts, there is the element of air.

Indeed, without the Muse and the bards throughout the ages, these sacred records in poetry, prose, and song would have been lost. Instead they remain, communicated naturally with the element of air. Had there been no language, though, these would have still been found, whispering in the winds.

Keynote for Air

The doors and windows of perception allow access to an inner theater and a stage upon which you may create, direct, rehearse, and perform your life. It is a private production if you choose or a public one if you require.

Spirit:
The Fair Ones

Honoring the Element of Spirit

If we are to define the element of spirit in terms of Celtic spiritual philosophy, we need to recognize the existence of the Otherworld.

In the Celtic sense, this Otherworld of spirit represented neither heaven nor hell, nor any form of netherworld in between. Instead, the Otherworld represented a realm that was richly alive and more real than surreal. This realm of spirit was the land of eternal summer—the Summerland. This view of the Otherworld placed its location as being a dimension closest to the elements and in an interwoven, continuous relationship with the powers of Nature.

This Otherworld realm was thought to be found on several of the legendary Mystic Isles. These were called by names of poetic beauty, such as the Isles of the Blest, the Isle of Apples, the Avalon Isle, the Happy Plain, the Land of Youth, or the Sacred Isles. The location of these Mystic Isles was said to be eternally toward the west, ever in alignment with the rays of the setting Sun. Mythic figures in Celtic lore were often allowed glimpses of the Blessed Isles and occasionally given an opportunity to visit these sacred realms of spirit.

There were also gateways to the Blessed Isles of the Otherworld. These appeared in Celtic myth often as *raths*, also called faerie mounds or barrows. Entering into these gateways of the Otherworld or even spending time in close proximity to them resulted in profound transformative experiences for those who were fortunate (or unfortunate) enough to do so. Tales such as these evoke other forms of mysticism. They say that those who returned from realms of spirit were greatly transformed, either with positive empowerment or with negative loss of self-identity. Those who were able to speak of their experiences were considered special and blessed. In Celtic myth, a surprising number of these figures did more than live to tell the tales of their experiences.

In Celtic mythology, there is a constant thread of connective relationship between humankind and the spiritual realms of the Otherworld. When those who had traveled into the Otherworld returned to the more material realms, they were often seen to have done so at the specific request of the rulers of those realms. Sometimes these requests included the communication of wisdom, blessings, judgments, or warnings. Other times, the requested purpose was the retrieval of people, powers, or possessions that had either been lost to the Otherworld realm or were simply required by those of that dimension. The persistent tales of *changeling* babies arise from this view of the retrieval requests of the Otherworld rules.

These rulers were, of course, none other than the faeries of Celtic myths. The Blessed Isles were considered to be the domains of the faerie rulers, also called the Fey, the Good People, or the people of the Sidhe. These were the de Dannan, transformed by the shape shifting of the mythic philosophy of the Celts. As time passed, many of these myths gelled into a view of one large Otherworld realm of faerie. This Otherworld was inhabited by all manner of multidimensional beings. This mythic view has persisted into modern times.

However, this view remains an all-too-convenient misconception. It is not borne out by the original myths, but grew out of the overlay of many forms of superstition. These forms were created in folk memories by the controlling factions of the conquerors and of the Church (sometimes these seemed to be the same controlling force).

It remains for us, in this new age of awareness, consciousness, and conscience, to seek deeper into the Celtic myths to uncover their clear message for us today. First we can sort out the superstitions that bind the Otherworld and its rulers into the all-too-demeaning diminutive forms of "fairy land." We do this to also dispel myths that reduce the splendid de Dannan to shady or capricious figures of superstition.

The de Dannan were never faerie. If anything, they ruled the realms of faerie; that is to say, the de Dannan had the keys to the wisdom and the magick of the elemental powers of Nature. If we are to find a true definition for faerie, it is as an elemental energy expressed in Nature and in self-nature.

The images of gnomes, dwarves, elves, sprites, leprechauns, and other little people that appear so often in Celtic folk myth are often symbols of humankind's conscious connection to the powers of Nature. Nature is alive. The very planet we inhabit appears to be a living system all its own. Humankind is (for the most part) aware and alive, as well. The relationship of humankind to Nature is one that reflects as spiritual or mystical images in consciousness. Images of this conscious connection are reflected in the forms of Nature spirits, *devas* and spirits of place (the *genus locurum*), the Sidhe, the little people (classically, the faeries). These images have come to include the Good People, the de Dannan. They are now imagined as faeries.

Faeries, I feel, are the multidimensional projections of our consciousness reflecting at least one aspect of the elements—spirit. These projected images provide a very real connection to the elemental powers of Nature. Faeries may well also be a projection on the part of Mother Nature herself, just as we are when we come to think of it. Regardless of the source of these images, it is our relationship to what they represent that remains of most vital importance to us now. This relationship is made up of ourselves as humankind in alliance with the energies of the Earth, and with reverent respect for the essential nature of this connection.

What we see as faeries are the reflected images of our own awareness of this essential relationship with Nature. What we see as faeries also reflect a projected image of our relationship with the many dimensions of our own mind and consciousness. This does not make what we call faeries either real or unreal. That would reflect a duality of consciousness. Faeries exist in the blended dimensions of our consciousness. Faeries exist in the Otherworld realms of tribal, cultural, and natural elemental consciousness. Faeries reflect in the Otherworld realms of our personal consciousness, and they do so multidimensionally. Faeries exist as the images of our essential experience of Nature. Faeries keep us reminded of our mystical connection to Nature and self-nature. Faeries reflect from the multidimensional elements of our minds. Images of faeries emerge from dimensions of mind and consciousness, which we have defined mythically as the Otherworld or the Mystic Isles.

Whether these, the Blessed Isles of Celtic mythology, ever existed corporeally or not is immaterial for us now. The Mystic Isles now exist within the dimensions of our own minds; these mystic realms are manifest as "islands" in our deep oceanic consciousness.

The Blessed Isles are reached by going into Otherworld dimensions of our mind. This is more than time/space travel. It is multidimensional linking. It is traveling to realms within the expansive dimensions of our Self in Nature.

Whether the Blessed Isles and the de Dannan exist in another tangible dimension related to time and space will continue to be a matter of much speculation. As with any dimension of spirit or any aspect of life reflecting the intangible element of spirit, it is a matter of personal belief. Whatever that belief might be, the Mystic, Blessed Isles, tangible or not, may only be accessed by the expanded dimensions of our own minds. When we actively develop the ability to work within the realms of imagination, we develop the capacity to cross the veils of consciousness and enter into realms yet to be explored.

We may now consider the Blessed Isles to be "patterns" or thought forms held in tribal and cultural memory strongly enough to retain a significant degree of energy. The Mystic Isles of magick and memory have a unique frequency, a vibrational rate all their own. The energy of these isles of consciousness parallels, approaches, and expands into matter through the form of our images and the shape of our lives. We reflect the magick, the mysticism, and the spirit we find within our Selves. We are the myth makers, and we live the myths we make.

The element of spirit reflects intangibly in our willingness to wake up to our fullest potential, to claim our natural heritage, to accept our personal gifts of power, and to assume responsibility for our lives.

The element of spirit manifests tangibly in the activated codes of our brain cells. Each cell of our brain contains codes to wisdom, memories, and realms we have yet to fathom. Each cell is like a crystal that amplifies the connection to Self, Nature, and spirit. Those of Nature wisdom have poetically told us, "Crystals are the brain cells of the Earth Mother." Each of your brain cells is a crystal of spirit. Use them wisely to amplify your access to the many dimensions of your Self.

Imagination is the key to wisdom. Wisdom maps the way to spirit. Spirit reveals itself through imagination. That's a Celtic knot.

❧ ❦ ❧

You will note that this chapter is already somewhat different than the previous four. This is for several reasons. One is that the experience of spirit is elementally sacred and personal. To attempt to structure this experience for others reduces its impact and can produce barriers to the realms of personal mind and consciousness. Also, the experience of spirit realms is quite Otherworldly and resists being described according to any set format or design. It is best for you to create images on your own with less help from external constructions, particularly with this element.

Finally, all of the material presented in the prior chapters has been designed to help you develop an elementally powerful relationship with your own mind and consciousness through the use of imagery and myth. All of the elements described before—fire, water, earth, and air—represent the more material frequencies. In all of these frequencies, the element of spirit vibrates eternally, yet is far more immaterial in nature.

As you shift your dimensions of consciousness to access the more immaterial dimensions, you enter the finest realms of your own mind and imagination. In this realm, magickally remembered, dwell the Wise Ones, the Old Ones, the Lordly Ones, the Shining Ones, and those called the Opalescent Ones.

181

The Wise Ones and the Old Ones often appear as reflections of your image of Celtic deities and of "spirit guides" of a druidic nature. These images are often quite similar, as shared experiences have revealed. With no intention to limit these Old, Wise Ones in any way, I will arbitrarily say that they represent our most mystically created inner guides. Whether these are entities with consciousness of their own or not is a matter of personal belief. Occultists such as Dion Fortune have described their spirit guides as "Secret Chiefs."

The wealth of wisdom received from spirit guides makes speculation on their origin and their nature also immaterial. The value of spirit guides must be determined by the value of their wisdom and the positive nature of their influence. The same holds true for the images and the guidance clearly designated as arising from your own consciousness.

Remember that this process is very much one of tuning in the right frequency or channel. Sometimes you just get static. Sometimes you get a clear reception, but that being picked up is just trash. If you pick up something trashy, just say so (out loud is bardically best). Then change the channel or turn off your "set." Use your remote control, if need be, when keeping your distance is wisest.

If you have connected with a source of guidance and wisdom that provides you with positive, enhancing material, then you have connected with something or someone sacredly kin to yourself. I call this "Working with the Wizardry." I have also heard this called multidimensional linking, which is self-descriptive.

Just remember that living is channeling. You do it every day; everyone does it, whether they know it or not.

Evoking Allies and Experiences of the Otherworld Realm: An Instructive Discussion

Let's now examine these mystical keepers of the element spirit. You may find it quite clear now that the realm and the element are one and the same. When you are seeking to define them they naturally resist. Best learn to be comfortable with all that spirit encompasses. It will become a clearer source of guidance if you can.

The Lordly Ones

The Lordly Ones are the more tangibly experienced allies from the elemental realms of fire, water, earth, and air. These Lordly Ones are mythically described as the de Dannan. Their images reflect the best aspects of our Selves in connection to the elements they favor. They are the archetypes of Nature as reflected in pure relationship with the archetypes of the Celts. Mythically, they are always seen to be the beautiful and the perfect reflection of humankind.

The Shining Ones

The Shining Ones are less tangible, even as they appear in our imagery or in myths. The famed Riders of the Sidhe (or the Silver Riders, as some call them) are a good mythic example of the Shining Ones. These Riders were allies of the de Dannan, particularly famed for helping Lugh battle the Fomorians. The Shining Ones have less tangibility, I believe, because they are made of past and future dimensions of our Selves. Their image is a dimension or so beyond the boundaries of our present, and thus more mystically projected.

The Shining Ones reflect the best of the best. They outshine the de Dannan, yet retain a similar quality. The Shining Ones are elementally more etheric. They reflect the element of spirit in its transcendent aspect. This we may understand as the "gestalt," the coming together of all the other elements in harmonious relationship. The gestalt is the transcendent quality that results from combining elements of Self or Nature, and finding that the whole (the gestalt) is far greater than the sum of its parts. The Shining Ones reflect the transcendent, the highly evolved—the gestalt of our consciousness.

The image of the Shining Ones also reflects one's personal view of the many dimensions of time and space. For some, the Shining Ones appear as what I call "space faeries," however, this tends to irritate those who define multidimensional beings as somehow alien.

If the Shining Ones appear in your imagery as futuristic, then so be it. If they reflect images of the past, so be that, too. More often than not, images of the Shining Ones include a blend of past and future that is naturally a reflection of the present. This, I feel, is their most shining aspect, "i-magick-ally" speaking. The images you find to describe your experience of the Shining Ones reveal a lot about how your own element of spirit reflects in your Self. It shows where your images of power find clearest conception. If the Shining Ones appear in your imagery as reflections of current times, the now, then be in that place. You are reflecting the current state or condition of the Celtic spiritual philosophy.

The Opalescent Ones

The Opalescent Ones are most classically represented as the gossamer-winged "fairy." Some have said that these are of the same dimensional quality as the Shining Ones, which I find to be partially the case. The Shining Ones represent all of the qualities of the Opalescent Ones (as well as the elemental Lordly Ones). The Opalescents are blends, but not gestalts.

The Opalescent Ones represent the more etheric aspects of our Self. They reflect the intangible spirit of our higher qualities as humankind, such as balance, peace, temperance, service, synthesis, renewal, love, truth, devotion, and other noble aspects of our nature.

I believe that the reason these Opalescent Ones appear so frequently as fragile, translucent, and winged beings is because they represent those extremely fine and rare qualities of humankind that arise from a certain inner light, a spirit of illumination, a higher aspect of Self. The wings are symbolic of these rays of spirit. They are the energy of the highest inner lights. This, I believe, is why angels appear as beings with wings of light, representing higher realms of spirit (the Christ consciousness). (Possibly that's another form of Shining Ones, suitably garbed to meet the spiritual expectations of our minds.) More *devic* forms could be called "Earth angels."

The Opalescent Ones are often described as beautiful beings, colorfully garbed and winged. The nature of these colors invariably is described as being of blended hues and luminous tones. The Opalescent Ones rarely appear in imagery in shades we found in our first box of eight crayons from elementary school. These more basic colors show up most often in images of fire, water, earth, and air. The different colors represent the differences of "tone" in our experiential images that are more material, and those that aren't. Also, the higher aspects or illuminated qualities of humankind begin with basic, natural traits, and become more refined as we blend experience and wisdom into more evolved forms. Personal evolution involves blending the many dimensions of our Self to create a harmonious relationship with life. The Opalescent Ones represent some of our more beautiful blends.

The following is taken from an experience I crafted using the blended ray colors of indigo, scarlet, peach, rose, turquoise, and golden green. I used these blended tones to evoke faerie images of the Opalescent Ones. I was astounded at how well it worked. I'll resist describing the images as completely as I saw them in my inner vision. I feel it's important for you to allow your own images of this realm to emerge first. Instead, I'll provide you with the notes I made with a little help from the wizardry.

For now, I suggest you work with these colors and these notes for practice. Note your own reactions, whether they agree or not. These are your images, your visions.

The Inner Voyage: Activating Images of the Faerie Realm

 This exercise will be helpful as you begin accessing the realm of consciousness we can still call faerie. Here is a simple format.

Either in your inner vision or with colored markers, focus on each of the suggested colors, one at a time. Note your reactions. Begin by creating an image of a "faerie" using the color with which you connect most strongly. Hold focus on the tone of the color you have chosen. This allows you to attune to the vibration of that color. Note your reactions to the tone—invigorating, calming, inspiring, healing, et cetera. Let your image reflect your reaction to the tone and the color vibration. Note the results.

Notes From An Inner Voyage

The following are notes and impressions from an inner voyage focused toward activating images of faerie realm and obtaining inner wisdom. The conversation recorded was neither "channeled" in the New Age sense, nor automatically written in the old spiritualist manner. Instead, it resulted from accessing the element of air and tuning in to that stream of deep thought, memory, and consciousness.

Please note that I refer to images that arose as I was "conversing" about faerie realm. It wasn't until I shifted out of intellectual processes into a more poetic, visionary realm of consciousness that I saw the image of the Opalescent Ones. From that I was able to gather enough information to make notes later. I've included this example so that you can see how delightful these experiences of consciousness journeys and multidimensional links can be. It's a true voyage into the Otherworld realms of mind and brain consciousness.

Finding the Faerie Realm

Q = Question or questor, A = Answer or alchemist

Q   Elemental energies seem to appear in such basic colors, particularly when not accompanied by faerie rulers. Is this more than just convenient classification?

A   When one is dealing with elementals, one is dealing with primitive energies, the primal forces.

Q   Except for fire, most of the other elemental faerie rulers do show variation in tone, but they're still very natural, very human in appearance.

A   When one is dealing with what you refer to as faeries, one is dealing with highly advanced multidimensional beings.

Q   But they're so human. Oh! We're a blend of both (elemental and highly advanced energies)?

A   Yes.

Q   Mostly one or the other?

A   This varies.

Q   Like faeries!

A   This blend is found particularly in cultures where faeries are a strong part of the collective consciousness.

Q   And the collective unconscious, like Jung's?

A   That becomes more difficult to reach for most.

Q   These faerie-conscious cultures—does this describe the Celts well?

A   I wouldn't suggest describing your modern-day Celt on the street as such! Could be dangerous.

Q   We will reclaim that word one day.

A   Spoken like a true Celt.

There followed a series of images without any sound. First an image of a crystal formed, then I saw it enter directly into my brain. An image of the neural pathways followed with crystals at every synaptic node.

Next I had a vision, very de Dannan in nature. With the de Dannan were twelve translucent, winged beings, classically faerie in form. The twelve beings were in six pairs, a male and female in each pair. Each pair reflected a different color in blended shades: indigo, scarlet, peach, rose, turquoise, and golden green. As I worked with this vision of faeries (then and at several later times), I found that each pair, each hue, had a different energy that corresponded to the color of the ray they reflected.

Briefly, so you'll have to "look it up" to find out more, here are the basic impressions I received of these six varieties of faeries (the Opalescent Ones I described previously).

- **Indigo:** These were serious, deeply reverent and priestly. My impression was that of Tibetan lamas or monks. I'm sure this will make those who stress the Arian, Indo-European origin of the Celts quite happy. These were rather remote, but powerful. They were focused inward.

- **Scarlet:** These were "Robin of the Greenwood" types, almost elfin. Their energy reflected a guardianship concerned with keeping the balance of the land and preserving the natural rights and rites. They were warrior-like, but more focused and thinking; ready for battle, but not looking for one.

- **Peach:** These were quite young and energetic. They were involved in the organized activities that concerned healing and prayers in a community sense. My impression was of maidens and young warriors whose role was a cross between spiritual service and social direction. They were powerful, but light and joyful, chattering constantly (seen but not heard by me).

- **Rose:** These were older versions of the peach in some respects. They were more oriented to the individual than the group. My impression was that of earth-bound, practical advisers—"older souls;" wise, calm, and loving. They felt like an active cross between a healer and a professor, with comforting energy fields, gentle but strong.

- **Turquoise:** These were feisty with quick motions, a dramatic sense, and fiery and zealous energies. My impression was that of a classic leprechaun because of their spritely energies. These were more tangible somehow than the others. They danced and played on pipes (again seen but not heard by me). They seemed to be making speeches between songs—a bit bardic, but more prose than poetry; less melodic than clear Muse energics, but inspirational and energizing. They were very friendly.

6. **Golden green:** These were the last pair to emerge. They were elaborately garbed, papal feeling, aware of their rank. My impression was of most important individuals, judges perhaps, with a spiritual role of great importance. They were a combination of healer, sacrificer, and confessor—holy, involved with essential forms of transmutation, communion, and the ceremonies of life and death. They were also remote, but focused toward Nature.

Personal Journey Account

The following journey material is based on imagery that emerged when working with the etheric, transcendent element of spirit. Spirit journeys are often quite intangible, in the sense that images are often not readily forthcoming. The tangibility of spirit journeys often comes experientially as a sense of having touched something extraordinary and divine within the realms of consciousness.

Spirit journeys often lead to experiences of the Otherworld, and sometimes produce an experience of the sacred void beyond images.

You may first glimpse the All as the Void. With devotion to that which you are seeking in the Otherworld aspects of your Self, continued experiences with the element of spirit will truly create new images and activate consciousness multidimensionally.

A ceremonial attitude is most helpful when working with the element of spirit. It also helps to do everyday, routine tasks (such as peel potatoes) afterward for grounding. Otherwise, you may find yourself behaving like a "space faerie" for days.

This journey actually represents two journeys that occurred a few days apart. The first part of this journey ran into an obstacle. It was stonewalled by my own attempts to structure the material as it emerged. In this case, too much of the element earth was at work. I had attempted to approach what I found within as a teacher, rather than as a student. Once I realized how that was limiting my experience, I was able to crack through the structures of my own expectations and begin the journey anew. Therefore, this journey account is the combination of two related journeys.

I feel that it is important to point out that all of the elements were present and active participants in this experience. A harmonious attunement with the first four elements ensured an experience of transcendent magick. It is advisable to be in balance with each of the first four elements before spending too much time traveling into the more transcendent element of spirit.

The Shining Ones: A Journey in Two Parts

Prelude: Widsom from the Old Ones

This is the time of the spirit journey, into the realms beyond and between the dimensions of clear definition.

I awaken in a time of spirit dreaming. I cannot tell if it is twilight or dawn. A thick fog covers the landscape with a mystical veil of light. No sounds come forth to signal activities that speak of the time of day or night.

From within the realms of my Self, I emerge from the mists riding a blue-white horse, bridled with a braided silvery cord. My horse is moving very fast, and I am just able to make out the shapes of the land through the mists. Above me, high, rocky cliffs tower like gray giants in the shadowy light. Below me, a rocky beach stretches out to meet a dark sea. I can hear the sound of small waves rushing softly up the sand. I see the sea foam fly up as my horse's hooves strike the beach.

The beach becomes rockier now, and my steed slows her pace. Large, round boulders loom in the mists like ancient sentinels, watching and waiting.

I stop the horse and dismount. I see a light emerging from a narrow space between two of the largest stones. As I peer through the space, I see a fire burning high. Its flames illuminate an alcove carved by sea and wind in the pale gray cliffs.

In the alcove, two white-robed figures cast stones across an altar top. The altar looks to be Nature-made. It is a large egg-shaped boulder whose topside has been shorn off, leaving a flat, strangely patterned surface. The altar looks to me as though it had been cleaved with a giant's battle-ax, then delicately carved with a faerie chisel. The pattern on the altar clears in my vision, and I see an intricately carved working of Celtic weavings and runic symbols, the *coelvains*. I have never seen its like before.

I am so compelled to take a closer look at the altar that I scarcely remember the two white-robed figures standing beside it. I realize with a slight shock that they have turned to look at me.

They are a man and a woman, both of an ancient age. Long white hair and cloudy-gray eyes are the first impressions I receive. The old man's beard is wispy and silver. It blows in the sea breeze and entangles itself in the long, woven chain around his neck.

Both he and the old woman wear medallions. I can just make out the design from my position behind the boulders. The medallions are bluish silver in color, perhaps platinum. Three inlaid concentric circles make up the design. The inner circle is a rosy gold, the middle circle a rich yellow, and the outer circle is a fine white gold. I am lost in the pull of these golden circles for a moment.

I have forgotten that I am not alone. A gentle cough from the old man reminds me of their presence. The old woman beckons to me, smiling patiently. The old man's eyes twinkle with amusement.

"Why don't you come closer if you want to know what's here?" the old man says wryly.

I suddenly feel quite childish standing there peeking in through the crack in the stones. "It's such a narrow space, I wonder if I will be able to pass through it," I call back.

"I wonder that, too," the old man chuckles. "Just how narrow have you made your passage?"

"Well, you can see for yourself that I can just barely squeeze my hands through here." I wriggle my fingers through the crack in the boulders.

"What we see from this side is a space as wide as you want to come into, or as narrow as you need to keep yourself out. Think about that." The old woman places her hands on her hips as she speaks. "Don't come in here, if you haven't made up your mind to do so."

"And if I have made up my mind?" I ask her through the crack in the boulders.

"And when you make up your mind to do so, you shall," says the old man, looking amused now. Both he and the old woman resume casting the runic stones across the altar.

I sit in the cool, damp sand and lean against one of the smooth stones. I ponder my resistance to entering this realm. The experience is deep and real. I know that it represents another realm of energy, another element of personal and natural attunement. I know it is another dimension of spirit. I wish to enter into it, but I am momentarily bound with a childish stubbornness.

"Is it really necessary for me to feel four years old?" I inquire. "Do I have to somehow live backwards like the Merlin to get here each time?"

I hear the old man laugh as the rune stones scatter across the altar. "It is only as a magickal child of light that you may enter here. You will have to accept that part of your Self without judgment, if you are to come closer."

I begin to feel the comfortable warmth of familiarity with these fine Old Ones. It is a remembrance, an ancient connection, an awakening to that always has been within.

The old woman stands up from her task and searches the deep night sky. With the fire at her feet and the moon above her head, she is suddenly all aspects of woman. She is all ages at once, and all experiences in one beautiful, wise old woman. I feel her shrewd gaze return to me.

"Many come here claiming to know just what they are and who they are. Of course, we've known them from the start. They don't need to tell us who they are, but they do. They always do."

The old man's eyes pierce me now. "And what shall you tell us you are, I wonder?" His kindly tone softens the sharp scrutiny in his expression.

I pause for a moment, pulling in all the magick I feel around me. I stand quickly and mount my horse. She rears up as I pull in on the reins. Her mane glistens in the moonlight as she shakes her magnificent head.

"I am a child of the universe," I call out into the night sky. I turn my horse away from the great boulders and ride down the beach, far enough away for a fast charge.

"I am the seeker, the student, the storyteller, and the sorceress. I am my Self. I am still that magickal child."

My horse gallops full force toward the stone barrier.

"I am the unlimited one!" I shout across the boulders. With a great burst of energy, the stones move apart as my horse and I jump through the now ample passageway between them. We land on the other side with a deft grace I had not anticipated.

I feel the heat of the fire against my legs. For the first time I notice that I wear a white robe, quite similar to those worn by the Old Ones I have encountered.

Only the medallion I wear is different. It is a simple cross of Celtic design, blue-silver arms reaching out equally in four directions from within a circle of gold. It feels strong above my heart. I notice the warm welcome in the Old Ones' faces, and I know that I have come home to a deeper, older part of my Self.

I get down from my horse and warm myself by the fire. It is a mild night, but my hands and face feel quite cold. The Old Ones watch me patiently. I realize that they are waiting for me to speak. I choose my words carefully, ceremonially.

"Old Ones, I have felt your presence many times and glimpsed your faces before. Yet never have I seen you together, thus, nor experienced your energies so clearly."

I pause to consider my next statement.

"Respectfully, I say to you that I am quite grateful for your presence, yet confused by it, as well. I began this journey into spirit with the intention of finding the realm of faerie. I had not expected to find you along the way. Neither had I expected to find great stone barriers to cross. I do not understand these things."

The Old Ones merely chuckle.

I feel a new kind of power beginning to flow into me. My body feels strong, my mind open and perceptive. My spirit seems to soar upward. I address the Old Ones with honor.

"I know that I must need something, some force that you are here to give me. I should only like to know what this is."

The old man takes a long wooden staff from a niche in the rocks and begins to draw a symbol in the sand. As he etches the lines, I recognize the same Celtic cross that I wear. The old man finishes the cross and circle, then speaks.

"We represent the full development of your natural potential. We are the elements of strength, intuition, sacred knowledge, and inspiration. We are experience. We are the portals through which you must pass into the other world that you call the faerie realm. We are ritual and ceremony. We are the Wise Ones, the Old Ones, the Magick Ones."

"How shall I pass through these portals you represent?" I cannot imagine charging my horse at these white-haired elder kin.

The old woman laughs at my thoughts. "You shall pass through by accepting all the elements of your Self in balance."

She motions for me to come close to the altar. As I study the runic coelvains there, she reaches into a basket half-hidden in the shadows. She takes out a flagon of wine, a heavy glass goblet, and a small, covered dish. Placing these upon the altar, the old woman begins to sing an ancient, haunting song. She pours wine into the goblet, pausing to wave her fingers over the rim. For a moment, her hands are smooth and supple as they draw symbols in the air above the goblet.

The old man steps forward and lifts the cover from the dish. He takes out a flat, wafer-thin cake and places it at the base of the goblet. With two fingers pointing out from his right hand, the old man begins to intone a series of sounds that shakes the stone altar with its vibrations.

I notice a shimmering mist has begun to move in slowly from the sea. Above me, the stars seem to shift their positions, some moving slowly, others cascading toward the ground. The mist thickens rapidly now. Each tone the old man makes sends silvery lights sparkling through the night air. Magical happenings seem imminent. Anticipation crackles through me. Patience fails me.

"Quickly, please, what shall I do?" I notice an eerie light illuminating the clouds on the horizon. Fingers of a "faerie" fog reach out toward me. They are gentle, but insistent. The mists sweep into the alcove, and I can no longer see the Old Ones.

"You must use the magick of your mind," the old man calls from the mist.

"You must use the purity of your heart." The old woman's voice sounds far away, lost in the fog.

The Encounter: Experiencing the Shining Ones

The mist drifts back out of the alcove, and I see that the Old Ones are gone. The fire burns low now. Its flames reflect with crystalline lights in the goblet. The wine is dark and thick. It looks like blood in the firelight, I think. I try to laugh at the shudder that passes through me. I pick up the goblet and drink.

"Sacred force of life, flow through me. Make me clear of mind and pure of purpose."

I pick up the wafer and break it in half. I eat one of the pieces slowly, and say, "Sustenance of life, strengthen my focus and manifest my resolve."

I take the goblet and the wafer to the water's edge. I pour the dark liquid into the sea foam at my feet, and I cast the wafer out into the mists.

"Realm of spirit, I resolve to reach you. I share these gifts with you as they were shared with me. Harken to the love in my heart and forgive my awkward fumbling manner. It is hard, being human."

A laugh, clear as silver chimes in the wind, carries across the mists. A shimmering flash crackles in a circle around my head.

From out of the mists step the Shining Ones. There are two of them, a male and a female. Their appearance indicates youth, yet their presence radiates a wisdom seldom found in the young. As they approach, the fire springs back to life, its flames dancing merrily. The air vibrates with an unusual pressure. It is as though there is too much air to breathe.

I steady myself against a huge stone boulder, and I notice that the rocks seem to be humming with energy. The rhythm steadies my shaking body and slows my racing thoughts.

Cool waves sweep far up the beach towards the altar and the alcove. The sea foam dampens the hem of my robes and drenches my feet. All the elements seem amplified by the appearance of the Shining Ones.

We study each other carefully, comfortably curious about sharing this presence. They assess me swiftly. I feel dimensions of my Self passing in review across the inner screen of my mind. They laugh with delight at my attempts to evoke images from them. They are misty and ethereal one moment, solid and manifest the next. The shifts begin to make me dizzy. I hold up a hand in protest.

"You are moving too fast for me. Remember, I'm made of denser energies, like those in Nature. Slow down a bit, could you, please? Find a less intense frequency. Pick another channel. Do something, so that I can really experience this completely."

The fire softens; the air reduces its electric charge; the stones settle down to a quiet droning; the water draws back into the sea. The mists clear completely, and the Shining Ones of the Otherworld become manifest in my realm of spirit dreaming.

They are tall, with builds that appear slight, yet convey great strength. Their hair is very light, a cool white blonde; silver ash or platinum, it could be called. Their eyes are crystalline and continue to shift color from time to time. I can see those eyes flashing the light blue of clear skies, the soft greens of seawater, the rich greens of Nature's foliage, and the deep blues found in the center of a flame.

In the direct light of the fire, their eyes become crystalline once more, translucent like frosted glass, or a mirror backed with old silver. I am fascinated with these magick mirror eyes.

I force myself not to stare. I admire their garments. Their cloaks are long and full, yet seem to lift with the slightest breeze or most gentle movement. The cloaks are made from a gossamer-light weave, a faerie fabric if ever there were one. Its rainbow hues are reflected in the iridescent threads of the fabric. Each movement of the cloaks sends out sparkles of light like the spectrum hues from a crystal prism, except the rays seem more like blends than basic colors. Perhaps this is because the energy these colors produce is moving at such a rapid rate, I think to myself.

The Shining Ones smile at me indulgently. I realize the extended analysis that I'm beginning to do must feel as strange to them as their rapid mind probe did to me.

I quickly note the clasps that hold their cloaks. They are eight-point stars. Each point is set with a clear crystal and a large rainbow-hued crystal forms the center. The bluish-silver hue of the metal makes me think it is platinum or possibly titanium, yet it feels different somehow from either of these. I resist the impulse to continue my less-than-subtle scrutiny of these magnificent beings. I wonder briefly why they don't have wings.

At this thought, both of the Shining Ones laugh, and I realize that they have known what I was thinking all along. Remembering that I had invited them, I strive to be hospitable.

"Excuse me for being so obviously curious. I fear I've remembered my analytic training but forgotten my manners," I offer by way of explanation.

"No instruments of your science can serve to reveal our substance," the male says in a voice both gentle and strong. "We are made of an etheric element. It is an element of pure light and energy that is transcendent in its aspect."

The female turns slowly toward the fire and speaks in her wind-chime voice. "We are as you expect us to be. Your belief creates our forms. You see us like this in your consciousness, and thus we appear as such."

"But surely others have seen you for countless ages," I reply. "Tales of the Shining Ones have come down to us from ancient times."

"It is so," she agrees with a nod of her shimmering head. "We would not say time or ages, though, but dimensions or realms of consciousness. We dwell in realms that few are willing or able to access. Yet to do so is quite simple, elementally speaking."

I smile at her efforts to explain such a complex creation as being simple. The male notes my amusement and contributes his own explanation.

"We dwell in a realm of such intense frequency, such high vibrational energies, that it is rarely reached by humankind except through the pathways of memory and deep mind. It is a realm that has never manifested in the mundane dimensions of this world. It is a realm that is purely what you call Otherworld. We dwell only in the mystic dimensions of conscious mind."

"And the mythic realms, as well?" I add. "What about all the tales of the faerie realms, the Mystic Isles, the stories of the Sidhe?"

"These emerge, as we do, from the deep consciousness of your tribal memories." He seems eager to share this information.

I feel a stupid lack of questions, but they answer what I need to know, yet cannot express.

"We represent a realm beyond the time and space constructs of your world. It is a realm you once knew and shall know again because stories have kept the awareness alive." The female wraps her cloak around her slender frame as she speaks. "We are the Shining Ones, as you have chosen to call us. We dwell between the realms of clear mind and pure spirit. We touch all of Nature, yet manifest in none of it in a material way."

The male leans forward from the rock on which he has seated himself. "We are of the Sidhe, of the spirit, yet our element is not manifest or material enough to sustain the vibrations needed for dwelling close to the Earth, as others of our kind can do."

"What others?" I interrupt, anxious to understand. I see that the Shining Ones are becoming somewhat translucent and beginning to fade into the mists once more. "Do you mean those who have appeared in the minds and the mythos for so long, and so frequently are of your kind, yet have some element that allows them, well, allows us greater access to them?"

"You have used the key word," he says, voice fading slightly into the wind. "Those of us with the elements of the material world reflect and connect much more clearly in the minds and the myths of humankind."

"That is because we are just that," the female speaks in a whisper, no louder than the waves. "We are the reflected images of the elements of your Self, your power, your very nature. Those of us reflecting the element of spirit most purely must remain ethereal. Those of us who dwell between the realms of the mundane and the mind can manifest more easily, if only in the magick dimensions of your lives. They are the Lordly Ones. They are the manifest images of Nature itself. They are the personifications of your natural, elemental Self."

"Would you say that the Lordly Ones are more like devas and the Shining Ones are more like deities?" I find myself calling into the mists as the Shining Ones fade into the shimmering glow surrounding the landscape once more.

The wind-chime tones of the female's voice send a soft melody out of the mists. "Neither devas nor deities have any more manifest reality than the dimensions of your mind will give them."

"How shall I know you better?" I speak to an empty image now, filled only with mists and clouds. Even my horse has melted away, fading along with my imagery. Yet, I wait for an answer.

"Journey along new pathways," the deep male voice cuts through the mists one more time. "Find the passageways to new dimensions of your mind. Follow the maps of myth and mystery. We will be there. We are eternally there, yet ever here in you."

Celtic Quest:
Crafting the Keys to the Realm

The time has come for us to enter into another dimension of this, our quest to reconnect with the natural elements of our Selves as Celts. Thus far, I have accompanied you on this journey as an instructor, guide, storyteller, and catalyst for your consciousness. Now I shift my shape somewhat and assume the role of a crafter of wisdom.

In this role, I shall travel with you side by side into the realms of symbols, myth, and the imagination, and reveal secrets that I have learned through my own journeys into history, myth, poetry, and magick. It is said of my Craft that it cannot truly be taught, only learned. Perhaps that is true, but some basics can be taught. Still more may be presented in sharing the tales of one's own personal journey. Real crafters of wisdom can only profess knowledge that they have gathered and experienced themselves. That is the true way of the druidic teacher.

The wisdoms I present is drawn from my own studies and my own shamanic journeys. They reflect my own experiences, my own system of wisdom. They represent the treasures I have accumulated on many travels into realms of magick and myth, and the knowledge I have gained in sharing with others and hearing the tales of their own journeys into the mythic realms of mind and consciousness. They represent the stories of a seeker, a quester, a crafter of wisdom. They represent the elements of my personal alchemy blended with the secrets of ages past, present, and future.

They are presented in this volume as a guide for you to follow only if you choose to do so. The journey and quest are for a personal connection to the natural elements of your Self. No one can tell you how to make that quest. There are many who would attempt to do so, but this advice is just ash of hastily consumed information with no more substance than smoke in the wind.

As we shall explore in this chapter, there are certain truths in wisdom, certain powers in symbols, certain magick in color and the sound of words. These may be shared, but must ultimately be experienced on a personal level. Ultimately they must be either accepted or rejected according to one's personal choice. Your experience of any given symbol, color, or word determines how personally meaningful and magickal it is for you. Create your own imagery. Make your own magick. The symbolic imageries that you create in accordance to your own experience provide you with keys. Use these keys to unlock the "doors of perception" and enter into the realm of magick, the expanded dimensions of mind and consciousness.

As a *ban drui*—a woman of wisdom, white oak druidess, white witch—I will endeavor to share my set of personally crafted keys. These keys are made of many elements shared by others. By my faith, they are crafted from the purest element of truth. I truly hope that they will help you craft keys of your own. Until that time, though, you are most welcome to use mine. I am honored to share them with you. I am also duty bound to share the great natural druidic laws of my Craft.

How you choose to use this wisdom is entirely up to you. I shall not judge you. However, by my Irish, I am bound to say that wisdom is a domain ruled by the Lady of Justice. This Lady carries a doubled-edged sword; one edge brings blessings, the other curses.

That being said, let us journey through the realms we have already explored. This time, as quester, you may gather the tools you need, collect the magick charms, accept the weapons, and activate your power more clearly.

Realm Quest:
A Guided Imagery to Quest for
the Powers of the Elements

 On this quest to the elemental dimensions of this Otherworld realm, your traveling companions will be that wizard with magick more of myth than fantasy, the great Lord Merlin, and me, the Ban Drui.

To ensure our safe passage, we also request the protective powers of "Teutates," the foresworn god of our people. To carry us along, we call for the mighty powers and protection of the Celtic horse goddess herself, Epona. She shall provide us with the proper steeds. With honor to the de Dannan, we shall use their fair gifts to expand our connection and empower our experience.

Let us begin.

Fire

Mounted on strong red horses, we enter first the realm of fire, the regions of guardians, and herein ruled by the Warriors of Fire. From our alliance with these mighty warriors, we learn about the magick powers of strength and physicality. We hear tales of courage, faith, and strength, and the battles for the protection of truth.

After we watch demonstrations of battle skills, we share the spare but sufficient fare of this fierce, fighting force. We enjoy ale from a drinking horn carved with Celtic knots. We break bread together and share a fine wheel of cheese.

It has been a warm day, but the chill of afternoon makes us gather close together around the center fire. As quester, you are given first a magick cloak to keep you safe, warm, and strong. Its colors are that of fire, ashes, and smoke—red, orange, and black.

As we sit around the fire, the Ban Drui tells of the magick properties this cloak brings you with its dramatic colors.

201

The red activates your strengths, empowering and fueling all that fire represents. The orange brings you vitality, guarding the physical processes of your body. The black transmutes your weaknesses and vulnerabilities, releasing your fears and doubts as you quest for the light of truth.

The Ban Drui gives you a talismanic brooch to hold your cloak. It is a Maltese Cross made of bronze, the alchemical metal that represents the ability to "test one's own metal" and blend power purely. It is set with carnelian, the stone of action, and smoky quartz, the stone that transmutes all challenges to your strength. It is symbolic of power in equal balance emanating from the center of your Self.

Next, the Lord Merlin presents you with magick runes. He draws these first in ashes on the ground and explains their powers.

Fire Runes

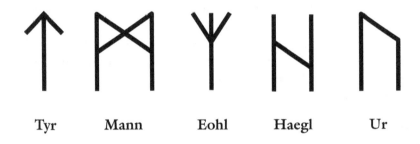

| Tyr | Mann | Eohl | Haegl | Ur |

- **Tyr**, the symbol of the warrior questing for the higher powers of truth.
- **Mann**, the rune representing the Self in full acceptance of the personal responsibility of power.
- **Eohl**, the sign of protection, the guardian barrier declaring your intentions to preserve the peace and safety.
- **Haegl**, the rune of disruption, a force to be used only for positive purposes.
- **Ur**, the solid power of strength, the essential element of a warrior.

Then the Lord Merlin reaches into his magick pouch and draws out five stones marked with these runes. You place them in a woven pouch of your own, a gift from the weavers by way of the Ban Drui.

Next, the Ban Drui adds a runestone of her own, symbolic of the faerie gift most purely matching the power of fire. It is the rune that represents the sword.

Cweord, the sword power to preserve and defend, to cut through bindings that impede your progress, and to enforce the positive power, the "might for right."

Cweord

With that, the Warriors of Fire present you with a sword of your own. It is crafted, faerily, of your own design. Its blade is double-edged, in keeping with the power of fire and the activation force of wisdom.

Then the Ban Drui presents you with one half of another symbolic weapon, fashioned of both fire and air (yet to come). She gives you the point of a spear, shaped and sharpened as though you had done so yourself. It is a primitive point of power and must be balanced by the advancement of your own intellect. For this, you are responsible. You save the spear point for a later phase of your quest.

Bidding fond farewell to the Warrior guardians, we make our way onward. We have exchanged our roans for new, fresh horses.

Water

On steeds of silvery gray we make our way into the realm of water, the regions of the Priestly Ones, ruled by the mystical healers of the sacred waters. From our alliance with these gentle healers we learn about the magick powers of intuition and emotions. We hear emotions expressed with honest feelings and secrets of searching within the heart to hear the voice of wisdom.

After we watch a performance of folk dance and juggling acts, we share in a snack of honey cakes and cool, refreshing water from the nearby stream. We celebrate the magick secrets of simply being happy with these compassionate priestly folk, so devoted to healing transformation. We share the simple pleasures, simply expressed and simply experienced. We share them openly amongst ourselves, whether in laughter or through tears.

As quester, you are given your second magick cloak, this one to make you feel better at all times. Its colors are that of water, cool and soothing—dark blue, lavender, and pale gray.

As you snuggle comfortably into your magick cloak, the Ban Drui tells of the magick properties this cloak brings you with its gentle colors.

The dark blue brings your emotions into a state of harmonious synthesis, and "pulls you back together" when you feel you're falling to pieces. It also opens you to inner wisdom. (The Ban Drui taps you on the center of your forehead as she tells you this.) Dark blue activates water. Lavender brings you the transformative power of self-healing by helping you transmute all disease and obstructions to health and positive emotional expression. It helps you release all the emotions you accumulated that need to be "thrown out," but not given away to others. Gray brings you flexibility, the ability to flow with your life cycles.

Next, the Ban Drui gives you a talismanic brooch to hold your cloak. It is a lunar crescent, symbolic of the cycles of your emotions and the phases of your personal growth. It is made of silver, the precious metal of receptivity, symbolic of the mystical lunar realms of inner, personal wisdom. It is set with moonstone, which has the power of absorbancy, and with pearls, which bring the wisdom of personal reflection.

The Ban Drui, being a woman of Nature wisdom, advises you on the ways you may choose to wear this lunar crescent.

Pointing up, it signifies the full moon, a time of celebration and ceremonies of empowerment. Pointing toward the east, it signifies the waning moon, a time for release. Pointing down, it represents the dark moon, a time for deep transformations. Pointing toward the west, it represents the new moon and new beginnings.

Next, the Lord Merlin presents you with magick runes of power. He draws these first on the floor using water from the stream to mark their shapes.

Water Runes

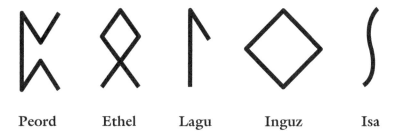

| Peord | Ethel | Lagu | Inguz | Isa |

- **Peord**, the symbol of initiation, marking cycles of transformations and gateways to wisdom through which you must pass.
- **Ethel**, the rune that represents the wisdom of personal retreats, the power gained from going inward.
- **Lagu**, the sign for the flow of wisdom, healing, and intuitive messages.
- **Inguz**, the symbol of the chrysalis, the womb of self-transformation.
- **Isa**, the signal rune for standstill, the inner calm, the peace, and the protective force for controlling overflows of energy and emotions.

As the water-fashioned symbols evaporate from the floor, the Lord Merlin gives you more smooth stones, marked with these runes. You place these in your woven pouch with the others.

Then the Ban Drui adds another runestone, symbolic of the faerie gift most clearly reflecting the power of water. It is the rune that represents the cup.

Calc, the cup power to receive and share personal wisdom. The holy cup to heal your Self with the purest powers of transformation and to reflect the sacred inner light.

Calc

With that, the Priestly Ones present you with a fine cup for you to call your own. It is fashioned, faerily, from designs received through your own intuition. Its bowl is large enough to be both a vessel for drinking and a basin from which you may bathe yourself with healing water.

We say goodbye to our devoted healing friends from the realm of water, and begin our quest once more. We have exchanged our graceful gray horses for other sturdy mounts, and we make our way onward through the shire.

Earth

Mounted on big, brown horses, we enter into the realm of earth. This is the region of the tribal planners, ruled by the Master Chieftain and Clan Mother. From our alliance with these determined folk, we learn about the magick powers of structured wisdom and practicality. We hear knowledge taught with skill and patience, and learn the methods and means by which prosperity and positive growth may be produced.

After we observe the systems that have been developed, and make notes recording the wisdom we have been instructed to know, we share in the abundant fruits of the harvest. We drink herbal tea and enjoy the rich nourishment of apples and nuts. We gather together as friends, connected by our common bond of Nature. We are honored as kin, and we return the compliment in kind. We discuss the prosperous potential that we may reach from this practical relationship and sacred connection.

As quester, you are given a third magick cloak, this one designed for practical purposes to serve you well. Its colors are that of earth, rich and natural—dark green, purple, and rust brown. As you adjust your cloak for a sure fit, the Ban Drui tells you of the magick properties that the cloak brings you with its rich colors.

The dark green activates the powers of growth, abundance, and prosperity. The purple educates you with the truth, the highest orders of sacred wisdom; it transforms the binding structures of false teachings and the limitations of dogma. The rust brown brings order to your life, and the power of centered, practical progress; it grounds your impulses and reduces chaos and confusion.

Next, the Ban Drui provides you with a talismanic brooch to hold your cloak. It is a fine, five-pointed, woven star, symbolic of the interwoven connection of humankind to all the elements of Nature and self-nature. It represents the sacred structures of wisdom and magick. It is made of copper, the practical metal of *devic* power, symbolic of Nature's sturdy, interwoven support.

It is set with amethyst, the spiritual stone in divine relationship to the source of all wisdom. It is also set with green marble, the foundational stone of luck appearing in practical forms, according to your needs.

The Ban Drui, being of the light weavers, reveals the often misunderstood meanings regarding the positions in which this wheel of Nature, the woven star, is worn. In so doing, she shares some secrets about its elemental power and its natural gifts.

One point up signifies a relationship with the source from which all elements derive their heritage—Mother Nature, the provider, the teacher, the spiritual connection. Two points up signifies a relationship with the guardian of the realm of Natural elements. Two points show the horns of the hunter, Lord of the Forever Forests, Lord of the Animals, the Herne.

Next, the Lord Merlin shares more sacred runes of power. He draws them first in the rich soil of the ground, then teaches you their properties.

Earth Runes

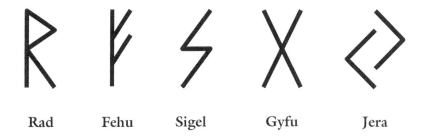

| Rad | Fehu | Sigel | Gyfu | Jera |

- **Rad**, the rune signifying journeys, the routes of progress, the maps of prosperous development gained by exploration and effort.
- **Fehu**, the sign for possessions in proper abundance, and of balancing needs and wants for practical purposes and continued prosperity.

- **Sigel**, the symbol of sacred power in its fullest, most abundant form creating the wealth of wholeness.
- **Gyfu**, the sign for gifts from the highest orders of power and truth, the sacred gifts of divine origin.
- **Jera**, the symbol of harvest, celebrating the assurance of cycles of growth.

When he finishes his lessons regarding the runes of the element earth, the Merlin gives you more stones marked with those sacred symbols. You add these to your collection.

Then the Ban Drui adds yet another runestone, definitely symbolic of the faerie gift that represents the power of earth. It is the rune that stands for the stone.

Stan, the stone power to structure sacred wisdom, to harvest the heritage of Nature, and to order one's life in practical, prosperous form.

Stan

With that, the Clan Leaders present you with two strong, practical gifts. The first is a stone marked with ancient symbols most faerily connected with your purpose, sacred in particular to your quest for truth and wisdom. The second is a shield, strongly crafted of sturdy material designed to symbolize the structure of your Self and your centered, grounded power. It is both a shield for wise, protective purposes and a banner of self-declaration. It, too, is decorated with colors and symbols that signify your Self and the way in which you choose to structure your image.

We take our leave from the Clan Leaders after conveying our appreciation and abundant gratitude for their lessons and their gifts. We leave our sturdy brown steeds to rest and resume our quest with horses that are refreshed and ready to go.

Air

Riding on fleet-footed steeds of a butter-cream color, we enter into the realm of air. This is the region of the bardic drui represented and ruled by the Muse Singers. From our alliance with these fair folk we hear mystically crafted music and eloquently spoken, illuminating poetry. We marvel at the magick these creative folk communicate. Their clear thoughts bring us new perceptions and focused awareness.

After we have heard the poetry-songs and prose of these fair folk, we gather in a sunlit meadow to exchange our inspirations, ideas, and philosophies. As we converse, we have a picnic of fine fresh vegetables from a spring garden and berries from the vines. We enjoy mead from cups made of porcelain, until we become quite heady from the light brew.

As quester, you are given your fourth magick cloak, this one to keep you enveloped in the power of your own perceptive awareness. Its airy colors are those of the sky, the Sun, and the clouds, bright, clear, and illuminating—light blue, yellow, and white. As you admire the delicate weave of your magick cloak, the Ban Drui tells of the magick properties it brings you with its light, clear colors.

The light blue activates your powers of communication, and enables you to craft and perceptively select the words you wish to express. The yellow provides you with the sharpened awareness of focus and the organizational abilities of your mind and thoughts. The white provides you with a valuable magick transmittal medium; it creates a veil of light to support the positive power of your thoughts and actions.

Next, the Ban Drui gives you a talismanic brooch to hold your cloak. It is symbolic of your abilities to activate your conscious mind and intellect. It is shaped like a set of wings with a harp at the center. It is made of fine white gold, the precious solar metal of activation and enlightenment.

The brooch is set with blue topaz, the crystalline stone of mental acuity, and with golden citrines, which bring focus and the powers of organization. The Ban Drui advises you to develop your perceptive skills before you attempt to take flight.

Next, the Lord Merlin shows you still more runes of power. He draws these out for you in the clear, sunlit sky. They sparkle in the air magickally crafted by his wizardry and drawn with his staff. He tells of their powers.

Air Runes

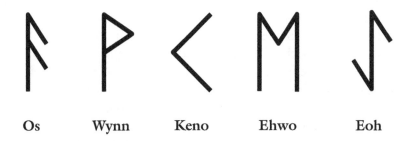

| Os | Wynn | Keno | Ehwo | Eoh |

- **Os**, meaning "God," signals from the highest source of light—the divine, the godhead—messages of power.
- **Wynn**, the symbol for joy, the magick of inspiration, the satisfaction of self-evolutionary thought processes.
- **Keno**, the rune of openings, new beginnings, new images of life, new ways of communicating one's Self to the world.
- **Ehwo**, the symbol of progress, the vehicle of the mind, body, and spirit developing toward a more conscious state of being; the method and the means of positive forward movement.
- **Eoh**, the rune of new perspectives, bringing thoughts and ideas into sharper focus, bringing new inspirations and power.

As the wizard-crafted runes fade into the air, the Merlin gives you these new runestones to include in your collection.

Now the Ban Drui adds yet another runestone, one that correlates clearly the power of air with the faerie gift it symbolizes. It is the rune that represents the spear.

Gar, the power of the spear to cast forth ideas, philosophies, and magick thought forms. This spear increases the power of communication and perception. It is a spear that never misses its mark.

Gar

With that, the bardic drui present you with a gift that puzzles you at first, until you give it some thought. It is a slender rod made from a long branch of ash wood. Its shape is straight, perfectly aligned, and feels balanced in your hands. With delight you realize its diameter is a perfect match for your spear point from fire.

As you fit the spear point onto the shaft, the Merlin nods his head with approval. Then one of the Muse Singers places a very special gift in your hands. It is a tiny wand crafted as beautifully as you have imagined it to be. At one end is a faerie cross, a staurolite; at the other end is a place where another stone has yet to be set.

With perceptive wisdom, you do not inquire about this wand with a missing stone. You know that you will discover its message along the way. With praise for your progress, the Merlin bestows another gift. It is a magick staff cut to just your height and bearing symbols of your personal power.

We bid farewell to the Muse Singers of air realm and begin the final phase of this elemental quest for symbols of power. We leave our beautiful butter-cream mounts with the fair folk and journey onward with horses of a more mystical nature.

Spirit

Borne on the backs of beautiful white horses, we make our way into the realm of spirit. This is the Otherworld region of the faerie folk, ruled by the Shining Ones. This is the realm of the Sidhe, shared with the de Dannan, governed by the goddess Danu, and ruled by the Celestial Creatrix, source of the universe.

From our alliance with this mystical, timeless realm, we obtain the purest power connecting us to all of life and Nature. We observe the spiritual crystalline web and see the interweavings of our lives, the evolution of our wisdom and the pathways to service. In the fibers of the crystal web, we see the flowing patterns of spirit and power moving through all the elements of Nature and self-nature. We see the highest, purest reflection of our Selves.

After we have received our visions of Self and spirit, we are shown others that tell of the triumph of creation forces over the oppression forces of entropy. We accept the truth of this spiritual vision and celebrate our alliance with this mysterious realm of light.

We are brought to a great hall elaborately decorated with luminous and iridescent colors. We take part in a communion ritual that empowers the connection of that which we call matter to that which we recognize as spirit. For those who choose to partake, there is wine in cut-glass crystal chalices and wafers on plates of translucent china. For those who prefer it, there is rose nectar in ornate long-stemmed glasses with tiny frosted patterns of flowers and stars. We enjoy the sustenance we choose as we listen to a discussion regarding the nature of this Otherworld realm. There are many fine folk to meet, many luminaries are here in this, the realm of faerie. Faerily, perhaps, we feel right at home.

As quester, you are given another special, magick cloak, designed to empower you with all the rights and privileges of this realm. Its colors reflect the full spectrum of the rainbow and all the blended hues between its bands. Its vivid hues vibrate with a higher tone. This cloak is a crystalline melody of color.

As you accept this cloak, you vow to honor its gifts and pledge yourself to the service of lights it represents. The Ban Drui comes forth to tell you of its full spectrum of power.

The rainbow tones and all the blended hues represent the powers of all the elements in harmonious perfection. It enables you to sense, feel, connect, and communicate power, light, and truth. It allows you to blend with others while retaining your self-identity, wisdom, growth, and image. It allows you to access the magick of multidimensional consciousness.

Next, the Ban Drui presents you with a brooch crafted in this Otherworld realm. It represents the wheel of druidic wisdom and the source of universal power, the great Star Mother, creatrix of galaxies yet to be discovered. It is an eight-point star made of platinum, the alchemical metal of multidimensional linking. It is set with clear crystal points, stones that amplify and clarify all that they touch. It is also set with rainbow crystals to represent the power of harmonic blending. The Ban Drui points out that no matter which way you turn this sacred symbol, it remains the same. It is the force of light and wisdom universally structured, reflecting in the cycles of Nature and of Self.

Then the Lord Merlin shares some rather spirited runes with you. He lays these out on an ornate altar in the great hall of the faerie realm. He crafts these from tiny, perfect crystals that sparkle in rainbow lights. Satisfied with his arrangement, the Merlin tells you of the powers in these runes.

Spirit Runes

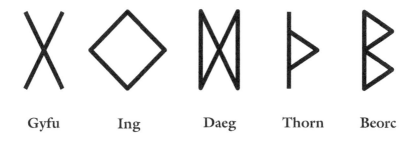

| Gyfu | Ing | Daeg | Thorn | Beorc |

- **Gyfu**, the rune for gifts from the highest realms of light and spirit, an acceptance of that which empowers purely.
- **Ing**, the symbol of perfection, the crystalline clear state accessed in the dimensions of divine light.
- **Daeg**, the rune signifying a breakthrough into higher dimensions of Self and spirit, a transmutational force opening to the light.
- **Thorn**, the sign of the gateway, the passage through which one travels on any quest or journey into the dimension of the Self. It is a gateway that provides access, but no direction as to the path to be followed. That remains, as ever, a personal choice.
- **Beorc**, the symbol of sustenance, the essential nourishment of body, mind, and spirit receiving fully from the source of all empowerment.

As he finishes telling you of the wisdom in these runes, the Merlin sweeps the crystals from the altar top and hands them to you along with runestones marked with the symbols in which you were just instructed. These crystals, he assures you, will amplify the power of all the runes you have collected.

You look expectantly at the Ban Drui, waiting for her to produce another rune symbolic of the faerie gifts. Instead, she tells you that runes of this nature have their greatest power when they are created personally. That is one key you must craft on your own. She suggests you work with spiritual symbols that have high significance for you to experience their sacred energies. Having done that for a time, you will then know, purely, how to create a personal rune symbolic of your unique relationship to the Otherworld realm of spirit. Crafted with positive intent, it will serve you well.

The bards sing out in praise of your courage, strength, wisdom, and perceptive abilities that have guided you on this quest. They sing out in praise of your spirit.

Then, from the far end of the hall come two white-robed figures, a man and a woman—the Old Ones, the Wise Ones. They present you with a tiny crystal that fits perfectly on your wand. It is clear and laser in its energy, and it sends out all shades of light and color. It is a tool of magick and a weapon of light. It amplifies your power purely, in line with your purpose and your intent. It shoots forth whatever forces with which you empower it. Its service is determined by you and your relationship to the realm of spirit.

We pledge ourselves to the preservation of this realm and its Otherworldly powers. We pledge ourselves to its service and to the activation of its light within the highest dimensions of our consciousness, reflected in the image we craft of its magick.

We leave our wonderful white horses in this realm of faerie and honor our allies for their many gifts of power. Then, as the mists rise slowly, we watch all images of this realm fade away, moving slowly into the west, yet never diminishing in our mind's eye. We find ourselves on a new path beginning another phase of our quest. Epona leaves us now, for we will travel on foot, marking our way step by step.

Dragons of Tara:
Taking Flight

Now you, as the quester, are accompanied only by the Merlin, representing the wizardry, and me, the Ban Drui. We journey to the realm of dragons, to castles built high atop sacred mountains. We journey in quest of the dragon power. We search for the magick to call forth the dragons. We travel to meet the dragon crafters. We quest for the secrets of the dragon masters. We travel to see the dragons of Tara.

We make our way up a steep winding path and reach the gates of a great castle hidden in the clouds that drift past the mountaintop on which it is built. We climb up the narrow stairwell leading to the tower and enter a chamber of magick. There we find our white-robed Wise Ones, once more waiting to guide us on our path to wisdom. They chuckle with amusement at all the magick regalia you have collected on your quest. They tease you lovingly and inquire if the weight of all this wisdom has become a burden.

The Ban Drui bids them be still and remember the times when they were still questers. She advises you to remember that all your tools and weapons of magick are no more or less than props to support your purpose and to catalyze the magick consciousness in your own mind.

She soothes your somewhat wounded pride by telling you that though these Old Ones have come to show you the powers of your mind, they too activate their magick with the powers of symbols, color, stories, and songs. They too employ the tools of their Craft, and to those tools, their magick responds.

The Wise Ones, the Old Ones of magick, bid you spread out all the gifts of power you have collected on your quest. As you do so, the Ban Drui tells you of the dragon power, the alchemy required to craft the dragons of Tara. When you have learned to craft these dragons in your imagination, you will be able to fly them into positively expanding dimensions of your life.

The Alchemy for Crafting Dragons: An Instructive Imagery

 First, take the power of a conscious mind and the will of a wizard or wise woman, and create thought forms crafted from a powerful imagination. Then blend three ingredients to taste: color, symbol, setting.

Add twelve ingredients from within your Self, beginning with consciousness and truth. Add intention, then motivation and sensation, communication and perception, orientation and connection, emotion and intuition, and finally, fold in a measure of transcendence.

You look somewhat puzzled at this, so the Merlin, on behalf of the wizardry, adds some alchemical secrets for crafting dragons as well. He tells you that from their conception in spirit, dragons are born of fire, borne on air, embodied by earth, dispersed by water, and guided by spirit.

Then the Ban Drui, duty bound to crafting wisdom for you on this quest, explains more thoroughly. She explains the crafting of the magickal images—thought forms of energy—shaped as dragons:

- Dragons are conceived in spirit, in the element of your intentions.

- Dragons are born from fire, the element of your motivations and sensations.

- Dragons are borne on air, the element of your communication and perception.

- Dragons are embodied by earth, the element of your structured orientation and connection.

- Dragons are dispersed by water, the element of your emotions and intuition.

Throughout this magick process, eternally present, dragons are guided by spirit, the element of multidimensional transcendence.

The Ban Drui repeats the wisdom for you, three times being the true charm of conscious manifestation.

Dragons arise from your consciousness, fueled by your desire, expressed by your inspiration, manifested by your efforts, and retired by your transformation. They are continually empowered by your quests for the gifts of truth and light. Dragons are the reflected images of your personal energy, your personal light. Dragon images enable you to focus, receive, activate, and manifest transformation in your life.

Now the Merlin draws a great circle on the floor of the tower with his magick staff, and marks the areas for south, west, north, east, and center. While he does this, the Ban Drui tells you more about crafting dragons with the regalia you have collected on your quest.

The cloaks represent the power of color, as do the vibrational "tones" of the stones and the hues of the metals. These have natural, elemental energies of their own, which support your purpose.

The brooches, the runes, and gifts (sword, cup/cauldron, shield, stone, wand, staff, spear, and crystal) represent the power of symbols to activate your consciousness, your magick, and your deep memory. These comprise your regalia, representative symbols of your power and the elemental power.

This symbolic regalia represents the reflected imagery of your conscious mind. Like your conscious mind, it carries the power to heal or to harm. Use it wisely. The way in which you use your personal power will affect your life. What goes around, comes around, through, and from you. Be responsible with what you activate within the magick dimension of you mind.

The setting is created by your active image and your arrangement of these colors and symbols. The setting is further empowered by the selection of sounds that match the elements, such as music that is fiery, flowing, rhythmically structured, lyrical, or mystical in nature. This you must craft by ear.

The Merlin bids you collect your regalia and place it in the areas that he drew to represent the elements. The Ban Drui reminds you that this druidic wizard, as those of his order before him, structured the plans and constructed the forms for the crafting of dragons and other magick wisdom.

If you choose to do so, you may place your regalia according to this simple structure, correlating directions with the elements' symbols and images. It is an arbitrary system, to be sure, but most useful.

South	Fire
West	Water
North	Earth
East	Air
Center	Spirit (as the place of conscious conception)
Circle	Spirit (as the transcendent guidance)

Place your spirit regalia in center to represent your Self.

As you work with your collected regalia, arranging it in imaginary, or in manifested forms, the dragon crafters amuse themselves with their arts. They summon all manner of dragons in unseen ways, using only the power of their minds. Only the shifting colors in the energy field around them give clues to what they're doing. Only their auras reveal their craft. While only a few can perceive that process, all can undertake it in their own minds. Here's a glimpse of this experience to give you a feel for the dragons of elemental energy.

Fire dragons burst into consciousness signalled by shades of flame. They are large, strong, fierce, and protective (or frightening, if that is the intention of the dragon crafter).

218

Water dragons flow into consciousness, gently reflecting cool, soothing hues. They are also large, but softly formed. They bring along a change of mood (also determined by the inner wisdom of the dragon crafter).

Earth dragons enter into consciousness at a measured pace, step by step, in rich, natural colors. They are of a moderate size and solidly structured. They come ready to build what you want to manifest (designed at the instructions of the dragon crafter).

Air dragons fly swiftly into consciousness, lyrically expressing light, inspiring tones. They are often small, sometimes large, but always fantastic to see. They shift their shapes most rapidly in tune with your images of them (according to the inspired philosophy of the dragon crafter).

Spirit dragons mystically merge into consciousness in luminous, translucent tones, reflecting the spectrum gently at first, then vibrantly later. They are any size you want them to be and are etherically formed. They bring gifts of pure power to the intended purpose (again, guided with positive wisdom by the dragon crafter).

The dragon crafters step into your circle to demonstrate their art. They bid you follow their example, which the Ban Drui spells out for you, once.

Calling Forth the Dragon: A Ceremonial Exercise

First, you face south, the place of the honored, senior element, fire. You acknowledge the powers of this element, then you acknowledge its aspects within your Self—strength, will, courage, guardianship.

Next, you face west, honoring water. As you did with fire, you acknowledge that element, then your Self—initiation, self-healing, transformation, emotional stability.

Now you face north, honoring earth. You acknowledge the element, then your Self—order, wisdom, practicality, productivity.

Then you face east, honoring air. You acknowledge the element, then your Self—creativity, perception, focus, expanded awareness.

Finally, you stand in the center, honoring spirit. You acknowledge the element, then your Self—transcendence, devotion, consciousness, compassion. You acknowledge the mystical guidance from spirit. You may stay in the center of your circle.

Now you request the harmonious presence of all elements of Nature and self-nature to empower your purpose.

You face the direction of the element you wish to work with to craft the dragon of your purpose.

(Note the following advice: try air first, if this is a fairly new process. Though often silly to start with, air is an elemental catalyst for imagination and rarely unpleasant. Earth requires some previous experience with elements for most to get the job done. Water can be too emotional for those who haven't practiced the detachment needed for observing images and visionary states of consciousness. Fire is almost guaranteed to bring immediate results, but is always intense and can be physically challenging. Spirit is elusive and sometimes will not allow itself to be seen or experienced clearly enough to work with until you have shown yourself to be of pure heart and purpose. To work with spirit, show your inner light clearly.)

State your purpose clearly, and poetically, if possible, being both sure and specific. Focus on the regalia you have collected, being certain to reflect it within your mind and consciousness. This is so, whether the regalia has manifest forms or imaginary ones.

Bring all the aspects, powers, energies, and gifts into the center of your Self. Merge with their energies. Reflect this in your consciousness. Call forth an active image of your dragons. Use a name if you have chosen one or wait until you're introduced.

Allow the experience of your dragon to emerge. Allow the image to develop strength, wisdom, structure, and forms of communication within your mind. Activate your image with the fantastic powers of your mind.

Craft the dragons of your imagination. Ride the dragons, master the dragons. Dismiss the dragons through the transformation of water's release. Let them flow away into transmutational realms of spirit. Dismiss them into the greater circle of spirit, harmony, and transcendent guidance.

The dragon crafters bid you to practice this art in the following way, step by step, if you please, and take notes if need be.

Dragon Practice: An Imagery Exercise

 I. Call forth images of "elementary" colored dragons, starting with air, if you care to. Create dragons one color at a time. Then blend the colors associated with each element, individually, one at a time. Concentrate on creating the image this time.

Air
1. Light blue dragons.
2. Yellow dragons.
3. White dragons.
4. All three tones in one dragon.

Earth
1. Dark green.
2. Purple.
3. Rust brown.
4. All three tones.

Water
1. Dark blue.
2. Lavender.
3. Gray.
4. All three tones.

Fire
1. Red.
2. Orange.
3. Black.
4. All three tones.

Spirit
1. Banded rainbow spectrum.
   (red + orange + yellow + green + blue + indigo + violet)
2. Blended spectrum.
   (scarlet + rose + peach + golden green + turquoise + indigo)
3. Both banded and blended tones together.
   (This is one fantastic dragon image!)

II. Repeat the process with one-color dragons only. This time note your response to the images you have created, using the following format. Focus on the first four elements only. Note the following:

- Your physical sensations.

- Your emotional states.

- Your connection or relationship with this dragon image. (Is it positive or not so positive?)

- Your ability to perceive this image and to communicate with it.

- The spiritual quality of this image. (Is it mystical? Hierarchical? Dogmatic? Enlightening? Natural? Unnatural? Light and pure? Dark and shadowy?)

III. Call forth images of the dragons from the element of spirit.

First, repeat the above process in regard to the rainbow spectrum dragon.

Next, select the blended colors, one at a time (scarlet, then rose, then peach, then golden green, then turquoise, then indigo) and repeat above process with these.

IV. Repeat process II with images of tri-colored dragons from each of these elements:

Dragon of Air	Light blue, yellow, and white
Dragon of Earth	Dark green, purple, and rust brown
Dragon of Water	Dark blue, lavender, and gray
Dragon of Fire	Red, orange, and black

Note the changes when colors are combined, but not necessarily blended. Note shapes, sizes, structures, and sounds. Always, always note the spirit each dragon image conveys to you. Even if you decide to send a dragon to someone else, it will come from and go through you. Of course, it will come back to you, as well. (More on this in the next chapter.)

V. Repeat all of process IV, this time "testing the metal" of your dragon image.

Air	Add white gold
Earth	Add copper
Water	Add silver
Fire	Add bronze

Then repeat process III with both banded and blended spectrum dragons, adding platinum (or perhaps titanium).

VI. Return to step I (yes, you can do it).

This time, concentrate on your image only and create dragons of a diminutive size. Create faerie dragons, so to speak. These may be imaged after the fashion of that wonderful wizard, Real Musgrave, whose art has shown us the wisdom of having "pocket dragons." Yes, even a red dragon can be made to fit in the deep pockets of your conscious mind.

Remember, if your mind can't assume complete charge over your creations, you'd best consider, carefully, what you're likely to cause.

Also, ask yourself this: if you're not in charge of the form of your images and the shape of your thoughts, who is?

The Ban Drui takes pity on you with all that dragon work to do. Remember that the druids put their trainees through years of work and practice. What you have been doing is more than exercising your dragons, you know. You've also been toning up your mind.

❧

The next process is to experiment with various items in your magick regalia and decide which ones are most effective in regard to your dragons.

For example, the shield may be more effective than the stone as a focusing symbol for the purple dragon. The green and rust-brown dragon may not respond as well, magickally speaking, to the shield. Also, certain runes and combinations of runes may evoke stronger images than others.

This is an experimental process. It is also an alchemical one. You will have to do a good deal of personal research to determine which keys (regalia, et cetera) work best for which images. These images, charms, and words can be personalized and used ceremonially as invocations.

As long as you remember that you are the master of your own dragons and the master of your active images, you will expand your personal power. When we externalize power, we deplete our Selves and the ability to master our own lives.

When you have become more practiced at dragon crafting, try creating blends of your own.

For example, call forth a fire dragon from out of the cauldron for intense transformation. Call forth an earth dragon with a sword of light to protect your home, business, investments, projects. Call forth an air dragon with the Grail to create sacred expressions of self-healing in your life. Call forth a water dragon with a spear to get at the heart of an emotional block. Call forth a spirit dragon with a wand or staff to really amplify your magick imagery.

Call forth dragons in combinations that you feel are needed in your life. Dragons are the elemental definitions of energy in our imagery. They are the energies we focus to create transformations in our minds first, then, with work, transformations in our lives.

As you learn to work with these dragons and other familiar images, it's helpful to personalize them with names. These can be pet names or names more properly referred to as power names. Remember, these dragons, as all do other images, truly reflect aspects and names that reveal your Self to you.

❦

Now the Lord Merlin and the Ban Drui leave you with the dragon crafters to practice your dragon work at home. (Actually, they beat a hasty retreat.) It's not that they don't wish to go through all this with you, but they each have lots of dragon work of their own, you realize.

Before the Ban Drui leaves, she gives you another faerie gift. It's one the dragon crafters may not remember, unless they are de Dannan. While they're drumming up more busy work, the Ban Drui tells you about the de Dannan-styled charms for calling dragons of the elements.

Fire

To call forth the dragon of flame,
Use fire colors and call this name: USEIAS.
Call forth this dragon with no trace of fear;
Summon with the sword and also the spear.
For powers befitting a warrior of true synthesis,
Add bright blue of flame and give it warm emphasis.
Repeat nine times the name of fierce USEIAS,
Then honor this winning dragon from FINIAS.

Call for your warrior/guardian allies from the realm of fire until you get used to this dragon of great elemental power.

Air

To call the dragon of air into consciousness,
Use sky colors and call on kind ESRAS.
Call forth this dragon of true delight;
You may use the spear, but keep it light.
For powers befitting a true bardic synthesis,
Add a heart color, rose, with bright, clear emphasis.
Repeat nine times the name of fair ESRAS,
Then honor the glory of this dragon from GORIAS.

Bardic allies from the realm of air make this an illuminating experience, to say the least.

Earth

To call forth the dragon of earth without stress-ah,
Use earth tones and call on MORFESSA.
Call for this dragon, with forms well known,
With sacred wisdom, use destiny's stone.
For powers befitting a leader with synthesis,
Add a golden tone and give it strong emphasis.

*Repeat nine times, unfailing, **MORFESSA**,*
*Then honor and hail this dragon from **FALIUS**.*

Nurturing allies from the realm of earth will help this develop properly and will give you greater patience to do so.

Water

To call the dragon of water into motion,
Use flowing tones and colors of the ocean.
For transformation with little fuss,
*Call on fine and gentle **SEMIAS**.*
Call with the cauldron—and even now, the Grail
For inner knowing and healing to prevail.
With a priestly notion of spiritual synthesis,
Add light healing green, and give it deep emphasis.
*Repeat nine times the name of **SEMIAS**,*
*Then honor this proud, pure dragon of **MURIAS**.*

Allies from water work gentle wonders with this when you use the image of the magick cup. The cauldron evokes a more intense experience.

Spirit

The Ban Drui bids you to hear her invoke
A dragon from spirit, imaged for fair folk.
Though not of de Dannan's mythic invention,
This dragon power summons most magick intention.

To call forth the powerful dragon of spirit,
To feel its magick, to draw closer near it,
Use your crystal to open the doors;
*Use all the aura colors and the name **AURABORES**.*
For powers befitting a druidic synthesis,
Add the light of pure crystal with magnetic emphasis.
*Repeat three times three, **AURABORES**.*

226

On transcendent wings it does fly
This enlightened dragon from the Ban Drui.

I leave you now to practice your Craft,
To call forth dragons on your own behalf.
Practice makes perfect, let it not give you pause.
We'll meet next the Maidens
At the Ring of the Laws.

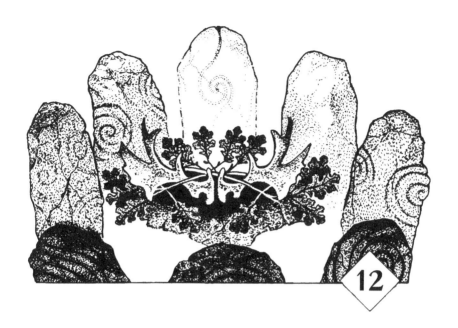

Che Wyrd:
Earth, Laws, and Craft

As we make our quest into the realms of Celtic myth and memory, we find the threads that connect us to the elemental powers within Nature and within our Selves. We find the patterns of natural laws that influence the structures of our lives. We find druidic systems designed to guide our growth and empower our progress.

These systems, though arbitrarily created, are based on the observation of natural patterns. They express uniformities found in Nature and in human nature. These systems describe patterns of natural phenomena as they relate to the patterns of our lives. They provide guidelines based on experiences in connection with these patterns. They are structures by which we may better understand our relationship with the elements of Nature, of Self, and of others who share the environment with us.

These structures are called laws, but are best understood as axioms or patterns of truth that influence the design of our lives.

These laws are not dogmas or doctrines that set fixed rules. They are descriptions of natural energies, elemental threads that interweave and connect with everything we do and are. These natural laws reflect the elemental structures with which we craft our lives. They are called, in current times, the Laws of the Craft.

The Craft we may define as being the active, conscious process of working with the elements of Nature and of Self to create our lives in accordance with our personal choice and in accordance with the powers of the Earth. This Craft is bound by only one essential law, expressed in various modern styles such as "And you harm none, do as you will."

This simple but profound law may be considered the center stone recently placed in the midst of a more ancient circle of stones. These stones represent the structures by which the many emerging Celtic forms of the Craft guide their work and create the active magick of their lives. The spirit of this center-stone law is also heard in the golden rule of the Christian spiritual philosophy: "Do unto others as you would have them do unto you."

This is particularly true when we add to the center-stone law and say, "And you harm none, do as you will, for the good of all in so far as you may see, in so well as you may judge."

Those who work actively with the elemental energies of the Earth are responsible for the transformations they make. The elemental energies of life and Nature may be seen as a vast, crystalline web of light and energy. This web is the essential, eternally active pattern of life. Its threads are pure energy, vibrating at different rates or frequencies, creating the patterns of Nature and Self. As part of these interwoven threads, everything we do affects the entire pattern of the web. The more experienced we become in working with the elemental-energy threads, the greater effect we have on this crystalline web.

As we change the patterns of our life, as we consciously or unconsciously shift our vibrational rate, we change our elemental frequency. This changes the threads of energy that our life represents in the greater web. Thus, we change the entire web. In the Celtic ways of Nature, this web and this interwoven process is called the Wyrd.

The word "wyrd" comes from the Anglo-Saxon term that means both "earth" and "law." This dual meaning shows the strong connection between the structures of our lives and the structures of Nature. "Wyrd" denotes the natural patterns of the Earth from which we must govern our lives. As part of the Wyrd, we craft our lives in accordance with the patterns of Nature. The laws of the Craft reveal this relationship and teach us about the elemental pattern of Nature and of our Selves.

As we become more proficient at working with the elemental energies, we find that we are more clearly connected to that wyrd, crystalline web. At first, it may seem that we are merely tangling with cobwebs between the threads of the Wyrd, and we may well be doing just that. In time, though, with perseverance and positive intentions, we find ourselves truly weaving with the essential threads, the elemental power of the Wyrd. We become both the weaver and the Wyrd itself.

The Way of the Woven Star: An Instructive Discussion

When we have reached that point in our active, conscious development, our responsibilities become magnified. They are amplified, as it were, by our connection to that crystalline web of light. Because this is commonly recognized in all systems that work with the energies of Nature, there are rules which describe the essential requirements for those who do so.

These are called the Rules of the Magus, the Rules of the Magician, and the Cornerstones of the Craft. There are four of these, and I add a fifth, as well, which I feel expresses the Celtic natural, active processes of the Craft and the Wyrd.

The Way of the Woven Star (Rules of the Magus)

1. To know = (primarily) the element of earth.
2. To will = fire.
3. To dare = air.
4. To be silent = water.

My addition to these is:

5. To weave = spirit.

I see these five rules as a circle of stones surrounding the center stone. These five stones are laid out in the shape of the five-pointed woven star of Nature. This circle we may imagine as the inner circle, because it reflects the individual requirements for those in the Celtic Craft of the Wyrd. I call these rules the Way of the Woven Star, and I relate them to the natural elements we have studied in this volume.

Here is the way that I relate these to the five elements of Self and Nature.

1. To Know

By fire, this means to sense, physically using your body awareness to protect and strengthen the knowledge you encounter. Your sensations of any knowledge are your best guardians of truth.

By water, this means to use your inner wisdom, to listen to your inner voice, to know through your emotional responses. Your intuition reveals the inner healer and teacher who guides your quest for knowledge.

By earth, this means to check the facts, to determine the validity and the practicality of whatever knowledge you are taught by others or by your Self. Your connection to truth provides you with the personal leadership to determine your own path to knowledge.

By air, this means to think, to use your head, to be perceptive, to be aware of your thoughts. Ask everyone, if you choose to, but think and decide for yourself about knowledge. Your thoughts are the bard communicating within your mind.

By spirit, this means to know, within the sacred realms of your Self, if the knowledge you encounter has truth and a positive light.

2. To Will

By fire, this means to use your physical strength, your will as a warrior to energize your work, your life, your Craft. Put some muscle behind your intentions and activate your will. This helps protect your purpose.

By water, this means to willfully express your inner emotions, to regulate your emotional stability, and control the flow of that which would either strain or empower your health. Will yourself to wellness.

By earth, this means to have the willpower to overcome limitations imposed by you or others. It also means having the will to judge what is practical and of positive potential—the will to choose wisely.

By air, this means to restructure your thoughts in accordance with your own will. It means having the power to express yourself, not willfully, but with the inspiration of inner will.

By spirit, this means being attuned to the light, the will of highest purpose, and having the willpower to quest for the best.

3. To Dare

By fire, this means to dare to take action. Fire up and get moving. This doesn't mean blood, sweat, and tears in the literal sense. It means simply to dance your dance, to walk your talk—not just talk your walk. Be an active warrior for truth and light.

By water, this means to dare to reach within and experience your emotions fully, to recognize the blocks that keep you emotionally bound, and to assume full responsibility for the health of your life.

By earth, this means to dare to assume leadership, to change structures and limitations that are wrong and damaging. It means also to dare to be successful, prosperous, and abundantly powerful.

By air, this means to dare to speak your mind and to dare to think for yourself. It also means using your intellect and perception to determine what you think and say. Think before you speak, and you will express yourself clearly. Dare to do that.

By spirit, this means to dare to live your life according to the guidance of your highest light. It also means to dare to seek the counsel of your own spirit.

4. To Be Silent

By fire, this means to show restraint, to be still and self-controlled. It means to have the faith and courage to hold yourself in check and to take charge of your actions and your reactions. When your sensations cause you to act and react without control, then you have lost the battle right away.

By water, this means to go within yourself, to enter into the silence. It means to make time for private self-healing, to retreat for transformative purposes, and to quietly receive what you require from within yourself.

By earth, this means to listen and receive from teachers and leaders—all those who bring you wisdom. Whether your choice is to accept the teachings of others or not, you must first listen before you can choose wisely. There is a time for questions and a time for simply hearing what is being said. It also means to silently observe all life, all Nature, all wisdom to receive truth.

By air, this means to develop the skills of silent perception, to have the quiet focus required for deep awareness. It also means to communicate with yourself, and to silently become aware of the unspoken messages in life.

By spirit, this means to be in that quiet state of spiritual attunement with your Self and with Nature. It means to leave the noisy static long enough to receive and experience the silent gifts of light. Grace of spirit enters quietly. Be silent, and you will know when it comes.

5. To Weave

By fire, this means to make the physical efforts needed to activate your Craft. It means making a physical commitment to be strong, to use your energy for your Craft. It takes strength to work with the energies of Nature. Even the threads of purest light (especially those) require physical strength and involvement.

By water, this means to weave, responsibly, the emotional energies of your life into a fabric that is self-healing and sacred. Weave the transformative experiences from your inner wisdom and the energies your emotions bring you.

By earth, this means to craft your work into structures of wisdom for the good of all. Weave a stable life with the threads of wisdom and knowledge you collect. Weave abundant energy for growth. Make it beautiful and enjoy your work.

By air, this means to express your Self and your gifts in a manner that creates harmony and empowers Nature. Weave your images and your ceremonies of power into magnificent, poetic melodies that celebrate life.

By spirit, this means to consciously connect with the Wyrd, to interweave your Self and your Craft with the crystalline web of light. It means to experience your Self as part of all life, all Nature. Weave with threads of light and attune with the experience of transcendent power.

That is my interpretation of the Rules of the Magus, which I call the Way of the Woven Star. It remains for you to make your own interpretation of this or any system of wisdom. It remains for you to activate the crafting of your life. As you do so, remember the wisdom of the center stone and keep your intentions clear, positive and for the good of all.

Working With the Laws of the Craft

From the center stone to the woven star, we expand our image to include another, wider circle of stones. There are nine standing stones in this circle. They represent the Laws of the Craft, which have also been called the Occult Laws or the Metaphysical Laws. This, I believe, limits their use somewhat. These are natural laws that affect everyone, whether they may realize it or not.

For those of us in the Craft, they provide structures of truth to guide our work. They are axioms for the way we work with the elemental energies of Nature. They are patterns for our weavings. They tell us the nature of the fibers we use. They tell us how the energies weave together elementally.

These laws appear in Celtic myth and wisdom in many forms. They are the nine Muses, the nine Maidens whose breath kindles the flame under the cauldron. The cauldron is the source of creation, transformation, sustenance, and inspiration. These nine Maidens are also the nine Priestesses of Brede, the senior aspect of Bridget. These nine Maidens kept the nine flames of life burning, eternally empowering the land.

Bridget, the Triple Goddess of Poetry, Smithcraft, and Healing, is the ancient Celtic goddess who has remained most intact in our tribal memory today. She is reflected in the many stories of St. Bridget and the nuns in her service, who also kept the flame alive.

As I describe these nine laws, I will tell you which aspect of Bridget I use to illuminate my understanding and empower my adherence to these sacred laws.

The name I give to this circle of stones is the Ring of the Nine Maidens. This interpretation was inspired by a current image of Robin Hood. This specific image came from a British Broadcasting Corporation (BBC) series, the film "Time of the Wolf," in particular. In it, Robin Hood must battle a clay man, a symbolic shadow of himself. He does this in a circle of nine standing stones called the Ring of Nine Maidens. This, I felt, was an inspired image created by the series writer (for most of the episodes) Richard Carpenter. Once again, we find the spirit of the ancient Celts finding expression in modern forms, with modern wizards, wise women, bards, druids, and warriors.

As I did with the Way of the Woven Star, I will tell you how I correlate these with the elements of Nature. These laws occur in many fine volumes on the ways of magick. They also occur in books on physics and science, which describe them as natural laws. Though their wordings vary, their patterns do not. The blending of ancient mysticism and modern science has brought new light and new energy to these ancient flames of truth. (Please see the bibliography, which I have carefully crafted to be a resource for your further explorations and your quest to activate your Celtic consciousness.)

As you learn and work with these laws, consider them as both external and internal, activated and received. Also consider that the Way of Wyrd requires you to be in a place of balanced, reflected power. In the words of the protector Herne (of the BBC series, "Robin Hood"), you must reflect "the powers of light and darkness in balance." This, for those who are familiar with the tarot, is represented by the Chariot. It may best be described as being in a state of awareness that reflects both the material and the immaterial dimensions of Nature.

This balance is represented by the two Celtic god forms: the solar/light/warrior king and the Otherworld/dark/tanist wizard. Light and dark are not symbolic of good and evil, but more of external and internal processes. Also, as you work with energy, it is important to develop a state of inner androgyny. This does not mean sexuality, nor is it gender-related in any way. It means being in a place of dynamic inner polarity, both active (often called male) and receptive (often called female).

This balance of light and darkness also means being aware that not everyone is as balanced as you are. It is idealistic to believe that everyone uses power for the good of all or is in the service of the light (the creation forces). It is pessimistic (and perhaps a bit paranoid) to believe that there are legions of people out there in the service of some dark force (the forces of entropy).

It is realistic to believe that most people reflect a varied blend of light and dark in the sense of being positive catalysts for creation, as well as benign contributors to the general chaos. Most people, if given the opportunity and the wisdom, would choose to be positive, active catalysts.

The Wyrd is about being just that. It is also about being aware of the chaos and working around it, not against it, for the purposes of positive evolution. The Wyrd is also about recognizing that negativity does arise, but always falls, as well, when blasted with laser swords of pure light.

We call these laws Maidens or Muses, to express their symbolic connection to and representation of the sovereign laws of Mother Nature. However, this terminology does not imply that women have greater power than men; that would not be a natural, Celtic point of view.

Since we will explore these laws in regard to several elements and aspects, I'll simply list them first. The order of this list and the titles given the laws come from Murry Hope's valuable modern work, *Practical Celtic Magic*. This is not a hierarchal structure, but a circular one. The interpretations reflect my opinion regarding the elemental properties of these laws.

The Ring of the Nine Maidens
(The Metaphysical Laws of the Craft)

1. The Law of Rebound.
2. The Law of Requests.
3. The Law of Challenge.
4. The Law of Equalities.
5. The Law of Balance.
6. The Law of Summons.
7. The Law of Polarities.
8. The Law of Cause and Effect.
9. The Law of Abundance.

1. The Law of Rebound

This law states that a stronger, superior force will always overcome a lesser force. That seems rather obvious until we examine its other aspects. Not only will a superior force overcome an inferior force, but the energy of both forces will rebound onto the losing force. This is akin to philosophies and practices in martial arts where the strength and weight of the opponent is used against him, to flip him over.

Superiority is measured in terms of intent, skill, and concentrated will. If you send energy and thought forms out to someone more skilled than you are, you will get them back with interest. If you send out in anger, that anger will fuel the response directed toward you. Of course, if you send courage, it strengthens your courage in return.

Consider what forms of imagery and energy you send across that crystalline web. They will be amplified in the process and doubly amplified as they return to you. If you are embattled with a superior force, your best offense is a good defense. Images (and representations) of mirrors will reflect the law of rebound, regardless of who sends the energy and thought forms first.

Beware, rebound happens faster than you think it will. Sometimes, sets of "matching mirrors" are constructed, one for each side, so to speak. This causes energy force fields to develop between people who are dueling. These energy fields, and sometimes the images (thought forms) that accompanied them, are often picked up by those caught in between (as well as by perceptive innocent bystanders).

The elemental energy used for the greater part in this law is fire. The symbol to activate it is the sword. The elements used to disperse these energies are water and spirit. Release with water, transmute with spirit. Use the Grail symbol to ensure the purity of your intent. Air will only feed the fire; earth is slow and may lead to further eruptions at a later time.

I call this Maiden of the Nine Laws the Protector. She teaches you to guard against biting off more than you can chew. She serves Bridget in her aspect as goddess of smithcraft, forging your weapon and forcing you to structure protective skills.

2. The Law of Requests

This law states that all requests made in the way of the Wyrd must be repeated in triplicate. These you may call the three magick wishes. This process involves activating three dimensions of your conscious mind. These are:

1. The awakened, Beta, alert, everyday state of consciousness.

2. The subtle, Alpha, receptive, meditative, deep-minded, "subconscious" states.

3. The expanded, Theta, psychic, soul force, and universal states of consciousness.

   (Note that Delta, which is a dream state, can be helpful for both 2 and 3.)

This means that you have to program the dimensions of your consciousness significantly in order to manifest changes in more than just your conscious mind. It takes an attunement of these three aspects to create cognitive restructuring that, in turn, leads to the change of structures in your life pattern.

This law is among the many representations of the sacred triplicities. This is why words of power are often repeated three times. However, if your mind isn't truly on your work or your Craft, this is just wasted air.

The elemental energy used primarily to create this conscious change is air. The staff is a useful symbol for focusing and making requests. Concentrate on the expression of your request and use the staff to direct and signal. The wand can be used to draw these symbols of your requests.

Fire is helpful to energize your request, as long as it brings the power of faith with it. Water is useful in activating the subtle states of consciousness through the use of emotions. Earth helps you be specific, which, in turn, creates the form of your requests and provides a foundation for your changes in thought, word, and deed.

I call this Maiden the Communicator. She inspires you to express yourself clearly and to act in accordance with your wishes. If you request a change, it helps to act as if it has already manifested, whenever that is possible. This is effective, even if you are only able to use your imagination. This Maiden, the Communicator, serves Bridget in her aspect as goddess of poetry. She teaches you that musing can awaken many dimensions of your mind.

239

3. The Law of Challenge

This law states that ideas, visions, images, energies, and even "spirit guides" that emerge and seem to be illogical or irrational must be challenged by you. This means that you need to be utterly clear about your own intentions and inexorably honest with yourself. You will need to use detached, perceptive awareness to determine the difference between a valuable vision and a destructive delusion. You will also need to express your power and your truth clearly, even if you are that proverbial "majority of one." This law lets you know for certain that you have the right, indeed the duty, to challenge whatever seems alien, negative, divisive, or simply a ridiculous waste of time.

Sometimes it takes a while for you to realize the validity or the real possibilities represented in your images and in your life experience. It is never too late to issue a challenge to test the potential of your ideas or those of others. So long as you stay in a balanced, yet imaginative reality-based state of awareness, your position in this is quite strong.

If an idea or image persists or is continually presented, and you think it is not right in some way, say so—if only to yourself. Then walk away. It is difficult to walk away from what we thought were our true dreams or true teachers. That is also one reason this law is called the law of challenge.

The element primarily used in this law is air. Use the wand symbol to imaginatively activate what is valid or vaporize what is not. The staff gives more strength if you should need it, as well as the support of earth connection. Spirit is an ally for this law, so long as you request the Wise, Old Ones. Do this at least until you have become accustomed to working with the Otherworld dimensions of mind and consciousness. If you're "living in a faerie tale," it's difficult to judge the potential, the purpose, and the reliability of what you experience as vision or inspiration. Come back to earth to make decisions about your great inspirations.

Fire may increase a sense of unrealistic expectations. Water may deepen delusions, but emotions are a good indicator of validity for your vision. If it feels right—really right—go for it. If it feels wrong—really wrong—go away from it or make it go away from you.

I call this Maiden the Illuminator. She sheds some real light on things so you may see more clearly. This also illuminates you to the fact that most ideas, images, or even people whose energies are mostly illusionary will simply go away at your direction. Be polite, and remember that rebound is always a possibility. Do this as three expressed requests, if need be.

This Maiden, the Illuminator, serves Bridget in her aspect as goddess of poetry. She teaches you to resist the lure of false inspiration.

4. The Law of Equalities

This law states that when equal forces meet, one will advance to a higher state as the result of that encounter; one will increase in force. The other force will remain as it was or decrease if there is resistance to the rise in power of the other.

This means that if two equal force fields meet, one will rise from the energy created by the encounter. It also means, in more human terms, that if two individuals of equal power, energy, or skill encounter each other, then one will achieve a "promotion" from the experience and the other will not.

This is a difficult process most of the time, since truly equal individuals attempt to maintain their equal relationship. However, if each can realize that these encounters are for the purpose of creating a catalyzing force for higher truths, then the distress is lessened.

To understand this is to realize why each individual must walk his or her own path alone. Each person is a unique part of the greater pattern. Sometimes we walk side by side with others whose powers are equal. This is making energies parallel. If we can keep that image of parallel paths, we can maintain our perspective about the direction in which we are going and the relative value of our journeys. It is inevitable that we change and grow, and it is inevitable that those we encounter do this also.

When those who experience the force of this law are comfortable with themselves, then this catalyst to a higher power is an occasion for celebration. Unfortunately, this is not always the case. Often when two individuals work equally on a project, only one will receive the lion's share of credit or honor. If the other one can accept this with grace instead of martyrdom, then the opportunity for his or her own rise in power will present itself sooner than he or she thinks.

The elemental energy most affecting this law is water. The element of water brings transformations that are often emotional, but ultimately are for the highest purpose of healing. Water enables both individuals to experience positive transformations, even if one seems to be in a higher or more powerful dimension than the other.

The symbol to use for this process, regardless of whether you have been "promoted" or not, is the Grail. This symbol reminds you of the higher purpose of life, which is to activate increased truth and to be healed even by what feels like a wound. Earth is helpful to establish new kinship. Fire won't help at all and may create anger. Air is useful, so long as the expression is positive. Spirit transmutes all unsettled feelings and fills empty spaces.

This Maiden I call the Partner. She reminds you that the only true partnership can be with your Self and with the divine source of light. She serves Bridget in her aspect as goddess of healing. She teaches you to accept your own transformations and those of others with equal grace.

5. The Law of Balance

This law states that there must be nothing in excess. It is the wisdom that counsels moderation in all things; it is the law of temperance. It also means that wasted energies are a violation of natural law.

This means that you are responsible for maintaining an even strain in your life. A harmonious relationship of body, mind, and spirit reflects a true adherence to this law. However, an indulgent, purist attitude toward this is, in itself, quite out of balance. It denotes an underlying attitude of negative judgment and a lack of self-acceptance.

Elementally speaking, this law advises you to activate and receive the elements in a balanced manner. Too much of any element imbalances the others, as does too little of any element. It is desirable to activate the energies of all the elements as soon as you have become used to working with them.

When you recognize the presence or absence of certain elements, you will be able to balance out any excesses or depletion. You may use one element to create a balance for another or a combination of elements to balance the remaining elements.

For example, too much fire is balanced by increased water. Let tears wash away rage. Too little fire is increased with more air. Let expressions of courage bring you the sensation of courage until it is truly activated within your conscious mind and in your life.

Too much water can be balanced by earth's energies. Give some structure to flowing emotional states. Too little water can be increased by air. Express your feelings verbally until your emotions respond.

Too much earth can be balanced with a combination of fire and water. Fire brings the motivation needed to change earth structures, and water helps in the transformation with healing energies. Too little earth is balanced by air. Expressed thoughts about needs and new ideas for what earth represents can attune you to these needed earth energies.

Too much air is balanced by increased earth, which centers and grounds air energies. Water can also bring peaceful silent retreat to erratic, chaotic air. Too little air is balanced by a combination of fire to activate and earth to connect with natural powers.

Spirit is the all-purpose balancer. Spirit amplifies according to your intention and will require a specific image. Otherwise, it may amplify the condition you are seeking to modify. That, too, will bring things into balance eventually. So if you're not certain of your imbalance, you can use the images and energies of spirit to help.

The element most primarily involved in this law of balance is water. Water transforms to create a healing balance. The symbol to use is the cauldron. The Grail may create a side effect of an increased purist attitude.

Fire gives you the willpower to bring your life and your Craft into balance. Air helps you create new images and mind changes to guide your balance. Air also helps you perceive imbalances sooner. Earth brings patience and perseverance.

I call this Maiden of the Ring of Nine Laws the Transformer. She will create the changes needed to bring balance and maintain it harmoniously. She serves Bridget in her aspect as goddess of healing. Balance is the prerequisite for all forms of healing. Without it, we are merely contagions, spreading our imbalances to others and to other elements in our life.

6. The Law of Summons

This law states that our earned rights determine the success of our work. This means that if you have not practiced working with some element or some system, then you cannot expect to have a perfect response when you do. Indeed, you may have no response at all.

This is particularly true for those who do not make the effort required to connect with the elements with which they are working. Instead, they play dress-up and pretend to have complete control. Sadly, most of these individuals do not even realize that nothing is happening. They are too bound up in their own illusions of grandeur, or, in worse cases, delusions. Often this creates chaotic energies, and results in various forms of confusion and mishaps. These are invariably blamed on someone else's lack of skill.

This may also be compared to riding a horse that you do not know well or that is not used to being ridden. It takes time and effort, as well as power, to develop the mutual respect and control of a skilled rider. An individual such as the one just described may get thrown from that horse. Unfortunately, others may be trampled in the process.

The Law of Summons requires the four P's: protocol, preparation, patience, and the paying of dues. This does not necessarily mean that someone who claims a higher skill, "degree," or rank necessarily earned it. These four P's are based on other P's, such as personal effort, positive intent, purity of heart, and pleasant manner.

The element primarily involved with this law is earth. Earth sets the standards for proper behavior and the rules for relating to the elements of Nature, Self, and others. The shield is the most effective symbol for this law. It declares your intent and your earned rights of power. Air is useful to create poetic, pleasant images and ceremonies. Fire can be a bit insistent. Water is helpful if it brings a soothing energy to your work.

This Maiden I call the Crafter. She helps you craft your wisdom with the right declared intentions. She serves Bridget in her aspect as goddess of smithcraft. She reminds you that the Craft is not for dilettantes and dabblers. The Craft is for diplomatic, self-determining individuals.

7. The Law of Polarities

This law states that there must be a dynamic relationship within the individual who works with the natural elements of magick. This means that aspects such as male/animus/active/external/overt must be in perfect balance with the female/anima/receptive/internal/covert aspects. This dynamic, balanced polarity must reflect in the individual who seeks a dynamic, balanced relationship with the elemental energies.

This is also called spiritual androgyny. The issue is not one of gender, but of energy balance. It is also not an issue of sexuality, but of spiritual balance. Regardless of someone's sexual preference, an inner androgynous balance is required to access the "finer frequencies," because all imbalances may be amplified as the higher dimensions are accessed.

For example, if an individual is already too receptive and not strong in the polar-active sense, then that receptivity can create an inability to take charge of what is being received. In this case, too much receptive flow can wash you out. If an individual is too active already, they could become hyper or manic. Too much emphasis on covert could result in introversion.

In these finer frequencies, all aspects are amplified in the ratio in which they exist. This is why an inner balance is so crucial.

The element that has the most influence in this law is spirit. Spirit can bring the synthesis required to pull all aspects into a dynamic, polar balance. This is the balance needed to access the creation force energies. All other elements can be helpful in accordance with the aspects they bring from Nature reflected in self-nature. Be sure to use them in balance with each other, in harmony together.

This Maiden I call the Synthesizer. She brings us the gift of inner balance if we are willing to create a dynamic relationship with our Selves and with Nature. This Maiden/Synthesizer serves Bridget in her aspect as the goddess of healing. She allows you to access the highest realm, so long as you are able to keep your Self in a state of synthesis. This state begins with inner androgynous balance.

8. The Law of Cause and Effect

This law states that for every action there is a reaction. Some say an equal and opposite reaction. However, this is simplistic and doesn't allow for the influences that affect all actions being made and all reactions as they are being made. This law also states in everyday terms, "what goes around, comes around." (To that I add, "and also through.")

This law is important for those working with the energies of natural elements. In this respect, I call this the boomerang law. So long as you can retain that image, you will be properly cautious and selective about what you choose to create and what you choose to toss out to others. This law advises us to use these same powers of selection and choice in regard to our Selves and especially in regard to Nature.

An image that you have activated and energized can come back to haunt you, so to speak, if you have been foolish enough to give it too much power. Don't confuse fantasy with imagery. Fantasy is fuel for imagery. Imagery is the fuel for self-transformation.

Fantasies can be quite functionally helpful in many ways, so long as you let them simply entertain you. Imagery is much more than entertainment. It is the crafting of mind and consciousness. Your activated images are very much like actions. They are subject to the laws of cause and effect, as well as to the other laws discussed here. Keep your intentions and your imagery clearly connected to your actions. Keep your fantasies to yourself.

The element most primarily involved with this law of cause and effect is fire. Fire is the catalyst of action and of reaction. The strongest symbol for this is the spear. When you use it to focus your imagery, your intentions, and your actions, remember the boomerang. Earth is a useful ally here because it grounds impulsiveness. Water can encourage emotions that lead to overreaction. Air is helpful so long as it makes you think before you act.

This Maiden I call the Ensurer. She ensures that you learn about the consequences of your Craft. She serves Bridget in her aspect as goddess of poetry. She brings you inspiration to create images and actions that will result in positive and enlightening reactions.

9. The Law of Abundance

The law of abundance states that like attracts like. This means that power has a magnetic quality that attracts other power of a similar quality. Though this law is usually presented as a way to create abundance, it can also create any condition that is empowered by the activation forces of your mind, your consciousness—your Craft.

To coin a phrase, what you weave with, you will have to wear. If you wish to weave prosperity, you will have to be giving, generous, and abundantly skillful in your use of prosperity. If you achieve what you set out to weave, you must not lose your perspective, for this would cause you to attract that aspect, and it would arrive with abundant energy. In other words, if you create prosperity in your life but become a miser or a spendthrift, then you will attract the elements related to those aspects and not retain those of prosperity. A miserly attitude would become abundant greed; a spendthrift attitude could result in a state of abundant need.

This magnetic attraction holds true for whatever we empower in our active conscious images and in the magick crafting of our lives. If you are sad, go out and help someone else create happiness in their life. That will make you happy, too. If you are in need of something, go out and help someone whose need is greater than yours. This is a law of abundant wisdom.

So long as you do not violate the laws of balance while you are trying to activate the law of abundance in your life, it will serve you well. The classic way that this law is taught is if you are down to your last dollar, share it with someone or spend it to attract the movement of "money energies."

This can give new students of the Craft a real misconception about this law. Instead, I say, if you are down to your last dollar, go sell something and give the money (or the something) to someone who needs it. This will bring results, so long as you don't overdo it. I believe this law could be retitled the law of magnetism.

The element most primary to this law is earth. Earth provides, so long as you provide for it. The symbol most connected with this is the stone. I use it to remember of the fine story of stone soup, which goes, briefly, like this:

Two soldiers were making their way home from the war. Their country had been ravaged, and there was famine in the land. The soldiers camped outside a small poor village. They were very hungry, but they knew the villagers had no more to eat than they did, which was nothing.

The soldiers lit a fire and placed their cooking pot over it. They filled it with water and put a few stones inside. They whistled and laughed until the villagers began to wonder what the soldiers had put in that cooking pot.

As the villagers came to investigate, they were told that it was stone soup being cooked in the pot. Each of the villagers thought this was just silly. No one can eat stone soup. The villagers gathered around the cooking pot while the soldiers continued to laugh and enjoy each other's company.

Soon one of the villagers said that she had an onion that would certainly help the taste of the stone soup. After all, what could she do with just one onion anyway? Another villager had a few carrots; some had potatoes. One even had a soup bone.

Soon the villagers were hurrying home to collect whatever they had to contribute to this mysterious recipe for stone soup. Just as quickly, they came back eager to share what little they had.

While they waited for the soup to cook, they all laughed and joked and felt grateful to have survived the terrible war. They felt grateful that they still had friends and family. They were glad that their village was still standing, even if it seemed a bit threadbare. They were glad to know that not only did they have enough to eat, they had enough to share.

That's a folk tale about the magick of the law of abundance.

All other elements provide support for this law, so long as they are in balance. Too much emphasis on any one would attract that one magnetically.

This Maiden I call the Quester. She gets what she goes out to find, and she knows how to attract what she really needs. She knows how to care and how to share. She serves Bridget in her aspects of smithcraft and healing.

Those who are "of the Wyrd" or "in the Craft" are often thought to be a law unto themselves. Yet now you know this is not so. Now you know the laws to which we are honor and duty bound. Now you know where to find us, at the Ring of the Nine Maidens.

Afterword:
The Far Hills of Remembrance

I walk through a narrow valley between two green hills. These verdant hills roll softly over a patchwork of fields and stone fences. They breathe with life. They rise and fall, almost imperceptibly, yet with a strong, steady rhythm. The hills are warm and comforting, the bosom of Mother Earth.

The path between the hills is strewn with small round stones. Perhaps these were left by an ancient river or an ice flow in time beyond memory. At intervals along this path are stone markers, carved with symbols that map the routes to many destinations. I gaze at the strangely familiar symbols and wonder if there can actually be a map of where I'm trying to go.

Ahead of me, just off the main path, is a white stone cottage with a thatched roof of thick reeds and woven straw. There are russet and golden-orange flowers planted in long, rectangular boxes. The flowers sun themselves beneath the two windows that border a green door. There are several vines climbing up the outer walls of this cottage. The violet and white blossoms on the vines around the doorway beckon with their welcoming beauty.

I step off the marked path and walk beside the long, low wall that runs along the front of the cottage. This wall is made of countless flat, gray stones that have been carefully stacked to create a solid structure without the use of mortar.

The wall winds around the side lands that surround the cottage. A long, low hillock, a barrow, forms the boundary at the back of the cottage. The ends of the gray rock wall seem to merge with the gentle green grasses of the barrow when they reach it.

I open a weathered wooden gate and walk up the smooth stone path leading to the cottage. Two ancient evergreen trees dominate the yard. Their rough, gnarled branches stretch out as though they were embracing this beautiful setting. Shiny, dark green needles give off a strong, rich scent of cedar and fir.

A hefty gray tabby cat drowses on the threshold of the cottage door, pretending not to notice me at all. A shiny-coated black-and-white dog rushes out to greet me. Its tail waves with welcoming delight as it licks my hand and barks to announce my arrival. A magpie flying over the thatched roof squawks in protest each time the dog barks. These animals and this cottage are quite familiar to me. I have seen them before, but never in such a pastoral light.

As I wonder about this changed setting, a woman appears in the doorway, and I notice that the cat is no longer there. The woman is somewhat short, with a pleasantly rounded frame. She wears her pale, sandy hair in a soft braided bun. She has a sturdy, maternal appearance, one that suggests a capability to endure all things gracefully. She is a woman accustomed to guiding the development of others with a firm hand whenever necessary. She wipes her hands on an apron and watches me with that shrewd expression I have come to know so well.

I wave in surprised recognition as I note the familiar amused twinkle in her clear blue eyes. She chuckles as she calls out to me from the doorway.

"Well, well, you didna' expect to find me in so fair and fine a place as this, now did you?" She smoothes the apron over her ample figure and waits for me to reply.

"Ah, Biddy," I laugh, shaking my head in mocked bafflement. "I'm no longer surprised to see you anywhere. I'm just well pleased that you continue to pop up whenever and wherever you do."

I look around at the beautiful green setting and the homey cottage. "I will say, this is an easier place to be than those cold, rocky cliffs where I usually find your cottage. Besides, that climb always makes me so tired when I get there, I can barely enjoy my visits with you. And the winds! The winds are so strong, blowing up the cliffs from the sea, that I can scarcely keep my feet on the ground at all."

I pause to consider the differences between this gentle landscape and the stark environment of the other.

"If I didn't feel such a connection to you," I nod my head at Biddy, "I would probably not be able to climb those cliffs at all. But here I feel connected to the land, almost as connected as I feel to you, but not quite."

"Well, that's only natural, girl," Biddy comments wryly. "This time you've come with a different way of being. You've set about this task openly, willingly, without the burden of your own resistance. And, because you really wanted to come, you haven't made the way so hard for yourself."

I compare my image of those sharp, steep cliffs with this one of gentle rolling hills. It is very much like comparing a quest to a retreat. I wonder if I'm really beginning to allow myself the luxury of learning about life in the gentle ways, rather than the hard ways to which I have become so accustomed.

Biddy has her hands on her hips while she watches me with an expression of amused appraisal.

"Biddy," I ask her, "how long does it take to learn how to roll along through life gently, like those beautiful green hills?"

She gestures toward the two hills bordering my previous path and replies, "Just how long do you think it took those soft green hills to transform from the cold stone they once were? And if you think you can answer that, then answer this as well." She continues smiling in gentle jest. "Just how long do you think it took for those stone mountains to shape themselves from the molten chaos they once were?"

I envision undefinable eons passing, each bringing the green hills another step along the way to becoming as I see them now.

"It is a time beyond true measurement, Biddy," I reply. "That is to say, we can date it, but we can't recreate it, so we really don't know."

Biddy continues her lesson. "Now suppose that you could do just that. Suppose you could create that soft hill from a whirling mass of molten chaos. How would you do it?"

"That's simple," I answer. "I'd bring in water, mostly as ice, probably, to cool the new formations cast out of that fiery molten chaos. Then I'd bring in the winds to sculpt a softer face on those fire-borne formations. Next I'd probably throw in a river just to give the creation process gentle pressure to keep it changing with the flow.

"Once in a while I'd set it all on fire to clear out the deadwood on its surfaces and make more soil for richer growth. I'd add a tremor or two every eon or so to shake some stones loose. These landslides would form another terrain at the base of the hills. The elements would soon provide a place where soil gathers in quantities sufficient to grow great, deep-rooted trees."

I motion toward the evergreens. "Like those fine elder evergreens," I say. Then I notice that these are the only trees of any size at all for what seems to be miles around. Biddy follows the process of my observation. She steps from the doorway and pats the wide trunk of the cedar tree. She poses another question.

"And what would you do when all the trees were cut down, and most of the stones were removed, and nearly all of the soil was carried away by the wind and the rain, and all but the sparest shrubs and grasses were gone, and the soil could no longer nurture itself in its natural ways? What would you do then?"

These soft green hills now seem to me to be solemn graves, memorials to the ravages of ignorance, destruction, and mindless consumption. For a brief moment I glimpse a vision of these hills heavily forested with a wide variety of trees. They flash through my mind in the famous forty shades of green, then they are gone. I grieve for the loss of the trees and the violation of this grand, green land. I turn to answer this, the old woman of Ireland.

"Biddy," I say, "if only I knew the ways of green witchery well enough, I would find some plant, some herb, or even some little-valued weed that would thrive in these conditions. I would weave these growing threads together and feed them with layers of new soil each time they reached another stage in their growth process. In time, the weaving would be strong enough to support new forms of growth.

Soon enough, the nurturing soil would have amassed a volume into which stronger, deeper roots could reach for assured sustenance."

I am astounded at the profound simplicity of this process. I see that the structuring of this regeneration would require only far-sighted patience to sustain the effort and thereby ensure that, in time, the land would prosper once again and forevermore. I cannot even imagine, nor shall I try, that this process would fail to re-create and preserve the land. Again Biddy reflects a question that I do not want to ask myself.

"What if, no matter what you did, or how long you did it, or how well," Biddy begins, "what if the land failed to sustain growth anymore? What if it were destined to lie fallow for all time?"

I know better than to try and deflect this question with only metaphysical mumbo jumbo about the power of faith alone. I have learned that this can be a blissful avoidance of mundane reality. I have learned that most miracles are manifested by hard work and humane management. Still, I must reply in defense of the land.

"It is not the land that has failed, Biddy. It is we who have failed the land, at least in some places. The true failure is our refusal to accept responsibility for reestablishing what we have brought to the edge of ruin."

I look across these oh-so-ancient hills once heavily forested with primeval growth and elemental power. I realize two fine things almost simultaneously. First, the hills are still pulsing with a steady unyielding power. It is a primeval force that has retained the elemental core of its energy. I also realize that, though barren and calm on the surface, this land is fertile and ever-changing at its center.

I know that the land is eternally regenerating herself. The process may be slow, but it is inexorable. I realize that Mother Earth, would regenerate herself if we would only stop what we are doing long enough to let her rest.

"I cannot believe that any thing or any place is beyond the redemptive grace of Nature's restorative powers," I say. I lift my chin with stubborn optimism and speak to the hills as old friends, as elders.

"You have sacrificed yourself for the slow but steady evolution of human knowledge. In realizing just what we have taken from you, we will learn to replace what can be, repair what is possible, and revere what still remains untouched."

I turn to Biddy and say, "If I knew that this place or others like it had indeed been destined to remain fallow, I would also know that it was for the purpose of our own growth, as it has always been.

"I would make these places into shrines of remembrance. Then the people could come reverently to remember their ancient connection to the abiding power of the Earth. These would not be places presented in order to rebuke humankind, but to remind us of our reliance on and our responsibility to the foundation from which we emerged. These hills, seemingly fallow, would become fertile ground in which the seeds of human awareness could grow and still produce a shared harvest of self-sustaining conscious conservation."

"And so it must be," says Biddy with wistful wisdom.

"And so it is," say I.

Glossary

aés dana — The Tuatha de Dannan, most specifically, the keepers of the arts and magick.

Celts — The tribe of European peoples of Indo-European origin who migrated into eastern Europe about 6000 BCE from the crescent area between the Black Sea and the Baltic Sea. These people, originally called the Battle Ax Aryans, blended with the tribes already in Europe and developed a unique culture called "Keltoi" by the Greeks and Romans. The Celts later divided into two distinct groups:

- **Gaelic Celts** — Those who migrated along a southerly route and settled in Ireland, Scotland, and France. The Gaelic Celts were also called the Chariot Warriors.

- **The Brythonic Celts** — Those who migrated across Europe somewhat later on a more northerly route and settled in Wales, Cornwall, and the Isle of Man. The Brythonic Celts were called the Ox Cart Aryans.

dragon — The symbolic representation of the alchemist's or magician's works of power. Also symbolic of the power of specific elements, places in Nature, or collective tribal energies. The shape and form of the dragon could have arisen from ancient humans' discovery of bones and fossils of massive, prehistoric creatures.

druid — The groups of highly trained priests and priestesses who practiced and taught the knowledge of healing, science, history, magick, natural laws, and universal wisdoms. The druids were divided into groups that specialized in various areas of knowledge. During the druidic revivals of the eighteenth century, these groups were given names to describe their roles. These names were derived from ancient oral traditions as well as more modern sources. These were:

- **Bards** — Singers, poets, genealogists, "political commentators," and preservers of the Celtic oral traditions.
- **Druids** (drui or draoi) — Those who observed and structured wisdom, and set up centers of learning called druidic colleges.
- **Equites** — The keepers of the Brehon laws, natural laws, and moral philosophies. From the knightly or royal classes, the equites served the chieftains and kings.
- **Vates** — Those who observed natural phenomena, and made diagnoses and divinations.

faerie — "Fey Sidhe" or Otherworld beings derived from a blend of Old Ones or ancestors, tribal dieties, and devic forces. Best understood as symbolic of humankind's conscious and/or subconscious connection with the powers of Nature. The realm of faerie is a part of mystical or Otherworld consciousness, encapsulated in tribal memories and genetic structures. Inhabitants of this expanded dimension or realm reflect human images of them. They appear in several distinct categories:

- **Wise Ones/Old Ones** — The elder mystical beings, some of whom inhabit the Otherworld realm, but are able to be accessed and communicated with by human beings. Also considered the spirits of the original ancestors or tribal deities of the Celts.

- **Lordly Ones** — Most tangibly reflect humankind and ancient archetypal Celts in elemental aspects. These are the most regal and perfect forms, thus their image reflects as the lord or lady of air, fire, water, earth, or spirit. In Celtic myth, these are most closely linked to images of the de Dannan, and may indeed be best representative of that ancient, pure breed of mystical Celt.

- **Shining Ones** — Also called the Riders or Riders of Sidhe. They are less tangible and more mystical than the other faerie, most likely representing realms of consciousness that are still expanding and evolving within the eternal present (that is, the past, present, and future). The Shining Ones are etheric and transcendent and reflect one's personal view of the many highly evolved dimensions of time and space.

- **Opalescent Ones** — Most classically reflected as the gossamer-winged, traditionally defined "fairy." Even more etheric than the Shining Ones, the Opalescent Ones seem to represent the energies from within our finest human qualities, and are thus projected from and illuminated by our development of these higher aspects of human nature.

faerie gifts (gifts of faerie)— The elemental gifts of the Tuatha de Dannan, symbolized by:

Spear (air)

Sword (fire)

Cauldron or cups (water)

Stone (earth)

These gifts symbolized all of the aspects and powers correlated with the elements, both in Nature and in human nature. To these we can now add the druidic, eight-pointed star of spirit.

Fomorians — A tribe sometimes allied with the de Dannan, sometimes not. Probably a less mystical tribe of early Celts (or proto-Celts) that inhabited the British Isles, particularly Ireland, Scotland, and Wales. Not to be confused with the Firbolgs, a much more primitive form and possibly vestiges of Neanderthalithic cultures.

genus locurum (geni loci) — The spirit of place or devic energy of a specific location in Nature. Sometimes seen to be attached to a certain tribe as a tribal deity.

Indo-European — Refers to the theory that the Celts and their ancestors originated in a region of what is now North India. Further connects the Celts to the ancient Siberian shamanic traditions.

Lord of Light — The Celtic god aspect who reflects the solar light or warrior king. Represented by Lugh, Nuada, and later by Arthur. The symbol of expressive and extroverted forces in Nature and humankind.

Lord of the Underworld — The Celtic god aspect who represents the mysterious, tanist wizard, such as in the Merlin, Taliesin, or the King of the Summerland. The symbol of the latent or introverted forces in Nature and human nature.

matristic — A culture or philosophy that emphasizes the importance of the Earth as the essential mother nurturer, the Earth as the Mother Goddess.

Ogham Script — A system of druidic writings, made up of a series of lines in various combinations, which further correlate with sacred trees and plants to have their own specific qualities or meanings.

Otherworld — Celtic term to describe the afterlife or the realm that paralleled the worldly realm. Considered to have been inhabited by mystical beings such as the Fey or faeries. Sometimes called the Summerland, the Happy Plain, Isles of the Blessed, the Mystic Isles, and other names.

shamanic steed — A symbolic representation of the vehicle that carries the seeker from the worlds of consciousness into the realms of Otherworld and mystery (the shamanic realms).

Sidhe (Shee) — Both the locations in which the oldest mystical and magical arts were preserved and the identity of the keepers of these locations. After the Milesian or Gaelic Celts entered Ireland, many of the de Dannan were given the regions considered most sacred and magickal. They were then blended in myth with the spirits of place in these locations. Therefore, the de Dannan became associated with the devic forces of Nature and the Otherworld. The Sidhe may be seen as being both the realm and its inhabitants, consequently under the dominion of the Tuatha de Dannan.

trois matres — The Celtic triple-aspected Goddess, traditionally, divided into Maiden, Mother, and Crone to symbolize the cycles of Nature as budding, growing, and fallow periods, as well as the cycles of a woman's life. Lunar traditions also relate the Triple Goddess to phases of the new, full, and waning moon times.

Tuatha de Dannan — The tribe or children of Danu, the Celtic Earth Mother Goddess. Often considered to be only mythic or mystical, the de Dannan were more likely the earliest tribes of Celts (or proto-Celts) that migrated into the British Isles. They were renowned for their phenomenal mystical and magickal skills.

Wyrd — A Saxon word meaning the web of life and the actions of the weavers or the Fates. Probably the original form of the modern English word "weird," which gives it an interesting aspect and defuses any negative connotations surrounding it.

Bibliography

I. Historical, Cultural, and Anthropological Sources

Alcock, Leslie. *Arthur's Britain: History and Archeology AD 367–634.* New York: Penguin Books, 1983.

Arensberg, Conrad M. *The Irish Countryman: An Anthropological Study.* Garden City, NY: The Natural History Press/American Museum Science Books, 1968.

Ashe, Geoffrey. *The Discovery of King Arthur.* Garden City, NY: Anchor Press/Doubleday, 1985.

Bonwick, James. *Irish Druids and Old Irish Religions.* New York: Dorset Press, 1986.

Bord, Janet and Colin. *Mysterious Britain: Ancient Secrets of the United Kingdom and Ireland.* London: Paladin/Granada, 1984.

Brennan, Martin. *The Stars and the Stones: Ancient Art and Astronomy in Ireland.* London: Thames and Hudson, 1983.

Condren, Mary. *The Serpent and the Goddess.* New York: Harper and Row, 1989.

Cunliffe, Barry. *An Illustrated History of the Celtic Race: Their Culture, Customs and Legends.* New York: Greenwich Press, 1986.

Ellis, Peter Berresford. *Caesar's Invasion of Britain.* New York: New York University Press, 1980.

Flower, Robin. *The Irish Tradition.* Oxford: Clarendon Press, 1979.

Gimbutas, Marija. *The Goddesses and Gods of Old Europe: Myths and Cult Images.* Berkeley and Los Angeles: University of California Press, 1982.

Green, Miranda. *The Gods of the Celts.* Totowa, NJ: Barnes and Noble, 1986.

Herm, Gerhard. *The Celts: The People Who Came Out of the Darkness.* New York: St. Martin's Press, 1976.

Johnson, Stephen. *Later Roman Britain.* London: Paladin/Grafton, 1986.

Lacy, Norris J. (ed.). *The Arthurian 'Encyclopedia.'* New York: Peter Bedrick Books, 1986.

Laing, Lloyd and Jennifer. *Anglo-Saxon England.* London: Paladin/Grafton, 1986.

———. *The Origins of Britain.* London: Paladin/Grafton, 1986.

Laing, Lloyd. *Celtic Britain.* London: Paladin/Grafton, 1986.

Leek, Sybil and Stephen. *A Ring of Magic Islands.* Garden City, NY: Amphoto Books, 1976.

MacManus, Seumas. *The Story of the Irish Race: A Popular History of Ireland.* New York: Devin-Adair, 1944.

Markale, Jean. *Women of the Celts.* Rochester, VT: Inner Traditions, 1986.

Newark, Tim. *Celtic Warriors: 400 BC–AD 1600*. Dorset, UK: Blandford Press, 1986.

O'Faolain, Sean. *The Irish: A Character Study*. New York: Devin-Adair, 1949.

Piggott, Stuart. *The Druids*. New York: Thames and Hudson, 1986.

Powell, T. G. E. *The Celts*. New York: Thames and Hudson, 1986.

Reilly, Robert T. *Irish Saints*. New York: Avenel Books.

Ross, Anne and Don Robins. *The Life and Death of a Druid Prince: The Story of an Archeological Sensation*. London: Rider/Random Century, 1991.

Ross, Anne. *The Pagan Celts*. Totowa, NJ: Barnes and Noble Books, 1986.

Savage, Anne. *The Anglo-Saxon Chronicles: The Authentic Voices of England from the Time of Julius Caesar to the Coronation of Henry II*. New York: Dorset Press, 1983.

Scherman, Katharine. *The Flowering of Ireland: Saints, Scholars and Kings*. Boston: Little, Brown and Company, 1981.

Sharkey, John. *Celtic Mysteries: The Ancient Religion*. New York: Thames and Hudson, 1987.

Sheane, Michael. *Ulster and the Lords of the North*. Cheshire, UK: Highfield Press, 1980.

Siochain, P. A. O. *Aran: Islands of Legend*. New York: Devin-Adair, 1967.

Thomas, N. L. *Irish Symbols of 3500 BC*. Dublin, Ireland: Mercier Press, 1988.

Wacher, John. *The Coming of Rome*. London: Paladin/Grafton, 1986.

Wentz, W. Y. Evans. *The Fairy Faith in Celtic Countries*. Gerrads Cross, Buckinghamshire, UK: Colin Smythe, 1988.

II. Mythical, Folk, and Faerie Tale Sources

Barber, Richard. *The Arthurian Legends: An Illustrated Anthology.* Lanham, MD: Littlefield Adams, 1979.

Caldecott, Moyra. *Women in Celtic Myth: Tales of Extraordinary Women from the Ancient Celtic Tradition.* Rochester, VT: Destiny Books, 1992.

Chant, Joy. *The High Kings: Arthur's Celtic Ancestors.* New York: Bantam Books, 1983.

Danaher, Kevin. "That's How It Was." Dublin and Cork, Ireland: Mercier Press, 1984.

———. *Folktales of the Irish Country Side.* Cork and Dublin, Ireland: The Mercier Press, 1988.

Danaher, Kevin. *In Ireland Long Ago.* Dublin and Cork, Ireland: Mercier Press, 1986.

Ellmann, Richard. *The Identity of Yeats.* New York: Oxford University Press, 1954.

Fitzpatrick, Jim. *Erinsage.* Dublin, Ireland: DeDannann Press, 1985.

———. *The Book of Conquests.* Surrey, UK.: Dragon's World, 1978.

———. *The Silver Arm.* Dublin, Ireland: Butler Sims, 1981.

Gantz, Jeffrey. *The Mabinogion.* New York: Dorset Press, 1985.

Glassie, Henry. *Irish Folk History: Folktales from the North.* Dublin, Ireland: The O'Brien Press, 1982.

Gose, Elliot B., Jr. *The World of the Irish Wonder Tale: An Introduction to the Study of Fairy Tales.* Toronto: University of Toronto Press, 1985.

Jackson, Kenneth Hurlstone. *A Celtic Miscellany.* New York: Dorset Press, 1986.

Jacobs, Joseph. *More Celtic Fairy Tales.* New York: Dover Publications, 1968.

Lenihan, Edmund. *In Search of Biddy Early.* Dublin and Cork, Ireland: Mercier Press, 1987.

Lynch, Patricia. *Tales of Irish Enchantment.* Dublin and Cork, Ireland: Mercier Press, 1986.

MacLiammoir, Michael. *Faery Nights Oicheanta Si: Stories on Ancient Irish Festivals.* Dublin, Ireland: The O'Brien Press, 1984.

O'Farrell, Padraic. *Superstition of the Irish Country People.* Dublin and Cork, Ireland: Mercier Press, 1982.

Porter, Jane. *The Scottish Chiefs.* New York: Charles Scribner's Sons, 1933.

Power, Victor O'D. *Some Strange Experiences of Kitty the Hare: The Famous Travelling Woman of Ireland.* Dublin and Cork, Ireland: Mercier Press, 1981.

Ryan, Meda. *Biddy Early.* Dublin and Cork, Ireland: Mercier Press, 1978.

Scott, Michael. *The Children of Lu.* London: Methuan's Children's Book's Ltd., 1986.

Simpson, Jacqueline. *The Folklore of the Welsh Border.* Totowa, NJ: Rowman and Littlefield, 1976.

Smith, Peter Alderson. *W. B. Yeats and the Tribes of Danu: Three Views of Ireland's Faeries.* Garrad's Cross, Buckinghamshire, UK: Colin Smythe, 1987.

Squire, Charles. *Celtic Myth and Legend: Poetry and Romance.* London: Newcastle Publishing, 1975.

Steinbeck, John. *The Acts of King Arthur and His Noble Knights.* New York: Farrar, Straus and Giroux, 1977.

Yeats, William Butler. *Irish Fairy and Folk Tales.* New York: Dorset Press, 1986.

III. Psychological, Symbolic, and Metaphysical Sources

Bates, Brian. *The Way of Wyrd: Tales of an Anglo/Saxon Sorcerer.* San Francisco: Hayes and Ron, 1983.

Bayley, Harold. *The Lost Language of Symbolism.* Secaucus, NJ: Citadel Press, 1988.

Bullfinch's Mythology. Distributed by Crown Publishers. New York: Avenel Books, 1979.

Byrne, Patrick F. *Witchcraft in Ireland.* Dublin and Cork, Ireland: Mercier Press, 1969.

Campbell, Joseph (ed.). *The Portable Jung.* New York: Viking/Penguin, 1985.

Campbell, Joseph. *Myths to Live By.* New York: Bantam Books, 1984.

———. *Occidental Mythology: The Masks of God.* New York: Viking/Penguin, 1984.

———. *Primitive Mythology: The Masks of God.* New York: Viking/Penguin, 1987.

———. *The Hero With A Thousand Faces.* Princeton, NJ: Princeton University Press, 1973.

———. *The Way of the Animal Powers.* San Francisco: Harper and Row, 1983.

Campbell, Joseph and Bill Moyers. *The Power of Myth.* New York: Doubleday, 1988.

Capt, E. Raymond. *Stonehenge and Druidism.* Thousand Oaks, CA: Artisan, 1979.

Cirlot, J. E. *A Dictionary of Symbols.* New York: Philosophical Library, 1983.

Elliot, R. W. V. *Runes.* Manchester, England, UK: Manchester University, 1980.

Goodrich, Norma Lorre. *King Arthur.* New York: Harper and Row, 1986.

———. *Merlin.* New York: Harper and Row, 1988.

Graves, Robert. *The White Goddess.* New York: Farrar, Straus and Girous, 1983.

Hall, Calvin S. and Nordby, Vernon J. *A Primer of Jungian Psychology.* New York: Signet, 1973.

Hawkins, Gerald S. *Stonehenge Decoded.* New York: Dell Publishing, 1965.

Hope, Murry. *Practical Celtic Magic: A Working Guide to the Magical Heritage of the Celtic Races.* Northamptonshire, England, UK: Aquarian Press, 1987.

Jung, Carl Gustav. *Aspects of the Feminine.* Princeton, NJ: Princeton University Press, 1982.

———. *Dreams.* Princeton, NJ: Princeton University Press, 1974.

———. *Four Archetypes: Mother/Rebirth/Spirit/Trickster.* Princeton, NJ: Princeton University Press, 1973.

———. *Mandala Symbolism.* Princeton, NJ: Princeton University Press, 1973.

———. *Memories, Dreams, Reflections.* New York: Random House, 1965.

———. *Psyche and Symbol.* Garden City, NY: Anchor/Doubleday, 1958.

———. *Psychology and Alchemy.* Princeton, NJ: Princeton University Press, 1980.

Knight, Gareth. *The Secret Tradition in Arthurian Legend: The Magical and Mystical Power Sources Within the Mysteries of Britain.* Northamptonshire, England: Aquarian Press, 1983.

Matthews, Caitlin. *The Elements of The Goddess.* Dorset, England, UK: Element Books, 1989.

Matthews, Caitlin and John. *The Arthurian Tarot: A Hallowquest Handbook.* Northamptonshire, England, UK: Aquarian Press, 1990.

Matthews, John. *The Elements of the Arthurian Tradition.* Dorset, England, UK: Element Books, 1989.

———. *The Elements of the Grail Tradition.* Dorset, England, UK: Element Books, 1990.

Michell, John. *Secrets of the Stones: The Story of Astro-archaeology.* New York: Penguin Books, 1977.

Pennick, Nigel. *Practical Magic in the Northern Tradition.* Northamptonshire, England, UK: Aquarian Press, 1989.

Rutherford, Ward. *The Druids: Magicians of the West.* Northamptonshire, England: Aquarian Press, 1984.

Starr, Kara. *Merlin's Journal of Time: The Camelot Adventure.* Solano Beach, CA: Ravenstarr Publications, 1989.

Stewart, R. J. (ed.). *Merlin and Woman: The Second Merlin Conference. London, June, 1987.* London: Blandford Press, 1988.

——— (ed.). *The Book of Merlin: Insights from the First Merlin Conference, London, June, 1986.* London: Blandford Press, 1987.

Stewart, R. J. *The Merlin Tarot: Images, Insight and Wisdom from the Age of Merlin.* Northamptonshire, England, UK: Aquarian Press, 1988.

———. *The Mystic Life of Merlin.* New York: Routledge and Kegan Paul, 1987.

———. *The Prophetic Vision of Merlin: Prediction, Psychic Transformation, and the Foundation of the Grail Legends in an Ancient Set of Visionary Verses.* New York: Routledge and Kegan Paul, 1986.

Thorsson, Edred. *Futhark: A Handbook of Rune Magic.* York Beach, ME: Samuel Weiser, 1989.

Wilde, Lady. *Quaint Irish Customs and Superstitions.* Dublin and Cork, Ireland: Mercier Press, 1988.

Wolfe, Amber. *In the Shadow of the Shaman: Connecting with Self, Nature and Spirit.* St. Paul, MN: Llewellyn, 1988.

Index